"Right or Wrong, God Judge Me"

"Right or Wrong,

God Judge Me"

THE WRITINGS OF
JOHN WILKES BOOTH

Edited by

John Rhodehamel
and Louise Taper

University of Illinois Press
Urbana and Chicago

© 1997 by the Board of Trustees of the University of Illinois
Manufactured in the United States of America
C   5   4   3   2   1

This book is printed on acid-free paper.

Library of Congress Cataloging-in-Publication Data
Booth, John Wilkes, 1838–1865.
 "Right or wrong, God judge me" : Writings of John Wilkes Booth / edited by John
Rhodehamel and Louise Taper.
   p.   cm.
   Includes bibliographical references and index.
   ISBN 0-252-02347-1 (alk. paper)
   1. Booth, John Wilkes, 1838–1865—Archives. 2. Assassins—United States—Archives.
3. Lincoln, Abraham, 1809–1865—Assassination—Sources. I. Rhodehamel, John H.
II. Taper, Louise. III. Title.
E457.5.B667   1997
973.7′092—dc21   96-51249
                                                                                    CIP

That affair in its philosophy, corresponds with the many attempts, related in history, at the assassination of kings and emperors. An enthusiast broods over the oppression of a people till he fancies himself commissioned by heaven to liberate them. He ventures the attempt, which ends in little else than his own execution.

—ABRAHAM LINCOLN ON JOHN BROWN'S RAID,
THE COOPER UNION ADDRESS, NEW YORK, 27 FEBRUARY 1860

It seems that uncontrollable fate, moving me for its ends, takes me from you, dear Mother, to do what work I can for a poor oppressed downtrodden people. . . . I have not a single selfish motive to spur me on to this, nothing save the sacred duty, I feel I *owe the cause I love.* the cause of the South. The cause of liberty & justice.

—JOHN WILKES BOOTH TO MARY ANN BOOTH,
NOVEMBER 1864

Our country owed all her troubles to him, and God simply made me the instrument of his punishment.

—JOHN WILKES BOOTH, APRIL 1865

CONTENTS

ILLUSTRATIONS FOLLOW PAGE 106

PREFACE

Nearly seventy documents written by John Wilkes Booth, some of them only brief notes or telegram drafts, are presented in the pages that follow. The meager documentary sum of Booth's life reflects not only the brevity of his twenty-six years but also widespread destruction of his letters and papers, motivated by both hatred of his crime and fear of being somehow implicated in it. While the doomed assassin dodged through Maryland and Virginia in his futile attempt at escape, the government was coming down hard on his family and friends, even his acquaintances and professional associates. Scores of people, almost all of them innocent of any complicity in the crime, were arrested and imprisoned. Even witnesses, who were not themselves suspects, were locked up until they could give their testimony in court. The harsh treatment mirrored the angry mood in the nation's streets, where those incautious enough to rejoice in Lincoln's murder or even to speak out in defense of the theatrical profession were likely to be jailed, beaten, or killed.

The homes, belongings, and papers of the Booth family were ransacked by government detectives. Booth's pregnant sister Asia was placed under house arrest in her Philadelphia home. Her husband John Sleeper Clarke was thrown into prison by federal marshals. Asia later wrote that "all information contained in criticisms, letters, playbills and theatrical records, has been lost in the general destruction of papers and effects belonging to Wilkes Booth. All written or printed material found in our possession, everything that bore his name was given up, even the little picture of himself, hung over my babies' beds in the nursery. . . . Not a vestige remains of aught that belonged to him; his books of music were stolen, seized, or savagely destroyed."[1] In Cincinnati, Wilkes's eldest brother Junius Brutus Booth, Jr., was nearly lynched by an angry mob. Edwin Booth, who would go on to become the greatest of American Shakespearean actors, believed at the time that the assassination had ended his theatrical career. He was sure that neither public resentment nor his own feelings of deep disgrace at his brother's crime would ever permit him to appear on a stage again.

In this atmosphere it is hardly surprising that the stricken family wanted to preserve some vestiges of their privacy by keeping personal papers out of the hands of imperious and vindictive investigators.[2] Johnny's letters went up in smoke. We know, for instance, because Mary Ann Booth chided another, less attentive, son with a comparison to her favorite boy's letter-writing habits, that Wilkes was a devoted son who, during at least some periods of his life, wrote to his widowed mother every Sunday.[3] Yet only two of what may have been scores or hundreds of Booth's letters to his mother are known to survive. At the same time, Booth's friends and associates were trying to rub out every trace of a connection between themselves and the assassin.

Other destruction in the days and weeks following the murder of Lincoln was doubtless prompted by hatred for the suddenly demonic J. Wilkes Booth. The urge to root out the very memory of the murderer was evidenced by an unenforceable government decree forbidding the sale of photographs of Booth, as well as by Secretary of War Stanton's suppression of Booth's diary and the secret burial of the assassin's corpse. Autograph manuscripts of John Wilkes Booth are consequently quite rare.[4]

This attempt to bring together and publish all of Booth's writings got its start when Lincoln collectors Barry and Louise Taper acquired a group of six passionate love letters written by Booth in the summer of 1864 to a seventeen-year-old Boston girl named Isabel Sumner. The newly discovered manuscripts are the only love letters of the handsome actor and accomplished ladies' man ever found. All were written less than a year before the assassination, during the summer of 1864, the period during which Booth resolved to capture Lincoln. The six letters, some twenty-one pages in all, as well as an inscribed photograph of the actor, a ring with the couple's initials ("J.W.B. to I.S.") engraved within the band, and other mementos of the long-hidden love affair, were acquired directly from the great-granddaughter of the girl who had so aroused the young actor's passions. They had been carefully preserved, and carefully guarded, by the family for one hundred thirty years. No outsider had ever seen the letters or learned of Isabel's mysterious romance with Wilkes Booth.

In the course of researching this one episode in the life of John Wilkes Booth, the editors were struck by the small number of his manuscripts that survive and by how many of those remained unpublished. We began to assemble, from every possible source and with the help of collectors, scholars, librarians, curators, and manuscript dealers, the texts and whenever possible facsimile copies (photograph or photocopy reproductions of original manuscripts) of every document that could be identified as having been written by Booth. With the exception of autographs, ownership signatures in

books, bank checks, signed photographs, and the theatrical promptbooks the
actor used and annotated, every document of any description that bears
Booth's handwriting or that can reasonably be attributed to him has been
included, even those known only from courtroom testimony or other reliable secondhand reports. The documents range from substantive texts, such
as autograph letters and manuscripts, to notes, telegram drafts dictated to a
clerk, and lost documents introduced into evidence at the trial of an assassination conspirator or published in secondary sources. Even some of the more
unremarkable autographic items, such as signatures on bank checks, stock
certificates, and hotel registers, have the value of establishing Booth's whereabouts on a certain date. These nonsubstantive documents are also recorded in the "Summary List of John Wilkes Booth Documents" that follows the
Introduction.

Booth manuscripts are found in a number of libraries, turning up most
often in Lincoln collections and in collections devoted to theatrical history.
The repositories include the National Archives, the Library of Congress and
the National Park Service, Princeton University Library, the Huntington Library, the Illinois State Historical Library, the Hampden-Booth Theatre Library at The Players in New York City, the Historical Society of Pennsylvania, Western Reserve Historical Society, the Massachusetts Historical Society,
the Chicago Historical Society, the University of Texas, the University of Tulsa,
and the Dallas Public Library. Many other autograph manuscripts of John
Wilkes Booth are to be found in private collections, and new pieces continue to appear in the market.[5]

NOTES

1. Asia Booth Clarke, *The Unlocked Book: A Memoir of John Wilkes Booth by His
Sister* (New York: Putnam's, 1938), 110.

2. Booth's sister lamented that a "calamity, without precedent, has fallen on our
country! We, of all families, secure in domestic love and retirement, are stricken des-
olate! The name we would have enwreathed in laurels is dishonored by a son,—his
well-beloved—his bright boy Absalom!" Asia Booth Clarke, *Booth Memorials. Passages, Incidents, and Anecdotes in the Life of Junius Brutus Booth, (the Elder.)*. . . . (New
York: Carleton, 1867), vii.

3. "Now Edwin writes to me every week unless he is sick—& John also he never
misses a Sunday." Mary Ann Holmes to Junius Brutus Booth, Jr., Baltimore, 3 February [ca. 1859], typescript of letter, Harvard Theatre Collection, Houghton Library,
Harvard University.

4. Because of their rarity and the fact that they are eagerly sought by collectors,

Booth manuscripts are quite costly. In 1992 a bank check Booth wrote for $100, containing only Booth's signature and a few words in his hand, was offered for sale at an amount equal to 150 times the face value of the check.

5. The largest single collection of Booth autograph manuscripts, public or private, is the one assembled by Louise and Barry Taper.

ACKNOWLEDGMENTS

The editors of this volume owe many debts of gratitude. We are grateful to Richard Wentworth, director and editor-in-chief of the University of Illinois Press, for his encouragement and patience. We are grateful to James O. Hall for sharing some of his unrivaled knowledge of and his exhaustive files on Booth and the Lincoln assassination. We are grateful to Arthur F. Loux for his generosity in making available the years of painstaking research contained in his unpublished manuscript, "John Wilkes Booth Day by Day." John Rhodehamel is grateful to the late William A. Moffett, director of the Huntington Library from 1990 to 1995, and to Mary L. Robertson, the Huntington's chief curator of manuscripts, for supporting the research necessary to complete this book. The editors also thank Jeannine Clarke Dodels for her research on Booth's 1860 speech; the late Harriet McLoone; Andrea Braver; Debra Kamphausen; Terry Alford; Michael W. Kauffman; William Hanchett, author of *The Lincoln Murder Conspiracies;* James M. McPherson; Dorothy and Howard Fox of Tudor Hall; Laurie Verge and Joan Chaconas of the Surratt Society, Clinton, Maryland; Raymond Wemmlinger, curator and librarian, the Hampden-Booth Theatre Library at The Players; Archie Motley, curator of archives and manuscripts, the Chicago Historical Society; Robert Eason, theater librarian, the Dallas Public Library; Thomas F. Schwartz, Illinois state historian and curator of the Henry Horner Lincoln Collection at the Illinois State Historical Library; Peter Drummey, librarian, the Massachusetts Historical Society; Peter J. Parker, director, the Historical Society of Pennsylvania; Jean Preston, former curator of manuscripts, the Firestone Library, Princeton University; Nicholas B. Sheetz, manuscripts librarian, special collections department, Georgetown University Library; Sidney Huttner, special collections librarian, University of Tulsa Libraries; Kermit J. Pike, director, Historical Library, Western Reserve Historical Society; Jeanne T. Newlin, curator, the Harvard Theatre Collection, Harvard University; and Sharon Herfurth, fine arts department, Dallas Public Library, Dallas, Texas. Finally, both editors affectionately acknowledge the support of their spouses, Barry H. Taper and Johanna Westerman Rodehamel.

INTRODUCTION

"Assassination is not an American practice or habit, and one so vicious and desperate cannot be engrafted into our political system. This conviction of mine has steadily gained strength since the civil war began. Every day's experience confirms it."[1] So wrote President Abraham Lincoln's secretary of state, William H. Seward, in 1862. Three years later, one assassin had killed the president and another had nearly killed Seward himself. It is the lot of those whose pronouncements are dramatically contradicted by subsequent events to have their erring words ironically recited, but Seward had not been so foolish in believing assassination a practice foreign to the United States. With the single exception of the deranged British house painter who tried to shoot President Andrew Jackson, there had been no attempt on the life of a leading American statesman in the Republic's history.

The gunfire that has disfigured our public life in the years since John Wilkes Booth's murderous encounter with Abraham Lincoln has done much to persuade Americans that assassination is after all a custom native to our shores. Now, however, a longing to deny that the violence is purposeful may be seen in the tendency to ignore the political dimensions of assassination in the United States. One study prepared by a governmental commission concluded that assassins of American presidents, including Booth, were for the most part "mentally disturbed persons, who did not kill in advance of any rational political plan."[2] That judgment is simply mistaken; most attacks on presidents and presidential candidates have been politically motivated.

John Wilkes Booth set the pattern when he killed Abraham Lincoln for clearly articulated political motives. Yet Booth has often been dismissed as a crazy, drunken actor—the son, after all, of a famously crazy, drunken actor. Some have enlarged their condemnations. In the final volume of his sprawling Lincoln biography, Carl Sandburg was compelled to reach deep into the supernatural to find words charged with evil sufficient for his portrait of the assassin. If the Good Friday murder had worked to transform Abraham Lincoln into a sort of American Christ-figure, a hero who gave his own life so that the nation might live, it wasn't hard to figure what that made of Booth himself: "the American Judas." "But who was this Booth?" Sandburg asked. "In what kind of green-poison pool of brain and personality had the amazing and hideous crime arisen? . . . he had now wrapped the letters of his name with a weird infamy synonymous with Enemy of Mankind. His name on a thousand occasions was to go unspoken with loathing for the unspeakable and untouchable: a pitiless, dripping, carnivorous, slathered, subhuman and antihuman beast mingling snake and tiger; the unmentionable . . . a lunatic . . . with an unstrung imagination, a mind deranged, a brain that was a haunted house of monsters of vanity, of vampires and bats of hallucination."[3]

In recent years, however, there has been increasing recognition that the shot from Booth's little pocket pistol was not a bolt out of the pathological blue, not an act of psychosis or drunken frenzy, and not the monomaniacal bid of a failed actor to win for himself a name that would belong to the ages, but rather a political murder that can be understood only in the context of the most violent period in American history and of Booth's beliefs and experiences. However misguided he may have been, John Wilkes Booth was not a monster. He was a highly successful actor and a Confederate secret agent. He was also an impulsive young man who shared the conviction of many, in the North as well as the South, that Abraham Lincoln was a malignant tyrant whose policies threatened to expunge the liberties that had long been the birthright of free, white Americans. Booth believed that he acted for his country and for his race, and he did so with the expectation that his act would make him a hero.

It is in the hope of advancing understanding of the first American presidential assassination that all the writings of John Wilkes Booth known to survive have been brought together in this volume. More than half of the material is published here for the first time. The nearly seventy documents that follow include a speech, letters, notes, and memoranda as well as Booth's several explicit statements of his political convictions, a series of love letters the actor sent to a seventeen-year-old Boston girl the summer before he murdered Lincoln, and the little diary he kept during his hopeless flight after the assassination. "Gentlemen: Allow me a few words" was the appeal with which Booth began his earliest political testament—the long, impassioned speech he composed in December 1860 in the midst of the secession crisis before the outbreak of the Civil War. If we allow John Wilkes Booth his words, we will discover the clear and authentic voice of a man convinced of the righteousness of his cause—the voice of a believer in a time when hundreds of thousands of American men were proving themselves willing to kill and to die for what they believed.

◇◇

Of course, Booth is not remembered for his speeches or his letter writing. Generations of Americans have known the story of the night of 14 April 1865, when the young actor fired a single shot into the back of Abraham Lincoln's head during a performance of *Our American Cousin* at Ford's Theatre in Washington, D.C. The mortally wounded president died early the next morning. Booth escaped the theater, rode out of Washington in the moonlight, and fled through Maryland and Virginia for twelve days before being hunted down and shot through the neck in a burning tobacco barn. "Useless, useless" was the dying actor's final line.

On 15 April a stunned nation woke to the "black Easter" of 1865. The North, which had been celebrating the victorious end of four years of war with illuminations and five-hundred-gun salutes, was suddenly plunged into mourning. Whole cities were draped in black, and hundreds of thousands of Americans filed past Lincoln's coffin for a last glimpse of the face on which they could see marks of the destruction worked by Booth's bullet. One hundred and thirty years after the explosion of the pistol, the assassination of Abraham Lincoln remains a defining event, one that, in the words of one of its ablest chroniclers, divided "as by the sweep of a knife . . . two eras of national life."[4]

J. Wilkes Booth, tragedian, son and brother of great tragic actors, had enacted at Ford's Theatre one of the great tragedies of American history. Lincoln's murder was the final, bloody act that marked the end of the nation's bloodiest war, a war that Lincoln's election as president had touched off four years before. One of the enduring legends of the Civil War era is the belief that Lincoln's death turned America away from the period of national healing envisioned by the magnanimous statesman, giving power instead to a clique of vindictive radical Republicans determined to use Reconstruction to scourge the defeated South. Although historians now question this interpretation, the assassination did achieve one result its perpetrator never dreamed of. For John Wilkes Booth had surely never reckoned that the murder of Abraham Lincoln would wrap a mantle of sainthood around the dead man and exalt him as the Republic's greatest hero. Booth believed Lincoln a guilty tyrant. Yet the unwitting assassin succeeded in projecting the tragic figure of Abraham Lincoln across the firmament of history in an apotheosis that was perfectly mythic in its grandeur and its symmetry.

◇◇

Much mystery, fable, and untruth attend the darkly beautiful person of John Wilkes Booth, but much is also known with certainty of him and his crime. He was born 10 May 1838, on a farm outside Baltimore, the fifth of six surviving children of Mary Ann Holmes and Junius Brutus Booth. His parents were British. They had taken passage to America in 1821, leaving behind in England the wife and young son that Booth had deserted there. Thirty years after coming to the United States, Booth finally obtained a divorce and married the woman who had long been his life's companion. The wedding day was also the birthday of the couple's favorite child, John, who had been born a bastard thirteen years earlier.[5]

Although eccentric and unpredictable, and haunted throughout his life by alcoholism and spells of madness, Junius Brutus Booth was acknowledged for three decades as the preeminent tragic actor on the American stage. And although their father tried to steer them away from the theater and into such conventional careers as surgery and cabinetmaking, three of the four Booth sons followed the old man onto the stage. Two of them—Edwin and John Wilkes—became actors of high distinction. Years later, long after the "mad tragedian" Junius Brutus Booth had passed from the scene, when Americans were trying to explain away his son's political murder of Abraham Lincoln as a meaningless aberration, as "one mad act" somehow outside of history, the father's reputation made it easier to declare that the son was crazy too.

Junius Brutus Booth died in 1852, when John Wilkes was fourteen. By then the boy had received a decent education at a series of private schools. At one military boarding school in the Maryland countryside, he wore a gray cadet's uniform and mingled with the sons of some of the Upper South's most distinguished slaveholding families. His sister remembered him as a slow but tenacious student; he learned with difficulty but rarely forgot what he had mastered. A loyal and generous friend who was always popular with his fellows, Johnnie Booth liked to sign his schoolboy letters "Thine till Death" or "Yours Forever." He would bring two of his boyhood friends into his plot against Abraham Lincoln. Both went to prison, and one died there.

Not long after his father's death he left school for good. He spent a couple of years working the family farm near Bel Air, Maryland, an occupation he called "trying to starve respectably by torturing the barren earth." But Booth had always dreamed big dreams—"I must have fame! fame!" he cried.[6] He longed to become a great actor like his father; he talked of winning undying fame with some prodigious feat; and he despaired at the prospect of being marooned in the countryside with his mother and sisters and little brother. He came to envy the two older brothers who had toured with the "Elder Booth" and had seen the actor's craft illuminated by their father's genius. Wilkes could only practice his elocution by declaiming to the field-hands passages he had memorized from *Julius Caesar*. Still, by August 1855 the seventeen-year-old felt confident enough to make his stage debut, playing the Earl of Richmond in a popular adaptation of Shakespeare's *Richard III*. However the performance may have gone that night, it is notable that Booth's first stage role was that of a hero who destroys a murderous tyrant, for that is exactly what the actor thought he was doing in Ford's Theatre ten years later when he squeezed the trigger of his derringer. Throughout Booth's short life, the line between the drama and the world was always a little blurred, and many of the plays he acted were violent, bloody spectacles studded with killings.

Two years would pass before Booth performed professionally again. His career really began in 1857, when he hired on as an eight-dollar-a-week supporting player in the stock company of a popular Philadelphia theater. The Booth name was an imposing property in the American theater at midcentury. Not willing to sully that shining name with poor showings or risk being accused of trading on the reputations of his father and brothers, the novice was careful to bill himself as Mr. J. B. Wilkes, or plain J. Wilkes. This was probably a wise move—the young player's early efforts were greeted with mixed reviews. He missed cues, forgot his lines, was struck dumb by stage fright, and, on at least one occasion, was laughed and hooted from the stage. But the theater was in his blood. Mr. Wilkes persevered, playing stock in Philadelphia for a year before joining the company of the Richmond Theatre in 1858. John Wilkes Booth came of age as an actor in Richmond, Virginia, and it was living there that confirmed his determination to be "of the South." He wanted, he said, "to be loved of the Southern people above all things. He would work to make himself essentially a Southern actor."[7]

Whatever kind of actor he might be, no one had the slightest doubt about the presence Booth brought to the stage. By the time he turned twenty, the dark-eyed mother's darling had grown into a figure many called "the handsomest man in America." Of Booth it was said that "women spoiled him," and it was small wonder that few were proof against the glamour and self-assured charm of the performer who could move an audience to tears with his readings of the maudlin poem "Beautiful Snow." One acquaintance concluded that "John Wilkes Booth cast a spell over most men . . . and I believe over all women without exception," while the actress Clara Morris resorted to a tender metaphor to suggest Booth's power over women when she recalled that "at the theater, . . . as the sunflowers turn upon their stalks to follow the beloved sun, so old and young, our faces smiling turned to him."[8]

"Seldom has the stage seen a more impressive, or a more handsome, or a more impassioned actor," remembered another who knew him. "Picture to yourself Adonis, with high forehead, ascetic face corrected by rather full lips, sweeping black hair, a figure of perfect proportions and the most wonderful black eyes in the world. . . . At all times his eyes were his striking features but when his emotions were aroused they were like living jewels. Flames shot from them. His one physical defect was his height, . . . but he made up for the lack by his extraordinary presence and magnetism."[9] Nearly everyone agreed that the young man was also charming, generous, and instinctively kind. And Booth possessed the gifts of a natural athlete—he was a fine horseman, an acrobat and swordfighter, and a marksman with pistol and rifle. With these formidable resources joined to his hungering ambition, John Wilkes Booth quickly fashioned himself into one of the most successful actors in the United States.

As he grew in stature as an actor and as a dashing, much-admired figure in the streets and drawing rooms of the city that would soon be the capital of the Confederate States of America, Booth was growing as well in his passionate, even fanatical, love for the South and its institutions, a love that was fully requited by both theater audiences and Richmond society. The Virginians had embraced Booth as one of their own. It was also during his days as an apprentice actor in Richmond that Booth had an adventure that deeply impressed him. In December 1859 he witnessed the execution of the abolitionist revolutionary John Brown. Donning the uniform of the city's elite militia regiment, the Richmond Grays, Booth stood in the ranks of armed men arrayed around the scaffold to guard against any last-minute attempt to free the condemned man. Although he later declared himself proud of the small part he had played in this battle against the forces determined to destroy slavery, Booth never forgot John Brown's courage or the old man's bold gamble at changing history with a single violent act. Five years later, the memory of seeing Brown die a criminal's death on the gallows must have strengthened the assassin's resolve not to be taken alive by the bluecoats who had brought him to bay in the Virginia tobacco barn.

❖❖

Booth played stock in Richmond for two years. By the fall of 1860 he was ready to make his first tour as a star. Success came quickly. Before long the playbills were hailing "J. Wilkes Booth" in bold capitals as "A STAR OF THE FIRST MAGNITUDE!—THE YOUNGEST TRAGEDIAN IN THE WORLD!" Critics praised him while theatergoers voted with their pocketbooks. Booth played to packed houses across the country. Within a short time, the young actor could boast of earning more than $20,000 a year, then an altogether spectacular sum. His first starring tour took him to Georgia and Alabama at the time of Abraham Lincoln's election, and there he must have breathed the fiery atmosphere of the secession winter in the Lower South. But in John Wilkes Booth, the fire-eaters were preaching to the converted. Booth already believed, as he was to write six months before he killed Lincoln, "that the abolitionists, *were the only traitors* in the land." While spending the 1860 Christmas holidays with his family in Philadelphia, Booth wrote a passionate, twenty-page speech in which he blamed all of the country's troubles on the abolitionists.

Growing up in Baltimore and on his family's Maryland farm, Booth had been born into a world in which slavery was a part of the accepted order of things. In 1864 he would describe American slavery as "one of the greatest blessings . . . that God ever bestowed on a favored nation." As a boy, he had come to regard African Americans with an affectionate condescension and to believe that their ancestral captivity was the happiest condition to which they could aspire. With most white Americans of his time Booth shared the conviction that blacks were an inferior people, incapable of living in freedom alongside whites. Booth had also adopted a patrician's attitude of easy contempt for working-class whites and the foreign-born. The young Southern gentleman would not allow his womenfolk to sit at table with the hired hands and once cudgeled a tenant farmer who had spoken rudely to his sister. Booth's earliest known political allegiance was to the American Party—the "Know-Nothing" Party—whose platform had been erected on the fear that a flood of Irish and German immigrants threatened to degrade the republican institutions of the United States.

There was a tradition of libertarian radicalism in Booth's family. His grandfather, a London lawyer, had once dreamed of fighting for liberty on the side of Britain's rebellious American colonists. John Wilkes Booth's own father had been named Junius Brutus in honor of the ancient heroes who overthrew the kings of Rome and fought to preserve the Roman republic. Junius Brutus Booth's best-known namesake was Marcus Junius Brutus, Shakespeare's Brutus, "the noblest Roman of them all," the heroic assassin of *Julius Caesar,* a tragedy all the Booths knew by heart. John Booth had also appeared in the play *Brutus; or, The Fall of Tarquin,* and one of his theatrical friends even claimed that the actor's admiration for the classical Brutus was the "mainspring" of the assassination.[10] "*Sic Semper Tyrannis!*" Booth shouted like a Roman a moment after firing his bullet through Lincoln's head. "Thus always to tyrants" was the translation of the defiant motto that adorned the great seal of the Commonwealth of Virginia. In some of the last words he scribbled into his pocket diary, a despairing, hunted Booth would identify himself again with the Roman Brutus, the tyrant-killer. After his death, an anonymous poem that circulated through the South eulogized Booth as "Our Brutus."

The assassin himself had been named for a famous eighteenth-century English radical the Booths claimed as a distant relative. His namesake, John Wilkes of London, had been an avowed enemy of the Crown and an agitator for the liberties of the people. Young John Wilkes Booth had every reason to see himself as heir to a great libertarian tradition of rebellion against tyrants. And the greatest of all history's tyrants, he would become convinced, was the usurper Abraham Lincoln—"Bonaparte in one great move," Booth called him, who aimed at nothing less than crowning himself king of America in the definitive repudiation of the ideals of the heroes of 1776. In the summer before Lincoln's reelection, Booth bitterly sang for his sister a popular song with the refrain "in 1865 when Lincoln shall be King." When in November 1864 Abraham Lincoln became the first president of the United States to win a second term since Andrew Jackson's 1832 reelection, Booth raged, "You'll see—you'll see that *re-election* means *succession*." Lincoln, he insisted, was "a false president yearning for kingly succession."[11] King or president-for-life, Booth said, it hardly mattered which.

Booth was not alone. Plenty of Americans, in the Union as well as the Confederacy, thought Lincoln had already made himself a sort of king. That Abraham Lincoln was while living the most hated president in the country's history will come as a surprise to those who know only the revered martyr-statesman. But during the Civil War many regarded Lincoln with anything but reverence. North and South, Lincoln's foes called him tyrant, gorilla, barbarian, "Abe the Widowmaker," and "King Abraham Africanus the First." With matchless eloquence Abraham Lincoln told his countrymen that the Union must be saved to keep alive for "man's vast future" the "last, best hope of earth"—the American experiment in self-government. His opponents, however, argued that the president himself was destroying the experiment by his dictatorial policies, systematic violations of civil liberties, and the consolidation of great new powers by the federal government. Lincoln was the nation's most controversial president, and his most controversial, and most detested, act was emancipation. There is no doubt that he wielded unprecedented executive power in fighting the nation's most costly war.

He began with the very act of accepting war rather than allowing the Southern states to "depart in peace." Lincoln's presidential predecessor James Buchanan was only one of the many who believed that although secession itself was unconstitutional, the Constitution gave the federal government no right to "coerce" the seceded states to return to the Union. Lincoln did not wait for congressional approval to call out troops or to draw on the federal treasury in attempting to put down the rebellion. Fighting his war from a national capital surrounded by disloyal slaveholders, President Lincoln moved to suspend the writ of habeas corpus within two weeks of the first shots at Fort Sumter. By the time the war ended, many thousands of civilians had been arrested without warrants, held without trial, or tried by military courts.

Certainly, the unyielding power of the U.S. government was strongly felt in Booth's native Maryland, and perhaps nowhere outside the Confederacy itself was Lincoln more hated. Four years of civil war brought down upon the Southern people sufferings on a scale unknown in the American experience. And although his administration had failed to achieve victory despite immense sacrifices of blood and treasure, Lincoln remained unwilling to negotiate on any terms but the restoration of the Union and the abolition of slavery. None of this was lost on John Wilkes Booth or the countless angry men who felt as he did. To them, Abraham Lincoln was not just the leader of a hostile power, but a man of real evil, a despot who aimed at nothing less than the destruction of free, white society and the erection in its place of some nightmare African despotism. "What shall we call him?" asked a Richmond newspaper, "Coward? assassin? savage? murderer of women and babes? Shall we consider these as all embodied in the word 'fiend!' and shall we call him that?—Lincoln the Fiend!"[12]

"This country was formed for the *white* not for the black man," Booth insisted in one of his passionate denunciations of the North. Racial hatred lay behind much of the malice toward Lincoln and his party. The Republican administration's policies of emancipation and the fielding of regiments of black soldiers were viewed by many as despicable acts of barbarism as well as explicit invitations to the apocalyptic race war Southerners had dreaded for generations. Jefferson Davis called the Emancipation Proclamation "the most execrable measure recorded in the history of guilty man," but his words seemed almost restrained alongside some of the howls of execration that greeted news that the Union army was being strengthened by tens of thousands of black men. Throughout the war, the Democratic opposition in the North denounced Lincoln and the Republicans with a savagery rarely equaled in American political history. Some Lincoln-haters even charged that the president himself was African American; John Wilkes Booth told his sister that Lincoln was a "half-breed."[13]

Abraham Lincoln had been in danger from the moment he was elected president. In the weeks following the 1860 election, the slave states seethed with hatred for Lincoln and his party of "Black Republicans" and race-mixing "amalgamationists." With wild hyperbole, one Southern newspaper swore that the Potomac River would be "crimsoned in human gore, and Pennsylvania Avenue . . . paved ten fathoms deep in mangled bodies" before the South would "submit to such humiliation and degradation as the inauguration of Abraham Lincoln."[14] Lincoln knew the danger he faced, as did his advisers and friends. The president was fatalistic. Although he eventually agreed to an escort of armed guards on some of his outings, Lincoln believed that nothing could protect him from a determined assassin, a man willing to trade his own life for that of the president.

President Lincoln and his protectors also knew that there were among the enemy those who plotted not to kill him but to take him prisoner.[15] The idea of seizing the Yankee president had suggested itself to Southerners even before the war began. By the fall of 1861, a Confederate magazine, *DeBow's Review,* could report that "were it not that Lincoln is so securely guarded, I have reason to know that he would have been brought a captive to Richmond ere this."[16] Of course a magazine piece does not represent government policy, but it does show that the capture of a head of state was considered a legitimate act of war. Indeed, United States General Order Number 100, dated 24 April 1863, stated that military necessity "allows the capturing of every armed enemy, and every enemy of importance to the hostile government."[17] The Confederate high command itself initiated, or at least approved, several plans to grab Lincoln and carry him south to Richmond as a hostage. Some scholars have argued that a Confederate grand strategy for retrieving Southern fortunes in the final months of the war hinged on Lincoln's capture or assassination.[18] What is known more certainly, however, is that one conspiracy to kidnap the president was led by a Confederate agent named John Wilkes Booth.[19]

◇◇

Booth had flourished during the war. On the road much of the time, he starred in a string of engagements that took him to New York, Boston, Philadelphia, Baltimore, Washington, Chicago, Detroit, St. Louis, and south to Yankee-occupied Nashville and New Orleans. His acting sometimes earned him as much as $1,000 a week. He needed the money. "My beloved precious money," he called it, "oh, never beloved till now!—is the means, one of the means, by which I serve the South."[20] Booth may have been serving the South since the first month of the war, when Marylanders had sabotaged railroads and fought pitched battles in the streets of Baltimore to block Northern troops passing through the city on their way to relieve Washington.

But if Booth was among the men who went out to burn bridges and cut telegraph lines in April 1861, it was to be the last such fighting he did. Many Marylanders who believed that justice marched with the Southern armies had gone to join the Confederates. Booth had followed a different course. Years later, Edwin Booth remembered a conversation with his younger brother. "I asked him once why he did not join the Confederate army. To which he replied: 'I promised mother I would keep out of the quarrel, if possible, and am sorry that I said so.'"

But Wilkes gave his sister Asia Booth Clarke another explanation, one that she recorded in her grieving tribute to her beloved brother, the memoir eventually published in 1938 as *The Unlocked Book*. The other Booths supported the North and, in the heat of a argument over the war, Wilkes had burst out, "So help me holy God! my soul, life, and possessions are for the South," prompting Asia to ask, "Why not go fight for her, then? Every Marylander worthy of the name is fighting her battles." "I have only an arm to give," her brother answered, "my brains are worth twenty men, my money worth an hundred. I have free pass everywhere, my profession, my name, is my passport." He went on to tell his horrified sister how he moved as a spy among the Union armies and mingled easily with the most distinguished society of the North, gathering intelligence. He told her how he smuggled precious quinine south. His hands were callused from nights of rowing small boats across the Potomac. He carried a pistol. When in Philadelphia he often stayed at his sister's house, sleeping in his clothes on a downstairs couch. Asia remembered that strange men called late at night for whispered consultations. Asia knew then "that my hero was a spy, a blockade-runner, a rebel! I set the terrible words before my eyes, for I knew that each one meant death. I knew that he was today what he had been since childhood, an ardent lover of the South and her policy, an upholder of Southern principles. He was a man so single in his devotion, so unswerving in his principles, that he would yield everything for the cause he espoused."[21]

Growing Northern might threatened to overwhelm that cause. By the summer of 1864 Booth had become convinced that he had to do much more to help his country. It was likely the Confederates themselves who told the actor just what he might do to help—capture President Lincoln. Booth apparently met with several Confederate spies at the Parker House Hotel in Boston in late July 1864. In October he spent ten days in Montreal, staying at the St. Lawrence Hall, a hotel "used as a headquarters for Confederate agents in Canada."[22] At these meetings the Confederates probably recruited Booth and gave him the instructions and support he needed to carry out the audacious plot.[23]

Booth virtually abandoned acting and began gathering a group to help him seize Lincoln during one of the president's carriage rides and carry him south out of Washington through lower Maryland and across the Potomac into Virginia. Booth was convinced that "if the North conquers us it will be by numbers only, not by native grit, not pluck, and not by devotion." In numbers the federals did enjoy the decided advantage. "The national resources, then," Lincoln told the nation in his annual message of December 1864, "are unexhausted, and, as we believe, inexhaustible."[24] The president was clearly determined to use those resources to secure a victory that would both restore the Union and destroy slavery forever.

Booth thought he had found a way to swell the Southern ranks, however. As a hostage in Richmond, Lincoln could be bartered for the thousands of Confederate soldiers held in Northern prison camps. The exchange of prisoners by warring powers was a common practice in the nineteenth century. A cartel to exchange U.S. and Confederate prisoners had been set up in 1862. But the agreement foundered on the divisive issue of Union enlistment of black troops. The Confederates threatened to treat captured African American soldiers as runaway slaves rather than prisoners of war. In retaliation, the North suspended all prisoner exchanges in April 1864. To some this policy seemed part of a calculated strategy to use the Northern advantage in manpower to grind the South inexorably to defeat. As Booth explained while recruiting one of his team of presidential kidnappers: "We cannot spare one man, whereas the United States Government is willing to let their own soldiers remain in our prisons because she has no need of them."[25] Another of the conspirators said that Booth was sure the capture of Lincoln would "produce the exchange for the President of all the prisoners in the Federal hands."[26]

Booth's first recruits were two friends from his school days, Samuel Arnold and Michael O'Laughlen. Both men had served as private soldiers in the Confederate ranks. Now, at a meeting in a Baltimore hotel room made pleasant by wine, cigars, and reminiscences, their famous friend was offering the two of them a chance at winning the war almost singlehandedly in a final, daring campaign.[27] Booth was as persuasive as ever. Both Arnold and O'Laughlen signed on. Booth explained that Lincoln traveled by carriage to the Soldiers' Home, a summer residence a few miles from the White House to which the president often retreated during hot weather. The plan was to fall on the unguarded carriage with a small party of mounted men. Some would seize Lincoln and secure him inside, while others would take the reins and, turning the horses' heads south, drive swiftly over the Anacostia River and on into Maryland. They would gun down the sentries on the bridge as they galloped the carriage across. With relays of fresh horses, they would race to the little town of Port Tobacco on the Potomac's Maryland shore. There a small boat would be waiting. A few hours of darkness would suffice to cross the big river. The route through a rural section populated by Confederate sympathizers was one used by Southern spies and couriers throughout the war. If all went according to plan, Abraham Lincoln would be a prisoner in Confederate Virginia within a day of his capture in Washington. It was a plan that shared elements with the other Confederate plots to capture President Lincoln.[28]

Next Booth made his visit to Canada. There was in Montreal a nest of Confederate spies plotting against the United States. Booth probably received from them both money and intelligence. When he returned to Washington to begin scouting the getaway route through southern Maryland, he had the names of reliable Confederate sympathizers along the way.[29] The young actor was meanwhile preparing to leave the North for good. He turned down offers from theater managers and disposed of his Boston real estate and his holdings in the Pennsylvania oil fields. He had even taken his valuable theatrical wardrobe with him to Canada and from there had put it, in several big trunks, on a schooner that would run the federal blockade to deliver a cargo to the beleaguered Confederacy.[30] At the same time, Booth bought a bill of exchange at a Montreal bank, telling the cashier that he planned to run the blockade himself. He evidently meant to resume his acting career, and, if he pulled off the capture of Abraham Lincoln, he could count on being the most popular actor in the South.

Returning to the United States, Booth added new recruits to his band of conspirators: Lewis Powell, a hulking, fearless Confederate veteran; David Herold, an inconsequential young man who knew the back roads of southern Maryland; a dashing Confederate courier named John Harrison Surratt; and a sodden German from Port Tobacco, George Andrew Atzerodt, to serve as boatman. Booth had to support most of them out of his own pocket. The out-of-work actor was spending himself poor buying supplies: horses and a buggy, boats, rations, handcuffs, rope, and weapons—knives, six pistols, and a pair of fancy repeating rifles. He had also acquired a derringer—a small, easily concealed .44-caliber pocket pistol that was usually loaded with a .41-caliber bullet.[31] It was a deadly weapon at close range. Booth and his men continued to explore the muddy country roads of southern Maryland. He practiced his marksmanship regularly at a Pennsylvania Avenue shooting gallery. Everything seems to have been in place by the end of January 1865. All that was lacking was the chance to get at Abraham Lincoln.

Frustrated by the delay, Booth considered abandoning the idea of catching Lincoln in his carriage in favor of a reckless plan to grab the president out of a crowded Washington theater during a performance. The new idea did not sit well with Booth's men, who believed they had signed on for a military operation, not a suicide pact. "I wanted a shadow of a chance for escape and success," one of them reasonably objected.[32] Significantly, Booth now hinted that if capture proved impossible he was prepared to kill Lincoln.[33] After some heated words, Booth backed down, and the conspirators went back to waiting for Lincoln to expose himself while traveling. A few days later, on 17 March 1865, about two weeks after Abraham Lincoln's second inauguration, Booth learned of the president's plans to attend a play at a soldiers' hospital near Washington. Lincoln would go by carriage, and the conspirators might be able to surprise him on a lonely stretch of road. But Lincoln changed his plans. Discouraged, some of the conspirators began to drift away. Booth hung on grimly in Washington, but he must have wondered whether his grand vision of saving the South had come to nothing.

Booth had attended the inauguration ceremony on 4 March 1865, apparently not much impressed by the speech that Lincoln considered his finest literary creation. Booth later exclaimed, "What an excellent chance I had to kill the President on inauguration day if I wished."[34] But as much as he hated Lincoln, Booth probably did not make the decision to murder him until sometime in April. That month brought a succession of spectacular events that signaled the final collapse of Southern fortunes: the capture of Richmond by Grant's armies on 3 April followed by Lincoln's visit to the conquered city the next day and Robert E. Lee's surrender on 9 April. News of the Northern victories fell like hammer blows on John Wilkes Booth. Furious, ashamed, and desperate, he began drinking hard, putting away brandy by the quart. Still the young actor refused to believe that the South was really defeated. Perhaps it was not too late. "For six months we had worked to capture," Booth would write after he killed Lincoln. "But our cause being almost lost, something decisive & great must be done."[35]

Booth may have finally given himself over to the idea of that "something decisive & great" on April 11, the night Abraham Lincoln made the last speech of his life. Booth, Herold, and Lewis Powell were in the crowd that gathered on the White House grounds to hear the president speak from a balcony. Herold identified this as the fatal moment in which Booth decided on assassination. One passage in the president's subdued victory speech touched on the place of African Americans in the reunited nation: "It is also unsatisfactory to some," Lincoln said, "that the elective franchise [in the new government of reconstructed Louisiana] is not given to the colored man. I would myself prefer that it were now conferred on the very intelligent, and on those who serve our cause as soldiers."[36] Booth was enraged. "That means nigger citizenship," he said. "Now, by God! I'll put him through. That is the last speech he will ever make."[37] The angry reaction to "nigger citizenship" sounds like Booth, but other testimony suggests that he may not have decided on murder until April 14, the day of the crime, when he learned that both President Lincoln and the Union's victorious lieutenant general, Ulysses S. Grant, would be together at Ford's Theatre that night.

Booth had been wild since the fall of Richmond, his family and friends remembered. He talked recklessly of riding through the streets of Washington and waving a rebel flag, he lamented that he no longer had a country, and, looking south across the Potomac, he sobbed, "Virginia! Virginia!" The soldiers of the Confederate armies accepted defeat a good deal more willingly than did Booth, who insisted that Lee should never have surrendered. It wasn't just the brandy. "If Wilkes Booth was mad, his mind lost its balance between the fall of Richmond and the terrific end," wrote his sister, but she never believed that he was mad.[38] Rather, Booth was supremely unhappy with history itself. He could not endure the outcome of one of history's greatest wars, and there was a kind of desperate pain in him that only death could mend. But when Booth heard that Lincoln and Grant would be sitting together in the state box at Ford's like a pair of shooting-gallery targets, he must have felt a surge of hope. He hurried to reassemble what remained of his gang and give them their new assignments. Together they would change history. In a single evening's bloodletting Booth intended to decapitate the government of the United States. If they succeeded, the conspirators would approximate the results of an aborted Confederate plot to blow up the White House with Lincoln and other high officials in it, a plot that may have been approved by Jefferson Davis himself.[39] Booth himself would kill Lincoln and Grant at the theater. George Atzerodt, the drunken German boatman, would kill Vice-President Andrew Johnson at his hotel, while the murderous Lewis Powell would take care of Secretary of State Seward, who was recovering at home from injuries received in a carriage accident. Atzerodt made no attempt to carry out his assignment, preferring instead to get drunk and pawn his re-volver. Powell failed too, although he nearly killed Seward and four other men he encountered in the secretary's home.

Booth was more successful. Naturally, the actor knew Ford's Theatre in-timately. General Grant had backed out at the last minute, but Booth had no trouble getting into the state box, where President and Mrs. Lincoln, accom-panied by a young army officer and his fiancée, made up a little theater par-ty. Timing his moves with the knowledge of a play he had often acted him-self in Richmond, Booth stepped into the box. Just a foot or two separated the muzzle of his little pistol from the back of Lincoln's head. Booth pulled the trigger, firing the half-inch leaden sphere out of the bore at four hundred miles an hour. The bullet crashed through the back of Lincoln's skull and tore across his brain. Throwing down the empty gun, Booth laid open the arm of the officer with a knife before vaulting from the box to the stage directly below. The twelve-foot jump should have been easy for the acrobatic actor, but in swinging himself over the rail Booth caught a spur on one of the flags draped from the box and landed awkwardly. He may have fractured the small bone in his left leg just above the ankle.[40] The actor recovered enough to deliver his *"Sic Semper Tyrannis!"* and make a final exit, stage right. The pres-ident slumped in the rocking chair, his head on his chest as though he were peacefully asleep. Mary Lincoln screamed. They carried the unconscious man to a little room in a boardinghouse across the street from Ford's. Anyone could see that the wound was mortal. Throughout that long, ugly night, the body on the too-small bed struggled to live. Finally, at 7:22 on the morning of 15 April, as a cold spring rain fell across the city of Washington, Abraham Lincoln died.

By that time John Wilkes Booth was resting in a doctor's house in south-ern Maryland, about thirty miles from Washington. He had made his way to his horse in the alley behind the theater and ridden out of town on the little mare, giving his true name when challenged by a sentry as he crossed the bridge. Over in Maryland, he met up with Davey Herold, in whose com-pany Booth would spend the rest of his life, all twelve days of it. His leg was an agony to him. With rest and proper treatment it was not a serious injury, but for a man on the run the fracture was a hindrance of the worst sort. Booth could just manage to sit a horse and hobble about with the aid of a crutch after the obliging doctor treated his leg, but he was reduced to a cripple. In the days to come the pain would only grow worse as his left leg swelled and blackened. Meanwhile, federal patrols ranged through the Maryland countryside, their eagerness to find the fugitives sharpened by a fierce appetite for revenge and the offer of a $100,000 reward.

Booth and Herold never had much chance. They hid out for six miserable days in a swamp before making it across the Potomac to Virginia in a small boat. But worse than the cold and hunger in the wet thickets, worse even than the pain of his swollen leg, were the reports of his deed Booth read in the newspapers a friend brought him. He was stunned to learn that the world, apparently even much of the South, condemned him as one of the most diabolical criminals who had ever lived. Booth could hardly believe it.[41] "After being hunted like a dog through swamps, woods, and last night being chased by gun boats till I was forced to return wet cold and starving, with every mans hand against me," he wrote in his little pocket diary, "I am here in despair. And why? For doing what Brutus was honored for, what made Tell a Hero. And yet I for striking down a greater tyrant than they ever knew am looked upon as a common cutthroat."[42]

◇◇

Running and hiding by turns, Booth and his boyish companion traveled the Northern Neck of Virginia and crossed the Rappahannock by ferry. There, however, the pair was spotted by witnesses willing to talk when the federal troopers came riding up. Booth was finally overtaken in the early morning hours of April 26, holed up in a tobacco barn on a farm not a dozen miles from the Rappahannock. Twelve days of flight had brought the assassin less than one hundred miles from Ford's Theatre. Thirty cavalrymen surrounded the ramshackle barn and ordered the fugitives to give themselves up. Davey Herold came out alone. Booth had no intention of dying with a noose around his neck like old John Brown. He prepared himself to die bravely. An officer threatened to fire the barn if Booth did not give up. The man inside had other ideas. "I'm lame," he called out. "Give me a chance. Draw up your men before the door and I'll come out and fight the whole command."[43] A handful of burning straw was thrown into the barn, and the building quickly took fire. The flames at Booth's feet flared like the footlights of the last act, and, so lighted, he was an easy target when, against orders, a veteran sergeant fired. The bullet passed through Booth's neck, severing his spinal cord and paralyzing him from the neck down but leaving him in excruciating pain.

They dragged him away from the burning barn. He died a few hours later, as dawn was breaking, on the porch of the nearby farm house. Booth suffered intensely, begging the soldiers to kill him at one point. "Tell Mother I die for my country," he gasped. Just before the end he asked that his lifeless hands be held up so he could see them. "Useless, useless," were Booth's last words. The body was sewn up in a rough army blanket and carried back to Washington.

Although popular fancy would find half a dozen living John Wilkes Booths in the next fifty years, the assassin was as dead as his victim. The government of the United States wanted the murderer of President Lincoln very badly, and the government made very sure that the dead man in the blanket was really Booth. Back in Washington, on a warship anchored in the river, the body was identified beyond doubt by witnesses who had known the man. Then, to assure that the assassin's grave would not become a rebel shrine, Booth was secretly buried beneath the floor of a government warehouse. In 1869 President Andrew Johnson finally agreed to return the body to the Booth family. At a Baltimore undertaking parlor the body was identified again, this time by his brother Joseph, friends, and a dentist who had filled one of Booth's teeth. The assassin's head, severed in the 1865 autopsy, was passed from hand to hand, and everyone agreed that this was all that remained of John Wilkes Booth. They bundled the wreckage into a coffin and buried it in an unmarked grave in the Booth family plot at a Baltimore cemetery. There it remains to this day.[44]

NOTES

1. William H. Seward to John Bigelow, 15 July 1862, in John Bigelow, *Retrospections of an Active Life* (New York: Baker and Taylor, 1909), 1:505.

2. James F. Kirkham, Sheldon G. Levy, and William J. Crotty, *Assassination and Political Violence: A Report to the National Commission on the Causes and Prevention of Violence* (New York: Praeger Publishers, 1970), 78.

3. Carl Sandburg, *Abraham Lincoln: The War Years* (New York: Harcourt, Brace, 1939), 4:301. But this passage, although irresistibly quotable, does not accurately reflect Sandburg's approach to the murder of Abraham Lincoln. As William Hanchett has pointed out: "More than any other Lincoln biographer to the present, Sandburg made an effort to put Booth and the assassination into their wartime context." William Hanchett to John Rhodehamel, 22 April 1994.

4. George S. Bryan, *The Great American Myth* (New York: Carrick and Evans, 1940; repr., with an introduction by William Hanchett, Chicago: Americana House, 1990), xi.

5. How heavily the burden of illegitimacy weighed upon the Booths and partic-

ularly on Wilkes, cannot be known. One scholar has suggested that the initials "J.W.B." that he crudely tattooed on his left hand as a boy were another attempt to prove that he was a real, legitimate Booth. Constance Head, "J.W.B.: His Initials in India Ink," *Virginia Magazine of History and Biography* 90 (July 1982): 359–66.

6. Asia Booth Clarke, *The Unlocked Book: A Memoir of John Wilkes Booth by His Sister* (New York: G. P. Putnam's Sons, 1938), 99; Stanley Kimmel, *The Mad Booths of Maryland* (Indianapolis: Bobbs-Merrill, 1940), 150.

7. Clarke, *The Unlocked Book*, 106.

8. Clara Morris, *Life on the Stage: My Personal Experiences and Recollections* (New York: McClure, Phillips, 1902). Actor John Ellsler said that Booth "had more than mere talent as an actor. In his soul the fire of genius burned brightly, and he promised to top them all in the profession to which he was born. He had by inheritance the fire, the dash, the impetuosity, the temperament, and the genius of his great father, and he more nearly resembled the elder Booth in those qualities which go to make up a great actor than any of the other sons of the eminent sire." In Francis Wilson, *John Wilkes Booth: Fact and Fiction of Lincoln's Assassination* (Boston: Houghton Mifflin, 1929), 17. William Hanchett observes, "It was impossible to see him and not admire him; it was equally impossible to know him and not love him." Hanchett, *The Lincoln Murder Conspiracies* (Urbana: University of Illinois Press, 1983), 37.

9. Wilson, *John Wilkes Booth*, 15.

10. The remarks of John T. Ford, owner of Ford's Theatre, were quoted in a letter (signed "A MARYLANDER") to the editor of the *Philadelphia Press,* 27 December 1881. This account was reprinted as appendix entitled "His Schooldays by a Classmate" in Clarke, *The Unlocked Book,* 151–58.

11. Ibid., 124–25. Booth's sister remembered, "Then he whispered fiercely, 'That Sectional candidate should never have been President, the votes were *doubled* to seat him, he was smuggled through Maryland to the White House. Maryland is true to the core—every mother's son. Look at the cannon on the heights of Baltimore. It needed just that to keep her quiet. This man's appearance, his pedigree, his coarse low jokes and anecdotes, his vulgar similes, and his frivolity, are a disgrace to the seat he holds. Other brains rule the country. *He* is made the tool of the North, to crush out, or try to crush out slavery, by robbery, rapine, slaughter and bought armies. He is walking in the footprints of old John Brown, but no more fit to stand with that rugged old hero—Great God! no. John Brown was a man inspired, the grandest character of the century! *He* is Bonaparte in one great move, that is, by overturning this blind Republic and making himself a king. This man's re-election which will follow his success, I tell you—will be a reign! The subjects—bastard subjects—of other countries, apostates, are eager to overturn this government. You'll see—you'll see— that *re-election* means succession. . . . These false-hearted, unloyal foreigners it is, who would glory in the downfall of the Republic—and that by a half-breed too, a man springing from the ashes of old Assanonthime Brown, a false president yearning for kingly succession as hotly as ever did Ariston'" (124–25).

12. Richmond *Enquirer,* 1 October 1862, quoted in *Nat Turner,* ed. Eric Foner (Englewood Cliffs: Prentice-Hall, 1971), 140.

13. Clarke, *The Unlocked Book,* 125. See also Adalbert J. Volck's print "Under the Veil" (ca. 1862), in which the Confederate cartoonist etched white supremacy's ulti-

mate nightmare: Under the veil, behind the speeches and the proclamations, Abraham Lincoln was an African.

14. The *Atlanta Southern Confederacy,* quoted in the *New York Times,* quoted in Michael Davis, *The Image of Lincoln in the South* (Knoxville: University of Tennessee Press), 13.

15. Louis J. Weichmann, *A True History of the Assassination of Abraham Lincoln and of the Conspiracy of 1865,* ed. Floyd E. Risvold (New York: Alfred A. Knopf, 1975), 56–57.

16. *DeBow's Review,* Oct.–Dec. 1861, cited in Davis, *The Image of Lincoln in the South,* 66.

17. Benn Pitman, comp., *The Assassination of President Lincoln and the Trial of the Conspirators* (New York: Moore, Wilstach and Baldwin, 1865; facsimile edition edited by Philip Van Doren Stern, New York: Funk and Wagnalls, 1954), 411. The order does condemn assassination.

18. Hanchett, *The Lincoln Murder Conspiracies,* 25–34; William A. Tidwell, with James O. Hall and David Winfred Gaddy, *Come Retribution: The Confederate Secret Service and the Assassination of Lincoln* (Jackson: University Press of Mississippi, 1988), passim; William A. Tidwell, *April '65: Confederate Covert Action in the American Civil War* (Kent: Kent State University Press, 1995), passim.

19. "Confederate plans to capture Lincoln and carry him off to Richmond began in 1864 and continued through most of March 1865. John Wilkes Booth was a party to the last such plan." Tidwell, with Hall and Gaddy, *Come Retribution,* 480.

20. Clarke, *The Unlocked Book,* 115.

21. Ibid., 115–25.

22. Tidwell, with Hall and Gaddy, *Come Retribution,* 262–65.

23. Ibid., 328ff.

24. Abraham Lincoln, *The Collected Works of Abraham Lincoln,* ed. Roy P. Basler (New Brunswick: Rutgers University Press), 8:151 (hereafter cited as *Collected Works*).

25. "The Rockville Lecture of John H. Surratt," in Weichmann, *A True History,* 431.

26. "The Confession of Samuel Arnold," in Weichmann, *A True History,* 381.

27. James O. Hall has concluded that the meeting at Barnum's Hotel took place some time in the first two weeks of August 1864. Hall to John Rhodehamel, 1989.

28. Ibid., 48ff.

29. Hanchett, *The Lincoln Murder Conspiracies,* 44.

30. The ship promptly sank in the St. Lawrence River. Booth's wardrobe, said to be worth $25,000, was ruined.

31. John K. Lattimer, "Good Samaritan Surgeon Wrongly Accused of Contributing to President Lincoln's Death: An Experimental Study of the President's Fatal Wound," *Journal of the American College of Surgeons* 182 (May 1996): 431–48.

32. "The Confession of Samuel Arnold," in Weichmann, *A True History,* 383.

33. "The Rockville Lecture of John H. Surratt," in Weichmann, *A True History,* 431.

34. Clara E. Laughlin, *The Death of Lincoln: The Story of Booth's Plot, His Deed and the Penalty* (New York: Doubleday, Page, 1909), 94.

35. See page 154.

36. *Collected Works,* 8:403.

37. Hanchett, *The Lincoln Murder Conspiracies,* 37.

38. Clarke, *The Unlocked Book,* 141.

39. Tidwell, *April '65,* 8–9, 160–75. Booth may have learned of the plot by way of John Surratt, who had met with Confederate Secretary of State Judah P. Benjamin in Richmond about March 31. Evidence that Booth knew of this, or a similar scheme to kill Lincoln and his cabinet by blowing up the White House, is provided by the testimony of one of the conspirators. Under interrogation after the assassination, Atzerodt stated that "Booth said he had met a party in New York who would get the prest. [president] certain. They were going to mine the end of the pres. [president's] house near the War Dept. They knew an entrance to accomplish it through. Spoke of getting friends of the prest. to get up an entertainment & they would mix in it, have a serenade & thus get at the prest. & party. These were understood to be projects. Booth said if he did not get him quick the New York crowd would." Tidwell, with Hall and Gaddy, *Come Retribution,* 418.

40. Lincoln assassination researcher Michael Kauffman has challenged the traditional explanation of Booth's broken leg, arguing that the injury was probably inflicted when the assassin's horse fell on him during his escape. Michael W. Kauffman, "Booth's Escape Route: Lincoln's Assassin on the Run," *Blue and Gray Magazine* 7 (June 1990): 17. See also Timothy S. Good, *We Saw Lincoln Shot: One Hundred Eyewitness Accounts* (Jackson: University Press of Mississippi, 1995), 18–20.

41. The assassin would have been reassured had he known about the rejoicing that greeted Lincoln's murder throughout much of the unoccupied South.

42. See page 154.

43. Bryan, *The Great American Myth,* 264.

44. Wilson, *John Wilkes Booth,* 291–98. In 1995, assassination conspiracy buffs filed suit in the circuit court of Baltimore City, seeking to exhume the "alleged remains of John Wilkes Booth" from the Green Mount Cemetery in Baltimore. Green Mount Cemetery opposed the exhumation. The petitioners hoped to unearth evidence to support the old fable that Booth had escaped, that another man had died on 26 April 1865, and that the government had conducted a cover-up and buried the wrong body. But the court denied the suit, stating that there was no compelling evidence that Booth had escaped in 1865 and that accurate identification of the remains might prove impossible in any case. Ruling of the Circuit Court of Baltimore City, 26 May 1995: Case No. 94297044/CE187741.

EDITORIAL METHOD

It has been noted that few documents survive from John Wilkes Booth's short life. It seems best to present Booth's writings as he wrote them. The texts published here retain the original punctuation (including dashes), capitalization, and spelling of the manuscripts, with the exceptions outlined below. Editorial insertions in the text have been kept to a minimum so that the printed page follows the original manuscript as closely as possible. These rules apply:

1. Words and letters in [roman type] within square brackets represent editorial supply of material not in the original manuscript. This includes editorial supply of words and expansions of abbreviations or contractions that might otherwise be incomprehensible, as well as editorial corrections of some names, places, and dates within the text that are wrong or misleading. This form can also represent editorial reconstructions of manuscript text lost, torn, or illegible. If doubt exists concerning the supplied material, a question mark precedes the closing bracket, for example: [reading?]. Missing or unrecoverable material—that which cannot be conjectured—is indicated by suspension points in square brackets: [. . .].

2. Material deleted by Booth is represented by ~~canceled type~~.

3. All insertions, both interlinear and marginal, are represented by ^roman type^ within carets.

4. Material written in superscript (frequently used as an indication of abbreviation) has been lowered.

5. Material underlined with a single line is represented by *italic type;* material double underlined is represented by SMALL CAPITALS; triple underlined by *ITALIC SMALL CAPITALS*. Booth also had an idiosyncratic practice of indicating emphasis by forming his letters more carefully and without giving the letters his customary left-to-right slant. Such material is also represented by *italic type.*

6. In the editorial note appearing at the end of each document, the form of the documents is described. An "autograph letter signed" is a letter in Booth's writing and signed by him; an "autograph manuscript" is in Booth's writing but not signed by him; a "document signed" bears only his signature.

This editorial note also provides the location of the original manuscript, if known, or the source of the text.

7. Endorsements: The recipient of a letter often made a brief note on the verso, recording such information as the name of the sender, the date of the letter's writing and receipt, and the date of any reply. This is an endorsement. The text of endorsements is supplied in the endnotes.

8. Whether or not the information appears in the body of the text, all documents are presented with a standardized heading giving the addressee and date and place of composition, if known.

SUMMARY LIST OF JOHN WILKES BOOTH DOCUMENTS

*[Documents marked with * do not appear in this volume.]*

1853

*JWB, autograph, October 1853, ownership signature in book, *The Pacha.*
Offered by American Museum of Historical Documents, Las Vegas, Nevada, 1989.

1854

JWB to T. William O'Laughlen, autograph letter signed, 25 January 1854, Bel
Air, Maryland. Maryland Historical Society.

*JWB, autograph, 1 February 1854, ownership signature and date within scroll,
in schoolbook: "John W. Booth Bel Air Harford Co. Md. Feb. 1st 1854." Private collection.

JWB to T. William O'Laughlen, autograph letter signed, 30 April 1854, Bel Air,
Maryland. Private collection.

JWB to T. William O'Laughlen, autograph letter signed, 8 August 1854, Bel
Air, Maryland. Private collection.

JWB to T. William O'Laughlen, autograph letter signed, 8 November 1854,
Bel Air, Maryland. Private collection.

1855

JWB to T. William O'Laughlen, autograph letter signed, 25 January 1855, Bel
Air, Maryland. Chicago Historical Society.

JWB to T. William O'Laughlen, autograph letter signed, 18 June 1855, Bel Air,
Maryland. Private collection.

JWB to T. William O'Laughlen, autograph letter signed, 14 September 1855,
Bel Air, Maryland. The Railsplitter Archives, New York City.

JWB to T. William O'Laughlen, autograph letter signed, 12 November 1855, Bel Air, Maryland. Private collection.

1857

JWB, two newspaper advertisements, summer, 1857, Baltimore. In *Pathways: The Journal of the Booth Family, Lincoln's Assassination and Historic Preservation Law* 1 (March 1985): 7.

1858

*JWB, autograph, [1858]. "John W. Booth, Feb. 4th, Arch St." in William Shakespeare, *Julius Caesar.* Taper Collection.

*JWB, autograph, April 1858. In auction catalog: Sotheby-Parke-Bernet, Sang sale, part 5, 4 December 1981. Catalog entry reads: "Clipped signature with address and date on portion of printed item, Arch Street Theatre, Philadelphia, April 1858."

JWB to Edwin Booth, autograph letter signed, 10 September 1858, Richmond, Virginia. Hampden-Booth Theatre Library, The Players, New York City.

*JWB, autograph, 1858, in promptbook,** *The Specter Bridegroom; or a Ghost in Spite of Himself. . . . by W. T. Moncrieff. . . .* (New York: E. Muren, 1821), Arch Street Theatre, Philadelphia. Taper Collection.

1860

JWB, autograph manuscript signed, 18 February 1860, Richmond, Virginia. Eight-line verse to "Miss White" inscribed in autograph album. Taper Collection.

JWB, autograph manuscript, December 1860–January 1861, Philadelphia, draft of a speech. Hampden-Booth Theatre Library, The Players, New York City.

*JWB, autograph, "John W. Booth, Richmond, Va., May, 1860," on "cover of play-book, 1 page, octavo." In C. F. Libbie and Company, Boston, *Catalogue of the Collection of Dramatic Autographs of the Late James F. Brown, Esq., of Malden, Mass. . . . to be sold at auction . . . May 11, 12, and 13, 1898.*

**A promptbook is a printed copy of a play annotated by a stage manager, a prompter, or an actor and used in conducting performances.

1861

JWB to Joseph H. Simonds, autograph letter signed, 9 October 1861, Philadelphia. Offered by Federal Hill Autographs, Baltimore, Maryland, 1981.

JWB to Fanny, autograph acrostic signed, 20 November 1861, Detroit, Michigan. Offered by the Gallery of History, Las Vegas, Nevada, 1991.

JWB to Joseph H. Simonds, autograph letter signed, 23 November 1861, Cincinnati, Ohio. In auction catalog: Christie's, 19 December 1986.

1862

JWB to Joseph H. Simonds, autograph letter signed, 10 January 1862, St. Louis, Missouri. Andre de Coppet Collection, Princeton University Library.

JWB to Joseph H. Simonds, autograph letter signed, 18 February 1862, Baltimore. In auction catalog: Sotheby-Parke-Bernet, Sang sale, part 4, 3 June 1980.

JWB to Joseph H. Simonds, autograph letter signed, 22 March 1862, New York City. Andre de Coppet Collection, Princeton University Library.

JWB to Joseph H. Simonds, autograph letter signed, 13 April 1862, Philadelphia. In auction catalog: Sotheby-Parke-Bernet, Roy P. Crocker sale, 28 November 1979.

JWB to Edwin Frank Keach, autograph letter signed, 25 July 1862, Philadelphia. Herndon-Weik Collection, Library of Congress.

JWB to T. Valentine Butsch, autograph letter signed, 3 August 1862, Philadelphia. Huntington Library.

JWB to Joseph H. Simonds, autograph letter signed, 6 December 1862, Chicago. Andre de Coppet Collection, Princeton University Library.

JWB to Edwin Frank Keach, autograph letter signed, 8 December 1862, Chicago. Gratz Collection, Historical Society of Pennsylvania.

1863

*JWB, autograph, 3 February 1863, Boston, signature on check of Edwin Booth. Anderson Art Auctions, W. Stilson Hutchins Collection sale, 12 January 1932.

JWB to Joseph H. Simonds, autograph letter signed, 28 February 1863, Philadelphia. Andre de Coppet Collection, Princeton University Library.

JWB to Joseph H. Simonds, autograph letter signed, 1 March 1863, Philadelphia. Andre de Coppet Collection, Princeton University Library.

JWB to Joseph H. Simonds, autograph letter signed, 3 April 1863, Philadelphia. Andre de Coppet Collection, Princeton University Library.

JWB to Benedict DeBar, autograph letter, 17 April 1863, Washington, D.C. Private collection.

JWB to Joseph H. Simonds, autograph letter signed, 19 April 1863, Washington, D.C. Andre de Coppet Collection, Princeton University Library.

JWB to R. J. Morgan, autograph letter signed, 22 June 1863, St. Louis, Missouri. Illinois State Historical Library.

*JWB, autograph in Tremont House Hotel register, ca. 1863, Boston. Offered by Joseph Rubinfine Autographs, West Palm Beach, Florida, Catalog 96, 1988.

JWB to John T. Ford, autograph letter signed, 17 September 1863, Philadelphia. John T. Ford Papers, Library of Congress.

JWB to Ben De Bar, autograph letter signed, 22 September 1863. National Archives.

JWB to John Adam Ellsler, autograph letter signed, 18 October 1863. Harvard Theatre Collection, Houghton Library, Harvard University.

*JWB, autograph document signed, 16 November 1863, Baltimore. In auction catalog: Stan V. Henkels, sale of 13 April 1906.

1864

JWB to Moses Kimball, autograph letter signed, 2 January 1864, St. Joseph, Missouri. Taper Collection.

JWB to Thomas Harbine, John L. Bittinger, P. L. McLaughlin, 4 January 1864, St. Joseph, Missouri. In Franklin Graham, *Histrionic Montreal: Annals of the Montreal Stage...*, (Montreal: J. Lovell and Son, 1902), 145–46.

JWB to John Adam Ellsler, autograph letter signed, 23 January 1864, Louisville, Kentucky. Western Reserve Historical Society, Cleveland, Ohio.

JWB to Edwin Frank Keach, autograph letter signed, 30 January 1864, Louisville, Kentucky. Swift Collection, University of Tulsa, Tulsa, Oklahoma.

JWB to Moses Kimball, autograph letter signed, 9 February 1864, Nashville, Tennessee. W. E. Hill Theatre Collection, Fine Arts Department, Dallas Public Library, Dallas, Texas.

JWB to Richard Montgomery Field, incomplete autograph letter signed, 9 February 1864, Nashville, Tennessee. Taper Collection.

JWB to Richard Montgomery Field, autograph letter signed, 22 February 1864, Cincinnati, Ohio. Andre de Coppet Collection, Princeton University Library.

*JWB, document signed, (deed), 22 February 1864. Private collection.

JWB to Richard Montgomery Field, autograph letter signed, 26 March 1864, New Orleans. Massachusetts Historical Society.

JWB to Richard M. Johnson, autograph letter signed, 28 March 1864, New Orleans. Huntington Library.

JWB to "My Dear Miss," autograph letter signed, 4 April 1864, New Orleans. Taper Collection.

JWB to Junius Brutus Booth, incomplete autograph letter signed, [ca. April 1864]. Private collection.

*JWB, document signed, rent receipt to George Heisler, 5 May 1864, Boston. Private collection.

*JWB, printed form filled out and signed, 30 May 1864, Boston, 1 page, oblong octavo, receipt for one dollar in payment for performance at Boston Museum, name of payer cut out. In *Manuscripts: The Quarterly Journal of the Manuscript Society* 36 (Winter 1984): 52.

*JWB, document signed, 30 May 1864, stock certificate for twenty-five shares of Boston Water Power Company. Taper Collection.

JWB, autograph document signed, 31 May 1864. In auction catalog: Charles Hamilton Galleries, sale of 25 May 1972.

*JWB, document signed, 1 June 1864, receipt. In auction catalog: Bangs Auction Company, Sawyer sale, 23 October 1902.

JWB to Isabel Sumner, autograph letter signed, 7 June 1864, New York City. Taper Collection.

JWB to John Adam Ellsler, autograph letter signed, 11 June 1864, Franklin, Pennsylvania. Harvard Theatre Collection, Houghton Library, Harvard University.

JWB to John Adam Ellsler, autograph letter signed, 17 June 1864, Franklin, Pennsylvania. Illinois State Historical Library.

JWB to Isabel Sumner, autograph letter signed, 17 June 1864, Franklin, Pennsylvania. Taper Collection.

JWB to Isabel Sumner, autograph letter signed, 14 July 1864, New York City. Taper Collection.

JWB to Isabel Sumner, autograph letter signed, 24 July 1864, New York City. Taper Collection.

JWB to Isabel Sumner, autograph letter signed, 26 August 1864, New York City. Taper Collection.

JWB to Isabel Sumner, autograph letter signed, ca. 27–28 August 1864, New York City. Taper Collection.

*JWB, signature in hotel register of St. Lawrence Hall, 18 October 1864, Montreal, Canada. Library of Congress.

*JWB to Dr. G. T. Collins, portion of a letter of 28 October 1864—"I have been in Montreal for the last three or four weeks and as no one (not even myself) knew when I would return home, my letters were not forwarded." In the *Cincinnati Commercial*, 1 May 1865.

JWB to J. Dominic Burch, letter, 14 November 1864, Washington, D.C. Transcription in David Rankin Barbee Papers, Georgetown University Library.

*JWB, autograph document signed, bank account check ledger, 16 November 1864–16 March 1865, Washington, D.C. "Jay Cooke & Co. in acc't with J. Wilkes Booth." Chicago Historical Society. The ledger records two deposits—$1,500 on 16 November 1864 and $250 on 5 January 1865—and seven withdrawals by check, providing the amount and date of the check but not the name of the payee. Five original autograph checks written on this account by John Wilkes Booth have been located. The two original checks that remain unaccounted for and for which the payee remains unknown are 20 December 1864 (for $100) and 9 January 1865 (for $750).

JWB to "To whom it may concern," autograph letter signed, November 1864. National Archives.

JWB to Mary Ann Holmes Booth, autograph letter signed, November 1864, Philadelphia. National Archives.

*JWB, document signed, 16 December 1864, check drawn on Jay Cooke and Company for $100, payable to Matthew W. Canning. Taper Collection.

*JWB, document signed, 24 December 1864, check drawn on Jay Cooke and Company and payable to JWB. In auction catalog: Bangs Auction Company, sale of 17 May 1902.

*JWB, document signed, 30 December 1864, rent receipt to George Heisler, Tudor Hall, Baltimore. Chicago Historical Society.

1865

*JWB, document signed, 7 January 1865, Washington, D.C., check drawn on Jay Cooke and Company for $150, payable to JWB. Louis E. Warren Library, Lincoln National Life Insurance Company.

*JWB, document signed, 14 January 1865, Washington, D.C., check drawn on Jay Cooke and Company for $75, payable to JWB. Taper Collection.

JWB to Junius Brutus Booth, autograph letter signed, 17 January 1865, Washington, D.C. Andre de Coppet Collection, Princeton University Library.

JWB to Orlando Tompkins, autograph letter signed, 9 February 1865, Washington, D.C. Private collection.

JWB to John Parker Hale Wentworth, telegram, 21 February 1865, New York City. Benjamin F. Butler Papers, Library of Congress.

JWB to T. Michael O'Laughlen, telegram, 27 February 1865, Baltimore. Benjamin F. Butler Papers, Library of Congress.

JWB, autograph manuscript signed, 5 March 1865, four-line verse to "Eva." In auction catalog: Parke-Bernet, the Oliver R. Barrett Lincoln Collection sale, 19, 20 February 1952.

JWB to Michael O'Laughlen, telegram, 13 March 1865. National Archives.

*JWB, document signed, 16 March 1865, Washington, D.C., check drawn on Jay Cooke and Company for $25, payable to JWB. Private collection.

JWB to Louis J. Weichmann, telegram, 23 March 1865, New York City. National Archives.

JWB to Michael O'Laughlen, telegram, 27 March 1865, Washington, D.C. National Archives.

*JWB, autograph in the Aquidneck House hotel register, 5 April 1865, Newport, Rhode Island. In auction catalog: Sotheby-Parke-Bernet, Sang sale, part 5, 3 December 1981.

JWB to Mary Ann Holmes Booth, autograph letter signed, 14 April 1865, Washington, D.C. New York *Herald,* 30 April 1865, 1, reprinted in George S. Bryan, *The Great American Myth* (New York: Carrick and Evans, 1940; repr., with an introduction by William Hanchett, Chicago: Americana House, 1990), 148.

JWB to Andrew Johnson or to Johnson's secretary, William A. Browning, autograph note signed, 14 April 1865, Washington, D.C. National Archives.

JWB to the editors of the *National Intelligencer,* text of letter written on 14 April 1865. Reconstructed from memory by John Matthews with the help of Philadelphia journalist Frank A. Burr in 1881, and published in the *Washington Evening Star,* 7 December 1881.

JWB, autograph manuscript, ("Booth's diary"), entries for 15 and 21 April 1865, written in a memoranda book, *Pocket Diary, . . . 1864.* Lincoln Museum, Ford's Theatre, National Park Service, Washington, D.C.

JWB to Dr. Richard H. Stewart, autograph letter, 24 April 1865, on leaf torn from pocket diary. Original lost; letter in House Judiciary Committee, "Impeachment of the President," *House Report Seven* (serial set 1314), 40th Cong., 1st sess. (Washington, D.C.: Government Printing Office, 1867), 676–77.

JWB to Richard H. Stewart, autograph letter signed "Stranger," 24 April 1865, on leaf torn from pocket diary. Original lost; letter in House Judiciary

Committee, "Impeachment of the President," *House Report Seven* (serial set 1314), 40th Cong., 1st sess. (Washington, D.C.: Government Printing Office, 1867), 676–77.

*JWB, autograph, in National Hotel register, 1865, Washington, D.C. Bates Papers, Library of Congress.

UNDATED

*JWB, autograph, ownership signature in *A Critical Pronouncing Dictionary, and Expositor of the English Language. . .* , by John Walker (New York: Collins and Hannay, 1825). Private collection.

*JWB to Blanche De Bar Booth, autograph note signed ("Dear Blanche— Excuse me this evening for not keeping my word. Will see you tomorrow. Your *Nunkie* John"). In Stanley Kimmel, *The Mad Booths of Maryland* (Indianapolis: Bobbs-Merrill, 1940), 374.

*JWB, autograph and notes, in a promptbook, *French's Standard Drama. Shakespeare's Historical Tragedy of Richard III.* Harvard Theatre Collection, Houghton Library, Harvard University.

*JWB to "Joe" [Joseph H. Simonds], autograph note signed ("Dear Joe. How are you. Tremont"). In auction catalog: Parke-Bernet, the Oliver R. Barrett Lincoln Collection sale, 19, 20 February 1952.

THE WRITINGS OF JOHN WILKES BOOTH

The Writings of John Wilkes Booth

The earliest surviving letters of John Wilkes Booth are the eight he wrote to his friend T. William O'Laughlen (1838–1915) in 1854 and 1855. Around 1965, a Baltimore woman cleaning out a desk in her basement suddenly realized that the old letters she was burning were signed "J. Wilkes Booth." The letters that survived the destruction, written when Booth was fifteen and sixteen, are the only writings known from the period before the young actor began his theatrical career.[1] These early letters were written from Tudor Hall, the Booths' country home near the little hamlet of Bel Air, in Harford County, Maryland, outside Baltimore. All but two of the Booth children were born in the log cabin hidden in the Maryland countryside. Junius Brutus Booth, Jr., born in 1821, was followed by Rosalie in 1823, Henry in 1825, Mary Ann in 1827, Frederick in 1829, Elizabeth in 1831, Edwin Thomas, born 13 November 1833, Asia, born 19 November 1835, John Wilkes, born 10 May 1838, and Joseph, born 8 February 1840. (The middle children—Henry, Mary Ann, Frederick, and Elizabeth—all died in childhood.)

Family chronicler Asia Booth Clarke described the Booth home in her memoir *The Elder and the Younger Booth,* published in 1882:

> In the summer of 1822, while the yellow-fever was raging in Baltimore, Mr. Booth purchased a farm twenty-five miles from that city, lying in Harford County, Maryland. This place became his constant resort when free from the excitement of his profession, and was the birthplace of his children. It was always known as "The Farm," but was in reality a dense forest, called the "Big Woods," which served as a free hunting-ground on moonlight nights when the whole place was rendered musical by the baying of the hounds and the call of the sportsmen. . . . The rough coach-road to the Farm was made picturesque and delightful in the summer by the massive trees which arched it. . . . From the road a crooked, narrow pathway wound to the Booth dwelling. . . . This was a log-cabin,

plastered and whitewashed on the exterior; the small square window-frames, and broad, plain shutters . . . painted red. Four rooms besides the loft, the kitchen, and the Old Dominion chimney, made up a picturesque and comfortable abode, standing in a clearing encompassed by huge oak, black walnut, beech, and tulip trees.

The cabin in its primal state, unpainted and unplastered, had been removed to its present locality across several fields. This proceeding caused great wonderment among the villagers, as every available man, ox, and horse that could be hired, were in requisition. . . . This costly removal had been effected on account of a spring of delicious water which Mr. Booth had discovered under the thickest trees.[2]

Shortly before his death, Junius Brutus Booth began building a gothic revival brick house to replace the old cabin. He called the new place Tudor Hall. The family also kept a town house in Baltimore, at 62 North Exeter Street, where they usually passed the winter. Across the street were the O'Laughlens at 57 North Exeter, and it was probably to that address that Wilkes directed his youthful letters to William O'Laughlen. Booth had attended a Baltimore grammar school with William and his younger brother, Michael O'Laughlen (1840–67). In the summer of 1864, when Booth was planning the abduction of President Lincoln, Mike O'Laughlen was one of the first recruits to his little band of conspirators. Convicted in 1865 as an accomplice in the Lincoln assassination, Michael O'Laughlen was sentenced to life imprisonment. He died during an 1867 outbreak of yellow fever at Fort Jefferson, a grim federal prison in the Florida Keys.

---

1. *Lincoln Log* 1 (April 1976): [6].
2. Asia Booth Clarke, *The Elder and the Younger Booth* (Boston: James R. Osgood, 1882), 65ff.

To T. William O'Laughlen
Harford County, Maryland, 25 January 1854

Harford. Jan 25th: 1854

My Dear Friend

I received your letter dated 15th: So now, I take my pen in hand (as the Lawyers say) to answer it. and believe me I was quite frightened when I saw the engraving underneath. and I hope that you will tell me who that happy fellow was that whent so far past his 63 rivels. I may—perhaps—come to town to learn a trade in the summer but I am going to school in Bel-Air to mor-row if nothing happens.[1] about the mederia. I can say nothing only that—his—nose is as bright as a chery. my respects to all, and excuse the shortness of this letter. but I expect you think it plenty long enough to answer, and excuse all faults. I still remain your Faithful Friend

John. W. Booth

Right soon

Autograph letter signed, Maryland Historical Society.

1. John Wilkes Booth received his earliest education at day schools near his Baltimore home. His first school was "kept by an old classical scholar named Smith. To this school he was sent while still in breeches, and here he was given the rudiments of an education" (David Rankin Barbee, "Lincoln and Booth," unpublished ms., Barbee Papers, Georgetown University Library, 211). In 1849, at the age of eleven, Booth began three years at Milton Academy, a Quaker boarding school in Cockeysville, Maryland. Located just twelve miles from the Booth farm at Bel Air, the school's three-story stone building contained a dormitory, school rooms, and a dining hall. A prospectus of the school survives in the files of the Maryland Historical Society. The *Circular of Milton Boarding School* states that the school's mission was "by a course of thorough instruction to prepare youths for college, or for a professional or mercantile life." Fees were $70 per term, with an additional $10 for Latin and Greek classes. In 1852 John Booth entered another boarding school, St. Timothy's Hall, in Catonsville, Maryland. At St. Timothy's, students wore the steel gray uniforms of artillery cadets. "The object of . . . St. Timothy's Hall," stated that school's prospectus, "is to make it an institution of strict discipline, of good morals, and, by the grace of God, a religious home for the young. [St. Timothy's is] a literary institution, for the education of young gentlemen whose appreciation of knowledge, and love of order, have made them diligent and patient of restraint." A year at St. Timothy's concluded Booth's education. He was fifteen years old.

To T. William O'Laughlen
Harford County, Maryland, 30 April 1854

Harford. April 30th: 1854

My Dear Friend

I was delighted to hear from you. I was thinking that I would receive a letter from you every day or else I would have written sooner. I am very sory that I cant come [to see?] the Hippodrome ~~But~~ ^For^ I have been from school so long that I have forggot how to spell and writght. so you must excuse it. There was a Ball in Bel-Air night before last. I was invited but did not attend on account of the storm. The country is beautiful now, evry thing is in blossom. and in about three weeks time Squirls will be fit for shooting. I should like you to come up then and give them a round. It was very stormy up hear all last week and the lightning knocked down ^nerly^ every telegraph post. There is no news that I can find, at present. I have got my eye on three girls out here. I hope I'll get enough. the next time you go to the Ne Plus drink my health and charge it to me. Indeed this is all I can find to say. but I guess you are tired of it already. I will now say good night. give my respects to all ~~th~~ ^who^ ask after me. and to those that don't, tell th[em] to kiss my Bumbelbee. Thine Till death.

J.W.B.
alias. Billy. Bow. Legs.[1]

P.S. ANSWER.SOON.

Autograph letter signed, private collection.

1. "There was a celebrated Indian Chief named Billy Bowlegs, and Wilkes went by this name among his companions at Catonsville." Asia Booth Clarke, *The Unlocked Book: A Memoir of John Wilkes Booth by His Sister* (New York: G. P. Putnam's Sons, 1938), 58. Like his father, JWB was conspicuously bowlegged.

To T. William O'Laughlen
Harford County, Maryland, 8 August 1854

Tudor Hall Aug 8th: 1854

My Dear Fellow.

In These last two weeks, I have had more excitement than I have had for a good while. First, and Foremost. I whent to a Champaign drinking. and you had better believe that the road (home) seemed longer that night than it ever did before. 2nd. we had a client on the place whom ^we could not^ agree with. we had several sprees with him in one he called my sister a Liar. I knocked him down, which made him bleed like a butc[he]r we got the Sherrf to put him off the place. he then Warrented me. and in a coupple of weeks. I have to stand trial. For assault. and battery. as you call it.[1] I paid another visit to the Rocks of Deer Creek[2] the other day. it looks just the same and sunday I whent to that large camp meeting[3] with the hope of seeing you there.

but I was dissipointed. I saw John Emlet there or that fellow that works in your shop. The Indian's where up here the other day with their great Bear. excuse my bad writing and excuse me also for not writing to you sooner. Give my respects to all who ask after me. I have nothing more to say.

Yours For Ever————John W. Booth write soon

Autograph letter signed, private collection.

1. JWB's sister describes this incident in some detail in the memoir of her brother she completed about 1874. Asia's memoir finally saw print as *The Unlocked Book* in 1938, a full century after the birth of its subject. Of John Booth's encounter with the surly tenant farmer, Asia recalled that "a man had the [Booths'] farm on shares. . . . He nearly ruined my mother [Mary Ann Holmes Booth, widowed since 1852] by purchases of guano, and then worked men, himself, and our beasts until her patience was exhausted. . . . Mother at last remonstrated, when he excitedly told her to 'mind her own business.' . . . [JWB was sent to secure an apology, which was not forthcoming.] 'Then,' said Wilkes, 'I'll whip you like the scoundrel you are.' And he let the stick fall heavily on the head and shoulders of the man who yelled out noisily that 'he was killed and murdered.'" Asia Booth Clarke, *The Unlocked Book: A Memoir of John Wilkes Booth by His Sister* (New York: G. P. Putnam's Sons, 1938), 99–101.

2. Rocks was a small town near Bel Air on Deer Creek, a tributary of the Susquehanna River. The Rocks themselves were a scenic attraction and a popular place for outings and picnics. Tournaments were held there each summer. Booth family historian Stanley Kimmel wrote, "On the announced day horsemen would appear at Deer Creek Rocks dressed in imitation armor of knights or ancient warriors. Bars were put up from which rings dangled and each horseman, carrying a long spear in his hand would rush his mount full speed towards the ring in an effort to spear them onto his lance." Kimmel, *The Mad Booths of Maryland* (Indianapolis: Bobbs-Merrill, 1940), 341–42. JWB probably attended these tournaments.

3. "On an occasion held to be of momentous interest to our Methodist people, everyone had been permitted to attend Camp Meeting. This was a sojourn in some woodland about ten miles distant [from Tudor Hall], and the whole congregation or community remained for a week or ten days, living and sleeping in tents or in camp. The religious exercises were of the most simple and unaffected kind, and these outdoor revivals were often productive of immense and serious good." Clarke, *The Unlocked Book*, 82.

To T. William O'Laughlen
Harford County, Maryland, 8 November 1854

November 8, 1854[1]

My Dear Friend

Indeed you must excuse me for not writting to you sooner, also for not calling on you when I was in the City. when next I see you I will give you my reasons for not calling on you . . . have had so much work all day and am so tired that I can not find time to write. It is very cold up here now, there was ice an inch thick the other day [. . .] Saw Jack King at the Fair [. . .] my Brother June[2] was here last week but he has gone back again . . . if nothing happens I expect to be in Baltimore in a few weeks [. . .] Remember me to all, and Believe me to be one of your best friends [. . .]

Autograph letter signed, full text not available, private collection.

1. JWB supported the American Party (the "Know-Nothing" Party) in the elections of November 1854. Shortly before he wrote this letter, JWB had served as a steward at an American Party rally near Bel Air. The principal speaker was congressional candidate Henry Winter Davis. Asia Booth Clarke, *The Unlocked Book: A Memoir of John Wilkes Booth by His Sister* (New York: G. P. Putnam's Sons, 1938), 106.

2. JWB's eldest brother, Junius Brutus Booth, Jr. (1821–83), was an actor and theatrical manager who was fully seventeen years older than Wilkes. June, who had been in California, visited Tudor Hall in the fall of 1854 with his wife, Clementine DeBar Booth, and their daughter, Blanche.

To T. William O'Laughlen
Harford County, Maryland, 25 January 1855

I should say the
home for travelers

Tudor Hall, Jan 25th: 1855

My Dear Friend.

I am at present seated in a very snug bar room by a comfortable log fire and the Poppular wood which is spitting and cracking and scending forth a merry blaze up the chimney puts me much in mind of home, and bye the bye it is home, but not my home. What I mean is that on the sign is ~~wrote~~ ^written^ the Home For Travelers. I don't know wether you are acquainted with the house or no, but I think you have past it, it is situate^d^ in Church Ville,[1] a very pleasent place, and I may say a very bad place, but no wonder, it has been an old saying (nearer the church nearer the devil). You said in your last letter that on Christmas day Bac[c]hus took the lead. Why my dear fellow, he always reigns in church ville ^either^ he or some other spirrit maker I don't know which. Bac[c]hus I believe was the god of whine but it seems that here Old Rye is the generel cry. the snow is about two inches deep on the ground now. I was passing here and it being very cold without I thought I would stop in a moment to warm myself. When I opened the door, I saw the same old thing a dozen fellows or more are around a sweet table, others playing cards. I did not want to play, borrow^ed^ Pen ink and Paper and write this to you. For Ever your affectionate Friend John W. Booth.

excuse my abrupt close but I am in a hurry.

Autograph letter signed, Chicago Historical Society.

1. Churchville, Maryland, was a village near Bel Air. Although JWB has headed the letter "Tudor Hall," he makes it clear that he is writing from a barroom in Churchville.

To T. William O'Laughlen
Harford County, Maryland, 18 June 1855

My Dear Friend.

I have been so taken up with pastimes and various amusements that I can scarcely find time to sleep, and it is something new to me, being a very late riser [. . .] The first week in June I was taken up by a Fair [. . .] I spent more time than money on it [. . .] for I was there night and day and you must not think I was blowing when I say I cut quite a dash. I saw pretty girls home from the Fair at ten o'clock at night, some at the distance of four or five miles [. . .] I have visited the Travelers home, or home sweet home[1] [. . .] The day after tomorrow I am invited to a strawberry eating and I promise you I will do my duty, and from then untill teusday I will do nothing but gun, ride, and sleep and eat [. . .] Then comes the grand affair. A Pick nick party to be held on the rocks of Deer crick.[2] Thirty-seven coupples to attend[3] [. . .] it is also an old saying that a Lawyer can lie like the Devil. I think they are like the devil also in making women content. The devil tempted mother Eve with an apple. I dont know wether Lawyers use apples or no, but they all tempt the ladies [. . .] for they have the means of revenge. hurah. I have wrote a long letter at last. try to answer it with one having as meny words and I am sattisfied. My Dear fellow I would finish this paper but my pen is so d—n bad, and by not writting for so long a time, I have forgotten how, but I will try and add I am your Faithful Friend, J. Wilkes Booth.

Autograph letter signed, full text not available, private collection.

    1. The Churchville tavern from which Booth wrote the letter of 25 January 1855.

    2. This "grand affair" apparently took place on 29 June. On 28 June 1854, JWB's sister Asia wrote to her friend Jean Anderson, "John is going on a picnic to the rocks tomorrow. Oh, those great rocks" (Asia Booth Clarke to Jean Anderson, Peale Museum, Baltimore).

    3. Here the description of the letter from the catalog of the 1966 Charles Hamilton auction at which the letter was sold adds that "Booth speaks enviously of local friends who have married wealthy girls."

To T. William O'Laughlen
Harford County, Maryland, 14 September 1855

Tudor Hall. Sept: 14th: 1855.

My Dear Friend,

    I received your letter the other day. I thought you did not intend to write to me, by your delaying it so long. I should have written long ago but I was waitting till I heard from you. I tried to see you on the night of my debut.[1] I saw Welch (I believe you know him) he said he would tell you to come out, but I expect he never did it. I am doing very well up here, but I am getting very tired of the country. I am thinking of moveing to Sebasterpol[2] you know there is some excitement there. and yet the country has been lively lately and next week there are two pick-nicks going on. and on the 25 there is a very large ball to be held in Bel-Air, and there are Plenty of Pigeons, Patriges and Sqrirrels for shooting. we are thinking of moveing to Baltimore in the winter but are not certain. I will be in Baltimore anyhow in October if nothing happens. you must excuse this dull letter, but I feel very low spirrited to day. Answer soon and try to write me a long letter. Give my respects to all who ask after me your Ever Affectionate Friend,

    J. W. Booth.

Autograph letter signed, the Railsplitter Archives, New York City.

1. John Wilkes Booth made his debut—his first professional appearance as an actor—on 14 August 1855 at the St. Charles Theatre in Baltimore. He played the Earl of Richmond, a major role, in Colley Cibber's popular adaptation of *Richard III.* He was billed under his own name and as the son of the great tragedian Junius Brutus Booth, who had died just three years before. Asia Booth Clarke remembered that after his first performance the young actor's "face shone with enthusiasm, and by the exultant tone of his voice it was plain that he had passed the test night. . . . Mother was not so pleased as we to hear of this adventure; she thought it premature, and that he had been influenced by others who wished to gain notoriety and money by the use of his name." Later, when he acted in Philadelphia and Richmond, Booth appeared under a pseudonym. Clarke, *The Unlocked Book: A Memoir of John Wilkes Booth by His Sister* (New York: G. P. Putnam's Sons, 1938), 107.

2. Apparently a reference to the Crimean War siege of the Russian Black Sea port city of Sevastopol.

To T. William O'Laughlen
Harford County, Maryland, 12 November 1855

Tudor Hall Nov 12th: 1855

My Dear Friend

It is too early yet for a light and too late to see without one, so you must excuse all, crossing the line. Allow me to appologise for not meeting you as was agreed on, you see I whent to the Fountain and found that Mother had Company so I was kept there till after nine Oclock and then had to show my galantry by going as far as broad Way. I returned to the Fountain, saw nothing of you. so with much disappointment I proceeded to the Holaday St:[1]

Things are going on fine in the Country. but I am getting tired—the excitement is all over. The Amer^ican^ ticket was elected by 1749 Majority in this County.[2]

Three Cheers for Amerrica.

    Yours truly

    J Wilkes Booth

Autograph letter signed, private collection.

1. These are Baltimore place names; "the Holaday St" is a reference to the Holliday Street Theater in Baltimore, where the Booths, father and sons, often appeared.

2. JWB had supported the American Party in the elections of November 1854, serving as a steward at an American Party rally near Bel Air. Two years later, during the 1856 presidential election, Asia Booth Clarke wrote that "men are all gone de-

ranged over their politics. We have two small flags crossed over the door, *Know Nothingism* of course. There was a meeting held opposite the shop a few days ago." Of the speeches she heard at this meeting, Asia continued, "I am afraid their delivery was like pouring water on stone, so little did the passionate orators seem to claim attention. I trust, like water, their influence may wash the filth from our country. Yes, I'm a know-nothing too, in its noblest and most ludicrous" (Asia Booth Clarke to Jean Anderson, 10 September 1856, Peale Museum, Baltimore).

Asia described the "Know-Nothing meetings" as "a so-called 'debating society,' where the question of putting a limit on white labor was contested. This, it was feared, would eventually supersede that of the blacks, and great privileges were falling too easily into the hands of the unnaturalized Irish immigrants." Although the American Party had virtually disappeared by 1860, nativist doctrines remained an important element of John Wilkes Booth's political thinking. He sounded very much like a Know-Nothing when he declared in 1864 that the supporters of Abraham Lincoln were "False-hearted, unloyal foreigners . . . who would glory in the downfall of the Republic." Asia Booth Clarke, *The Unlocked Book: A Memoir of John Wilkes Booth by His Sister* (New York: G. P. Putnam's Sons, 1938), 75, 125.

Newspaper Advertisements, Summer 1857, Baltimore

FOR SALE

THE SUBSCRIBER has for sale two valuable horses—one about 7 years old, and the other 8—both excellent work horses, working well in a single or double harness. One of them is a fine buggy horse. They will be sold on reasonable terms if early application is made to Alvin Herbert, Esq., Churchville.

JOHN BOOTH

FOR RENT—The splendid and well known residence of the late J. B. Booth, in Harford County, about three miles from Bel Air on the road leading to Churchville. This place will be rented to a good tenant if immediate application be made. There is 180 acres of land, 80 of which is arable. Address.

JOHN BOOTH
Baltimore, Md.

Two notices published in Pathways: The Journal of the Booth Family, Lincoln's Assassination and Historic Preservation Law 1 *(March 1985): 7. The only information regarding the source is a sentence reading, "The following ads were placed in a local newspaper in the summer of 1857 by John Wilkes Booth."*

To Edwin Booth
Richmond, 10 September 1858

Richmond Sept: 10th: 1858[1]

Dear Ted[2]

I would have written to you before this, but I have been so busily engaged, and am such a slow writter that I could not find time, I am rooming with H Langdon.[3] he has stoped drinking and we get along very well together. This climate dont agree with me. I have felt ill ever scince I have been here. I called on Dr. Beeal[4] soon after I arrived here. He and his Lady seem a very nice couple. I like them very much. He has put me under a course of medicine, the same I have been subject to before. I understand it is that, that makes me so languid and stupid. I have played several good parts. scince I have been here, Cool in London Ass[urance][5] last night. I believe I am getting along very well. I like the people, place, and management, so I hope to be very comfortable. There is only one objection and that is I believe every one knows me already. I have heard my name—Booth—called for. one or two nights, and on account of the *likeness*[6] the papers deigned to mention me. How are you getting along. I had hoped to hear from you before this. Give Mother my love. For I may not be able to write to her this week. as they are casting Miss Mitchells peices.[7] and I will have much to study. Excuse this dull letter. God bless you. write soon. And believe me I am ever your affectionate Brother.

John

Autograph letter signed, the Hampden-Booth Theatre Library at The Players, New York City.

1. This is the only letter known to survive from the period of John Wilkes Booth's theatrical apprenticeship from 1857 to 1860. His professional stage career began in 1857, when the nineteen-year-old son of one of America's most celebrated theatrical families joined the stock company of William Wheatley's Arch Street Theatre in Philadelphia. Philadelphia was then the most important theatrical city in America. The theater season usually began in late summer, running through the winter to end in early summer. Performances were not attempted in the hottest months. Booth played one such season as a stock actor in Philadelphia, from August 1857 to June 1858. In September 1858 he joined the stock company of the Richmond Theatre. He played stock for two seasons in the Virginia capital—September 1858 through May 1859 and September 1859 through May 1860. One Virginian remembered Booth during his Richmond period as "a man of high character & social disposition & liked by everyone with whom he associated. Was considered very handsome having coal black hair and eyes, and frequently wore, . . . a fur trimmed overcoat" (George Crutchfield to Edward V. Valentine, 5 July 1909, Valentine Museum, Richmond).

2. JWB performed twice with his brother Edwin in *Richard III* shortly before and after the date of this letter: at the Holliday Street Theatre in Baltimore on 27 August and at the Richmond Theatre on 1 October 1858. In both appearances JWB played Richmond to his brother's Richard III; in both instances he was billed under his true name—"Wilkes Booth." Of Wilkes Booth as a performer in 1858, Edwin Booth wrote, "I don't think he will startle the world . . . but he is improving fast and looks beautiful on the *platform*." Francis Wilson, *John Wilkes Booth: Fact and Fiction of Lincoln's Assassination* (Boston: Houghton Mifflin, 1929), 17.

3. Henry ("Harry") A. Langdon was then the leading man with the stock company of the old Marshall Theatre in Richmond, Virginia. JWB played supporting roles to Langdon's leads.

4. Dr. James Beal was a prominent Richmond physician. JWB was a frequent guest at his house, located on the same block as the Richmond Theatre, and there the young actor met the cream of Richmond society. JWB is said to have given a ring to Beal's little daughter, Mary. After news of Lincoln's murder reached Richmond, the ring was buried in the garden for fear that it might reveal the family's friendship with the assassin.

5. JWB played Cool in the play *London Assurance* on 9 September 1858. The comedy was written by the British actor and dramatist Dion Bouicault, whom Booth had supported in one of the latter's star engagements in Philadelphia. Gordon Samples, *Lust for Fame: The Stage Career of John Wilkes Booth* (Jefferson, N.C.: McFarland, 1982), 22.

6. JWB refers to the resemblance to his famous brother Edwin, noted by the newspapers despite the fact that the novice actor appeared under a pseudonym during his first season in Richmond. In October 1858 JWB's mother wrote that "Edwin is playing now in Richmond . . . John is in Richmond too & Edwin thinks he will get along first rate—he plays some very good parts—he played Richmond in Baltimore to Edwins Richard—& he acted very well—& looked well & his Voice is so like Edwins you could scarcely tell them apart." The proud mother also noted that her favorite son was earning $11 a week. (Mary Ann Holmes Booth to Junius Brutus Booth, Jr., 3 October 1858, Taper Collection.)

7. Margaret Julia ("Maggie") Mitchell (1837–1918) was one of the leading actresses of the day. She made a starring appearance at the Richmond Theatre for two weeks in the fall of 1858, opening on 13 September. The stock company of the theater, including JWB, supported her. Although born in New York, Maggie Mitchell was a Confederate sympathizer. During the Civil War, she liked to dance on an American flag. She and JWB became close friends in 1858 and often appeared together over the next few years. In December 1860 Maggie Mitchell gave JWB his first benefit (a special performance from which most proceeds went into a star actor's pockets).

To Mary C. White[1]
Acrostic verse inscribed in an autograph album
Richmond, 18 February 1860

Miss White.
May all good angels guard & bless thee.
And from thy heart remove all care.
Remember you should ne're distrest be.
Youth & hope, can crush dispare.

Joy can be found, by all, who seek it.
Only be, *right,* the path, we move upon.
Heaven has *marked* it: Find & keep it
Ne're forget the wish of—John.[2]

Richmond Febth: 1860
He who will ever be your friend

J. Wilkes Booth

Autograph manuscript signed, Taper Collection.

1. Mary White is probably the actress identified in a brief notice in T. Allston Brown, *History of the American Stage, Containing Biographical Sketches of Nearly Every Member of the Profession Who Has Appeared on the American Stage, from 1733 to 1870.* (New York: Dick and Fitzgerald, 1870), 391: "Attached to the Richmond, Va., Theatre for some time. Died 1860, in that city, June 20." The first page of the album contains an ownership signature: "Mary C. White, Richmond, December 10th 1859." There are no entries in the album after June 1860, the month of Mary White's death. The album also contains verses signed by actors Samuel K. Chester and George W. Wren, who were, like JWB and Mary White, members of the stock company of Richmond's Marshall Theatre during the 1859–60 season.

2. The first letters of the two stanzas obviously spell out the names of Mary and John.

"Allow Me a Few Words!":
John Wilkes Booth's Secession Crisis Speech of December 1860[1]

In the silence of three o'clock on a winter morning in 1873 Edwin Booth and a servant boy descended into the basement furnace room of Booth's Theatre in New York City. Waiting there was a trunk filled with belongings of John Wilkes Booth. Edwin Booth had chosen this secret time to destroy by fire these remnants of the dead brother of whom the great tragedian never spoke.

Over the next three hours, he and the boy fed into the furnace all the trunk's contents—costumes from *Hamlet, Othello,* and *Richard III,* wigs and jewelry, stage swords and daggers, a photograph, and a packet of love letters. Finally, they broke up the trunk with an axe and burned the wreckage, too. Sparks flew from the furnace, and the heat scorched the boy's face as he worked. It is hardly surprising that he never forgot the night. While the world slept, Edwin Booth gave over to fire what little remained of his brother, with the hellish glare of the subterranean furnace as it consumed the assassin's things suggestive of the perdition to which his memory had been consigned.[2]

But there was one important relic of Wilkes that Edwin Booth did not destroy, that he chose to preserve for the judgment of a future that he must have realized would always be fascinated by his brother's crime. That relic is the manuscript of a remarkable speech that John Wilkes Booth wrote, but probably never delivered, in Philadelphia during the last days of December 1860, less than two months after the election of Abraham Lincoln and a few days after South Carolina became the first of the Southern states to secede from the Union. A note in Edwin Booth's hand on the first page of the manuscript reveals that the speech was deliberately saved, not merely overlooked. Although unsigned and undated, the speech is entirely in the hand of John Wilkes Booth and can be dated with some exactness as having been written between about 22 and 27 December 1860.[3] Edwin Booth not only held the speech back from the flames, but he also kept it until his death in 1893 and saw to it that the manuscript was preserved at the actors' club and museum he founded in New York City—The Players. The manuscript is today a part of the collection of the Hampden-Booth Theatre Library at The Players.

One can only guess at Edwin Booth's motives for saving his brother's speech. In 1881 Edwin wrote that the Booth family regarded Wilkes "as a good-hearted, harmless, though wild-brained boy, and [we] used to laugh at his patriotic froth whenever secession was discussed. That he was insane on that one point, no one who knew him can well doubt. When I told him I had voted for Lincoln's re-election he expressed deep regret, and declared his belief that Lincoln would be made king of America; and this, I believe, drove him beyond the limits of reason. . . . All his theatrical friends speak of him as a poor, crazy boy, and such his family think of him."[4]

By revealing the almost hysterical fervency of John Wilkes Booth's passion for the cause of the South and that passion's wild, often disordered expression in the speech, Edwin Booth may have hoped that some day people would be able to see his brother as one misguided, unlucky, or insane rather than a figure of unalloyed evil. Here, more than a century after the death of Edwin Booth, John Wilkes Booth's secession crisis speech of 1860 is published for the first time by the kind permission of The Players.

◇◇

Booth probably wrote the speech while staying with his mother and sister Rose in a Philadelphia boardinghouse.[5] He had just made the all-important advance from a stock player to star, but his first star tour had been marred by an accident. His agent, Matthew Canning, had arranged for Booth to appear in Columbus, Georgia, and Montgomery, Alabama, supported by a stock company from New York.[6] Booth would star in roles that included *Romeo and Juliet, Hamlet,* and *Richard III.* But on 16 October 1860, in the dressing room of the Columbus Theatre, Canning was playing with a pistol. The gun went off, wounding the young star. The point at which the projectile entered Booth's body was variously described as "in the side," "in the fleshy part of the leg," "in the thigh," and "in the rear." Wherever it struck, the bullet inflicted an injury that prevented Booth's playing many of the roles scheduled for the rest of the tour. He spent more than a week recuperating at his hotel in Columbus before continuing on to Montgomery, Alabama, on 23 October.

Booth remained in Montgomery for more than a month, all through the intense excitement over the 1860 presidential election. (Lincoln was elected on 6 November, and Booth left Alabama to travel north to Philadelphia about 4 December.) The actor was undoubtedly caught up in the excitement. Montgomery was the home of William L. Yancey, a fire-eating secessionist and an influential defender of Southern rights. Booth may have heard Yancey deliver a fiery call for secession to a Montgomery audience the day before Lincoln's election, and he mentioned Yancey's views in his own speech. He may have also heard two other statesmen speak on the national crisis in Montgomery: Georgia Senator Robert Toombs, another fire-eater, and Democratic presidential candidate Stephen A. Douglas.

Booth wrote the twenty-page manuscript of his speech in a gathering of blank leaves stitched together into a thin booklet, a form in which stationers sold writing paper at the time. The main body of the speech is followed by several pages of material to be inserted into the running text and some fragments that Booth must have meant to work up into additional text. At more than five thousand words, the manuscript is by far the longest surviving document written by the actor. It is also the earliest, the most dramatic, and one of the most revealing of the handful of political testaments that John Wilkes Booth left behind. The manuscript is clearly a rough draft, which leaves off abruptly in midsentence.

Behind the soaring wildness of its words is the lofty presumption of a man who may have believed in 1860, as he would in 1865, that he, acting alone, could change history. But the views he expressed were shared by a good part of the population of the slave states, where so many were then raging, like John Wilkes Booth, for "equal rights and justice for the South." There were also many in the North who also believed that the crisis had been brought about by the systematic violation of Southern rights by Northern antislavery forces. First among those so convinced was the outgoing president, James Buchanan, who would remain in the White House until Lincoln was sworn in on 4 March 1861. Buchanan's last major state paper—his annual message to Congress of 3 December 1860—could have served as a text for portions of Booth's speech.[7]

The actor dramatically structured the address with a chorus of responses from his imaginary audience. "Gentlemen," he boldly began, "Allow me a few words! You every-where permit freedom of speech. You must not deny me now." Booth would have had little trouble imagining himself addressing a crowd; he had, after all, appeared before a good many large audiences over the previous five years. The audience he imagined may have been suggested in part by the "Grand Union meeting" that was held in Philadelphia on 13 December 1860, a week or so before Booth drafted his speech. The speech also shows the influence of the plays of Shakespeare, particularly *Julius Caesar*.[8] The words are sometimes ordered in Shakespearean cadences and driven by the furious, ranting language of the mid-nineteenth-century American theater. Although self-conscious about his limitations as a writer—he often appended to his letters the apology "excuse this hasty scrawl"—Booth was at times capable of language of some power. There are such passages in his 1860 speech. The speech has been described by some as Booth's plea for the preservation of the Union, but it is actually a call to counter-revolution, a demand to restore the old supremacy of slave power in the federal government that had prevailed through much of the first half of the nineteenth century.

The Union rally held in Philadelphia on 13 December 1860 figures importantly as one of the inspirations for the speech. Booth had just concluded his tour of Georgia and Alabama when he arrived in Philadelphia in mid-December to spend the Christmas holidays with his mother and sisters and his brother Edwin. Philadelphia, like the rest of the nation, was in turmoil over the extraordinary constitutional crisis provoked by Abraham Lincoln's election and the probable secession of the Lower South slave states. Pennsylvania bordered two Upper South slave states, Maryland and Delaware, and many Pennsylvanians regarded their state as a sort of bridge between the country's two antagonistic sections.

Philadelphia was also a mercantile city with longstanding economic ties to the South. Despite the fact that Lincoln had carried both the city and the state in the presidential election in November, there remained considerable sympathy for the South. Many Philadelphians despised the abolitionists, whose ideology seemed to threaten to destroy trade. By the end of 1860 Philadelphia merchants were already losing their Southern customers, and they feared worse to come. When an antislavery leader proposed making a speech in Philadelphia, the threat of riot caused his appearance to be canceled. Instead, Philadelphia Mayor Alexander Henry called for a "Grand Union demonstration" on 13 December in the square near Independence Hall, the venerable building that had been the scene of the signing of the Declaration of Independence and the drafting of the Constitution.

Now the great republic framed by those documents was about to break apart. Outraged by Lincoln's election, South Carolina would declare its independence from the Union on 20 December. Other slave states seemed sure to follow. The Philadelphia rally was called because of the "serious peril of the dissolution of the union of these states, under whose protection we have grown to a great and prosperous nation." Citizens were urged "to counsel together to avert the danger which threatens our country." Businesses and stores would close for two hours, and delegations of factory workers would march. More than ten thousand people showed up. John Wilkes Booth may have been among them. Even if he did not attend the rally, Booth could have read the day's speeches in Philadelphia newspapers.

If he was there, Booth would have heard the speakers—who included Mayor Henry, Theodore Cuyler, Joseph R. Ingersoll, and George W. Woodward—condemning Northern extremists for driving the Southern states out of the Union. (A banner reading "Concession before Secession" summed up the aim of the rally and the tone of the speeches.) "Many good citizens still believed that Philadelphia's duty was that of an arbitrator between the extremists of both North and South," one writer explained.[9] But the rally's leaders seemed to believe that it was the South that had been wronged. They pushed through resolutions urging strict enforcement of the fugitive slave laws, opening the federal territories to slavery, and calling for an end to "all denunciations of slavery" and slaveholders as "inconsistent with the spirit of brotherhood and kindness."[10] The resolutions were forwarded to South Carolina, but the citizens of that state, by then committed to secession, took no notice.

Some of those attending the rally were disgusted by the pro-Southern tone of the speeches, and some must have been puzzled to hear that toleration of human slavery was in keeping "with the spirit of brotherhood and kindness." John Wilkes Booth, on the other hand, would have been well pleased. It must have appeared to him that most Philadelphians agreed with him in blaming the secession crisis on abolitionists and Northern extremists.

When he wrote his own speech a week or so later, Booth used many of the ideas and some of the language of the speakers on the platform that day. It is easy to imagine that the twenty-two-year-old actor was inspired by the notion of himself addressing some kind of mass rally like the 13 December meeting. It was a time in which oratory was much admired, and young men studied the master speeches of American statesmen such as Daniel Webster, Henry Clay, and John C. Calhoun. Booth's sister wrote that the "oratorical powers of the cadets at St. Timothy's [the boarding school Booth attended] were, without doubt, encouraged and cultivated; stump-speaking was the delight of those youths who longed to make their voices heard throughout the country. It was almost a bad school for fostering the wild ambition born in Wilkes Booth."[11]

John Wilkes Booth also had personal knowledge of two of the most divisive episodes of the decade of growing sectional antagonism that preceded the Civil War: the fugitive slave "riot" in Christiana, Pennsylvania, in 1851, and John Brown's raid on Harpers Ferry in 1859. Both had sharpened Booth's indignation over the injustices he believed the North was visiting on the South. He referred to both violent events in his speech.

The Christiana riot was a sensational incident in which a group of abolitionists and escaped slaves defied the federal Fugitive Slave Act of 1850 by violently resisting a U.S. marshall and a posse of slave-catchers who had pursued four Maryland runaways into Pennsylvania. Confronting the abolitionists, Maryland farmer Edward Gorsuch, the owner of the four fugitives, vowed that "my property is here, and I will have it or perish in the attempt."[12] But the armed and defiant black men he confronted insisted that human beings could not be another's property, and they were prepared to defend that proposition with their lives. A few minutes later Edward Gorsuch lay dead on the ground—shot, stabbed, and bludgeoned. When the men who did the killing, brought to trial for treason by federal authorities, were acquitted by a Pennsylvania jury, the South reacted with outrage.

Edward Gorsuch's youngest son, Thomas, was a good friend of John Wilkes Booth. Young Booth must have heard from his friend how a gang of "nigger abolitionists" had murdered his father only to be set free by a Yankee jury. To Booth, the Christiana riot and the acquittal of the accused were injustices that called out for revenge. Throughout his speech, Booth calls again and again for "justice for the South." Among other things, "justice" meant the strict enforcement in the North of the fugitive slave law and the speedy return of runaways to their Southern masters.

In October 1859 John Brown led his little band of followers on the famous raid on the federal arsenal at Harpers Ferry, Virginia. Brown hoped to seize thousands of muskets and incite a slave rebellion with a guerrilla army fighting from mountain strongholds. He was overwhelmed and captured by federal troops, swiftly tried and condemned of treason by Virginia, and sentenced to be hanged. Brown's raid galvanized the nation and greatly increased Southern distrust of the North. As the date of Brown's execution approached, the Virginia militia was called out to thwart any attempt to save the old man. Booth talked his way into one of the militia companies, the Richmond Grays, and spent about two weeks on duty. He witnessed John Brown's hanging. Although Booth differed so radically from Brown in his convictions, the abolitionist became a kind of hero to John Wilkes Booth. "John Brown was a man inspired," Booth told his sister, "the grandest character of the century!"[13] In his speech Booth fiercely insisted that all abolitionists were traitors like John Brown, and that, if they did not cease their agitation against slavery, all of them deserved Brown's fate.

---

1. The editors are indebted to the research of Jeannine Clarke Dodels on Booth's 1860 speech: "Water on Stone: A Study of John Wilkes Booth's Political Draft Preserved at the Players Club NYC," unpublished manuscript, copy in possession of Louise Taper; and Dodels, "John Wilkes Booth's Secession Crisis Speech of 1860," in *John Wilkes Booth, Actor: The Proceedings of a Conference Weekend in Bel Air, Maryland, May 1988*, ed. Arthur Kincaid (North Leigh, Oxfordshire: Published privately, 1989), 48–52.

2. Otis Skinner, *Footlights and Spotlights: Recollections of My Life on Stage* (Indianapolis: Bobbs-Merrill, 1924), 179–84. The contents of the trunk included some of the theatrical props and costumes Booth had sent in late 1864 from Canada on a blockade-runner bound for the Confederacy. After the ship sank, the trunk's ruined contents were sold at auction; most of the material eventually came into the possession of Edwin Booth. Stanley Kimmel, *The Mad Booths of Maryland* (Indianapolis: Bobbs-Merrill, 1940), 189.

3. The speech was written after "Crittenden's Compromise" (a proposed constitutional amendment aimed at placating the South by legislatively protecting slavery) was rejected in Senate committee on 22 December, because Booth refers to that event. It was probably written before 27 December, when the country learned that Maj.

Robert Anderson, commander of the U.S. garrison in Charleston, S.C., had secretly shifted his command from Fort Moultrie to the more defensible Fort Sumter in Charleston harbor. The news of Anderson's move was momentous enough that it seems likely that Booth would have made reference to it had he been writing after it took place. Dodels, "Water on Stone," 14–15.

4. Edwin Booth to Nahum Capen, 28 July 1881, in Edwina Booth Grossman, *Edwin Booth: Recollections by His Daughter* (New York: Century, 1894), 227–28.

5. "John Booth is at home. He is looking well but his wound is not entirely healed yet—he still carries the ball in him. . . . Mother & Rose are boarding in Marshall Street at a private home. John also" (Asia Booth Clarke to Jean Anderson, Philadelphia, 16 December 1860, Peale Museum, Baltimore).

6. Matthew W. Canning, a Philadelphia lawyer, had given up the law for the theater. By October 1860 his Canning Dramatic Company, with John Wilkes Booth as star actor, had engagements at a pair of theaters in the Deep South: the Columbus Theatre in Georgia and the Montgomery Theatre in Alabama. Canning met JWB in July 1860. In July 1863 he made several engagements for JWB, but Booth backed out and their relations cooled. Booth wrote a $100 check to Canning on 16 December 1864. Ten years later, a sketch in the *National Republican* described Canning as "a good-natured looking man, although his stock of patience sometimes gives out, and his temper becomes more easily 'riled' than that of the manager. Canning is a blonde, wears a nice goatee, brilliant diamonds and neatly-fitting clothes. He is scrupulously neat, and his shirt bosom presents a spotless appearance. His hat and boots shine like the white of a colored 'gemmen's' eye, and his hand is always full of bills, which he never pays out without first scrutinizing in the closest manner. Canning is an experienced manager, and has done a good deal of business with many eminent artists, . . . he is a master of details, very active, and an enthusiast in his profession" (16 February 1874).

7. James Buchanan, *The Works of James Buchanan*, ed. John B. Moore (Philadelphia: J. P. Lippincott, 1910), 9:7–54.

8. JWB had performed Mark Anthony's speech from *Julius Caesar* as recently as 20 October 1860 at the Columbus Theatre in Columbus, Georgia.

9. Frank F. Taylor, *Philadelphia in the Civil War: 1861–1865* (Philadelphia: Published by the City, 1913), 11–12.

10. In 1860 Philadelphians had returned a fugitive slave to his Southern master, the attempt of which had provoked riots in other Northern cities. Russell F. Weigley, ed., *Philadelphia: A Three-Hundred-Year History* (New York: W. W. Norton, 1982), 392; Ellis P. Oberholtzer, *Philadelphia: A History of the City and Its People* (Philadelphia: S. J. Clarke, 1912), 2:357.

11. Asia Booth Clarke, *The Unlocked Book: A Memoir of John Wilkes Booth by His Sister* (New York: G. P. Putnam's Sons, 1938), 59–60.

12. Jonathan Katz, *Resistance at Christiana: The Fugitive Slave Rebellion, Christiana, Pennsylvania, September 11, 1851* (New York: Thomas Y. Crowell, 1974), 90–100.

13. Clarke, *The Unlocked Book*, 124.

[Draft of a Speech]
Philadelphia, late December 1860[1]

Gentlemen

Alow me a few words! You every-where permit freedom of speech. You must not deny me now. My fellow countrymen Can I use the liberty of speech among ye. If so hear me. I will not keep you long. So be patient, silent and indulgent, to one, who deeply feels his countrys woes, And would give his life to ~~save~~ ^help^ her. So hear me conservatives of the North,[2] And fellow Countrymen from whatever section you may come, or to whatever party you may belong.

I wish to speak, not for the sake of being looked at, ~~and~~ ^or^ talked about. But to vindicate myself in the steps I intend to take. I am a northern man.[3] But unlike most Northerners, I have looked upon both sides of this question. I am confident that you are not afraid to hear the truth, however bitter it may be. And all I ask is that you will hear me to the end. And then if need be, I will answer one and all. I don't intend to argue, but to speak clearly ^of^ what I ~~think and~~ know, and what I intend to do. I will not fight ^for^ cesession.[4] No I will not fight for disunion. But I will fight with all my heart and soul, even if theres ~~are none~~ ^not a man^ to back me, for eaqual rights[5] and justice to the South. As I would do for the North in the like position. So hear me without interruption to the end, and then you can do with me as you please.^[6] Now, Mr. Thedore Cuyler[7] in his speech of Dec 13th: says that liberty of speech and licence of speech are very different things. I agree with him and can safely say, It is that very liberty of speech *abused,* which has brought us to the brink upon which we stand, You will all admit my liberty of speech does not extend to my speaking my mind freely in society, or I should be kicked out. No more does it warrant my useing profane language in a church. Then why should free use of speech have license to destroy a country, What, think you, Would our revolutionary fathers have said & done if during the childhood of their dear bought liberty ~~If~~ men with false views stood forth to cry down freedom. And applaud a King. Would they not have considered all such men (if such there were) as torys & trators who could even harbor a thought hurtful to their country ~~and~~ ^or^ their ^countrys^ freedom, Were such men allowed to go through the land spreading their seditious opinions among our patriotic fathers, trying to instill in those noble hearts a love for slavery & contempt of liberty. No, would those Old defenders have alowed a Trator to hiss his poisonous breath within their very homes, Answer me my countrymen. *No.* Then where was ~~his~~ ^their^ liberty of speech. And yet my

friends I regret to know that we have such men in our midst. who unmindful of the benefits they have derived from the great boon our fathers left us.
Unmindful of that liberty which cost them years of toil and blood to gain.
who are continually preaching and crying. O we cannot govern for ourselves
we ought to have a great central government. Others (a little more moder-
ate) say the Presidents term is too short, they he should be elected for life,
bah! such men would throw away their great birthright and kiss the feet of a
King to morrow.[8] Heed me, there are such of whom I speak. Aye. both north
& south. Is our liberty less dear to us now, than it was to our fathers of 76?[9] I
should hope not, for freedom is a star ~~what~~ ^that^ should never dim. Then
what should be done with such men who are cold to all the blessings of ^the^
freedom ^they possess?^ who laugh at our country as it is. Scoff at her institutions as they are, And who not only would cry for a King, but endeavor
to lead others in their views and spread their d—d opinions throughout the
land. Now I call it treason to our common country, and it should not be
alowed. dont you, my friends. Aye. then where is their liberty of speech. I tell
you that liberty of speech can be abused and should not be tollerated to the
abuse thereof. Men have no right to entertain opinions which endanger the
safety of the country. Such men ~~who~~ ^I^ call trators and treason should be
~~crushed~~ ^stamped to death^ and not allowed to stalk abroad in any land. So
deep is my hatred for such men that I could wish I had them in my grasp
And I the power to crush. I'd grind them into dust! My friends I will not tire
you but answer what I ask you in one word. Ay, or no. Do you not call it treason for men to entertain & advocate opinions which are hurtful to their country. which will destroy her peace and her prosperity.[10] Do you not call it treason, *Aye.* Then what are they who preach the Abolition doctrine who have
in doing so ^nigh^ destroyed our country. I call them trators. So do you, but
you dont like to use so harsh a term, for there are many in this state, why do
you allow them to abuse the liberty of speech freedom of opinion. Is it because they are Penslavanians, and their opinion and actions interfere not with
their own state ^or her institutions^ Of course it is or you would soon find
away to stop them. Now I never could understand this sectional feeling, (if I
may so call it) True in time of peace it may be a blessing, as it stimulates a
generous rivalry to make our country great, But in times like these it is a heavy
curse. Now Yancy[11] says if his ~~country~~ ^state^ goes out ^of the union^ he
must go with her, of course he means if ^she's^ right or wrong. I spoke with
some New Yorkers in the south,[12] and men from other states, who said of
course they would abide by the desision of their ^individual^ states. I expect they meant ^to do so^ even if their state had a majority of (what I call

trators). Now I believe in *country* right or wrong, but gentlemen the whole union is our country and no particular state. We should love the whole union and not only the state in which we were born. We are all one people, and should have but ^one wish^ one object, one heart. Thank God I have a heart big enough for all the states. If Main was wronged by her sister states, and struck for justice, Id fight for Main. If Florida was wronged by her sister states, Id fight for Florida. If Delaware was wronged by her sister States, I'd fight for Delaware, And so for all the rest, though I struck the first blow at my own dear Maryland. If this sectional feeling is so strong we may as well say we will only fight for the house in which we first drew breath. Or only for the mother that bore us, or in fact we wont fight at all. No gentlemen the whole union is our country, And the Cry for justice should be heard & heeded from whatever extremity it may come. The south wants justice, has waited for it long, she will wait no longer. You have not aided her or even heeded her cryes, because you have thought I am not a Southern man, it hurts not me. But you find now that it dose. You have commenced to feel that you are southern men. You find now that your interests are as much South as North, what destroys her institutions & happiness will destroy your own. ^The^ Laws have not been enforced that would protect southern rights, others have been passed to enfringe ~~those~~ rights.[13] She has ~~cryed~~ called for justice in vain; we of the North have promised & promised but that has been all. At length she pleads no more so again we promise, will she have faith in our empty words, can she trust them without a proof they will be kept. No and if she can she deserves her fate. You Philadelphians have acted nobly! True you have done much to reconcile her.[14] But she cannot be reconciled. She cannot live, while the republican principals[15] still exist! Oh my friends you think not of their situation. You are troubled but will not act. It would be otherwise if you had a plauge [plague] among you and knew the cause from which it came. You'd root it out! If a foe did wrong, you'd be revenged. Why not then use justice and revenge to right the states, and save the Union. My friends, do not misinterpret my words, but understand me clearly. I would not have you violate our country's laws. I would not have you break our city's ordinance. But I could wish you would prove to the south, with deeds, instead of words, that she shall have those rights which she demands, *those rights which are her due.*[16] I tell you Sirs if the south does not cecede. If she stays in the Union and the abolition principles are not entirely swept away, why we have but smoothed our troubles o're, which in a few years will burst forth with redoubled horror. Now that we have found the serpent that madens us, we should crush it in its birth. Not wait for time and peace to give it strength & courage to destroy. We should act with coolness and judgment, all should be done in peace. For God be my witness that I love peace, that I would give my all to maintain it, but Gentlemen there is a time when peace becomes a burden. There is a time when men should act for themselves and not under the guidance of a few political leaders who use ^them^ only for their own ends, I tell you Sirs when treason weighs heavy in the scale, it is a time for us to throw off all gentler feelings of our natures and summon resolution, pride, justice, Ay, and revenge, to take the place of those nobler passions in the human heart, respect, forgiveness and Brotherly-love. O. God, what a dismal future have we before us, If our *curse* can be smoothed over only for the time, to break forth again when ere it will, dark, dark, indeed. Yet some there are, who lightly think and say. There's naught to fear. all will be bright soon. As if the future was but to morrow. Who is there here can look towards that aweful page and say to himself there, there is peace & happiness waiting to embrace us. Who, who is there, my friends that does not shudder when he contemplates what a few years may bring to light. When he sees this once glorious republic on the decline to ruin and disgrace, and a portion of its sons becoming trators, not only to their brethern, their children and their truth, But to the memory of their Sires, their country and their God. Can you with unmoved souls see the land, where once dwelt love and Joy, fretted by internal dissentions? To see the land where dwell *our fathers our mothers, our hearts, our loves, our all,* upon the fearful brink of self-distruction. O what a triumph for the crowned world will it be to see this once proud union bend its head unto the dust! To see the bird that is the emblem of our freedom and our strength break its majestic pinions and fall fluttering to the earth. To see this glorious fabric shivered into atoms and each weak part (like Greece in days of Yore) entreating the protection of some foreign power. *Must this be so.* Can we but aim at self-aniallation, can we only carress our foes & fight our friends? Will you. Will You my brothers destroy this union. Can you tear down this great temple of civilation. This Monument of our father's greatness. The banner that has marked our freedom, that has protected our infancy, encouraged our youth, and sheltered our age for a set of deluded fools. An Abolition crew, who have naught to lose—No—not even love of country- in this great crush of states.

The South is leaving us. O would to God that Clay & Webster[17] could hear those words. Weep fellow countrymen, for the brightest half of our stars upon the nations banner have grown dim. Once quite out my friends, all will be dark and dreary. Where once reigned shuch a dazzling & celestial light to strike with awe the enthronéd Monarchs of the universal world. I tell you sirs it is now the time to act, not to think. Or do we love our warm firesides, more than our country. if so, we should stay in doors & let things take their course. No indeed, we do not. I feel that your country is foremost in your hearts, and you love her institutions more than aught in life, something must be done. We cannot condemn the faults of our brothers in the South till we pick out the beam from our own eyes. You all feel the fire now raging in the nations heart. It is a fire lighted and faned by Northern fanaticism.[18] A fire which naught but blood & justice can extinguish. I tell you the Abolition doctrine is the fire which if alowed to rage—will consume the house and crush us all beneath its ruins. Shall we my Brothers be destroyed on account of these Abolition leaders, (It is the leaders not the mass..) the mass! why ^they^ are nothing, they know nothing, they go it blind, they are fed only by that word freedom and understand it not. They see not that *such freedom* is slavery for ourselves. That it is breaking up our peace, our union, and our power.

My fellow Countrymen, I am no pollitician nor did ever speak in public on the present subject. I may perhaps have leaped (in my speech) the bounds of prudence. But I am a great lover of my country and cannot curb my feelings when I see her (as I see her now) sinking slowly into ruin. And in sooth my friends, I have been in constant dread scince my speech began, lest some mouthing pollitician should call upon me to answer questions, or argue this, or that subject. I cannot argue. I am gifted with no such powers. But I can tell you the truth which is better than argument all the world over. I can tell you the truth, shuch as you know it to be yourselves! I can use my weak voice and perhaps *vain endeavors* to call you back to reason. To fan the dieing embers of patriotism now slumbering in your hearts. To wake that love of country which I know you to possess. Indeed *I* love her so that I oft mentally exclaim, *with Richelieu.*[19] O my native land let me but ward this dagger from thy heart! and die upon thy bossom. ~~Indeed I love her so~~ Such is my love that I could be content to crawl on to old age. With all the curses, that could be heaped upon me, *to see her safe from this coming tempest!* If there is any man here who can lay his hand upon his heart and say he would not do the same, *that man* I deem unworthy to hear me. But I am sure there is no such man. Would you not all die to save your country. Yes. I know you would. Why then will you allow her to destroyed. The cesessionists of the south say that all argument has been exausted, that they can and will use it no more. ~~If~~ we have been deaf to the voice of justice. We cannot blame them. What is to be done? If argument has no more resources, it is time for all good citizens who are, or would be conservative to their country, in, this, her hour of need to come to action. And not stand Idly by hoping to save a country by *fast* and *Prayer.*[20] O, my brothers, think of the peaceful dead who for years have been moldering in their shrouds. Think of the lives nobly spent and lost in rearing aloft this great temple of liberty. Think of all the blood spilled to cement the work. Think upon the actions of our fathers, who endured evry privation, who even died to secure to us (their sons) this glorious heritage of freedom. A heritage unstained by injustice, unstained by treason, unstained by any wrong, a heritage upon which God smiled and poured his blessings. A heritage which the memory of our fathers, *Commands us to maintain.* Do you think my brothers that the spirit of those peaceful dead will smile upon us when this union is destroyed. No No this union must and shall be preserved.[21] We'l all stand by her, And keep her in her original purity, or die. Grant but impartial justice and our country will stand the shock of ages. Ay, grant love to all, justice to all. With death to trators and she can never die. I would go on but know not what to say ^to^ you, you are all better judges of this subject than I, I am ~~gifted with no power of oration~~ unused to speak upon the spur ^of^ the moment. I am gifted with no powers of oration but am a mear child a boy, to some I see around me. A child indeed and this union is my Mother. A Mother that I love with an unutterable affection. You are all her children, and is there no son but I to speak in its Mother's cause. O would that I could place my worship for her in anothers heart, in the heart of some great orator, who might move you all to love her, *to help her now when she is dieing.* No, No. I wrong you. You all do love her. You all would die for her. Yet hesitate upon the way to save her. God grant, it may be done in a peaceful way. If not, it must be done with blood. Ay with blood & justice. The South is leaving us. She has been wronged. Ay wronged. She has been laughed at, preayed upon and wronged. Tis I a northern man that tells you so for I have no interest in the south more than in all the union. She must be reconciled. How can she. Why ^as I said before^ with naught but justice. The Abolition party must throw away their principals. They must be hushed forever. Or else it must be done by the punishment of her aggressors. By justice that demands the blood of her oppressors. By the blood of *those,* who in wounding her have slain us all, with naught save blood and justice. Ay blood, in this case, should season justice. You may not agree with me. Yet ~~John Brown was executed~~ thousands do. The whole South does. For John Brown was executed (yes, and justly) by his country's laws for attempting in another way, mearly what these abolitionists are doing now. I saw John Brown hung[22] And I blessed the justice of my contrys laws. I may say I helped to hang John Brown and while I live, I shall think with joy upon the day when I saw the sun go down upon one trator *less* within our land.[23] His treason was no more than theirs, *for open force is holier than hidden craft. The Lion is more noble than the fox.* O My friends would I had the eloquence of a Dimothanies or a Ciciro[24] that I might speak what you would heed. O would I could tell you the result of things, If left to take their course (as I fear they will be) And I would try and picture to you the miserys we all must suffer. I would try ~~and~~ to show ~~to~~ you the desolation of the north. The vessels in our ports rotting to decay, riots in our streets growing to rebellion. Our working men with naught to do but starve & quarrel. Our poor labouring & factory girls who's only dowery *now* is their truth and industry. O what a fate is theirs. Will they not dayly pray to God. with sunken cheeks & hollow eyes for curses upon them that have torn away their dayly bread. Many will say this is not so. for let the worst come to the worst it will be a peaceful cesession. bah there is no such thing.[25] Did not our great Webster himself affirm it.[26] Others may think at all events trade will be preserved. Ay, But how Europe will have the advantage of her trade. We will have to pay at double the rate for things which are now too high. A dirth of industry will infest the land. Famine will range around, Banks will fail. Familys ruined. Poor widow's who want their little mite to rear their children, will point to the famished stricken forms of their dear infants, And look towards you with water-standing eyes. And say to you, *You might have prevented this.* I *hope* may I never live to see that day, even should it follow soon, when we are no more a united nation. When our flag must submit to insult and bow to scorn. Such misery would soon make us realise the blessing of the heaven we had lost! Remorse would be so keen you could not live, You would hate and envy the confederation of the south. You would say she is weak in numbers, we are strong. We will force her to submit and once more restore the union. The South will call in the powers of Europe. Fearce Civil War will follow. And then, what then. *Why God alone can tell the rest,* even if this be true. Say it is not my countrymen say the picture's false (as I hope it is) Say that you will be rich and prosper in everything, and the South be weak & poor, that she would crawl in the dust before you. Is that a cause you should deny her equal rights & justice. Is that a cause for her to be trod upon. *Is that a cause for you to slight the constitution & the countrys laws. Is that a cause for you to allow men to break the union & destroy your countrys peace. No God forbid it No, You are too wise, too good, too just. Ill speak no more, think upon what I have said. For we can not live without the union as it was. The Union our fathers made. The union which God has blessed, And the flag of that union forever*

Now I don't mean to admit ~~the right of~~ ^that the south should^ ceceed nor do I believe a state can ceceed without revolution & blood-shed. But gentlemen ~~this great union~~ the foundation of this great union was justice &

eaqual rights. Our fathers ~~fought for justice & eaqual rights~~ ceseeded in a measure from the power of England. They fought for justice and for eaqual rights. They freed themselves, this country which they built was founded upon justice. Sweep away that foundation: deny that justice and anything Ay even cession is warrantable. For that *Treasure* gone it is then no longer the union ^that^ they ~~have~~ pledged themselves to maintain. Gentlemen I am no alarmest. But I am surprised to see men look on with so much indifference at a sinking count[r]y Meny laugh at the cesession of South Carolina thinking that she will come back or that we will force her back or that if she stays out, we will never miss her. It is shear folly, to reason so, And then again there are meny who are for instant coercion. That is madness. The first attempt at force will be the cue for every southern state to aid her. South C[aroli]na could wish for nothing better than an attempt at coercion, for it would speedily link togeather the southern states in one vast confederation Besides gentlemen she is fighting in a just cause with God himself upon their side. We must not use force against her. if we do then are we greater tyrants! Than George the 3d: ever was towards our fathers! Yet she must be brought back and it must be done with compromise. The only ^Mr. Critenden's^[27] compromise that could ^have^ saved us has been laid upon the table, to be rejected by whom? why, by northern men. Gentlemen, I don't believe that any ~~northern state~~ of us are represented truly in Washington. For if that compromise was put to the vote of the people it would be carried by an overwhelming majority. The men there are abolitionist and are determined to gain their ends regardless of the consequences! South Ca[roli]na is not lost ^yet^ when She is the whole south is lost with her, What has been the cause of all this why nothing but the constant agitation of the slavery question.[28] Much. Too much has been said upon that ~~question~~ subject. I'll touch it lightly, yet enough to show my views. First I ~~think~~ know that the South has a right according to the constitution to keep and hold them. And we have no right under that constitution to interfere with her or hers. And instead of looking upon slavery as a sin (mearly because I have none) I hold it to be a happiness for themselves and a social & political blessing for us. Yet say it is a sin how can it hurt you. You are free of it! The guilty only must be answerable to God for their respective guilt! He can not condemn me for the crime of anothers. Nor a nation for having in it a few bad men. Friends can sin and happiness ^live together in^ the same brea[s]ts. A sin—a lame excuse; It is not a sin. I have been through the whole South and have marked the happiness of master & of man. Take every individual and you will find the happiness greater there than here. True I have seen the Black man w[h]ip[p]ed but only when he deserved much more than he received. And had an abolitionist used the lash, he would have got double. You know it is not a sin. and if it was. The Constitution forbids you to interfere with it. Now what should we call men who break the constitution.

My friends, I wish to tread on no mans corns if I do tis in my countrys cause and his corns should yeald. Yet would I enquire if that is the only sin you will have to answer for. Have you grown so good so gospell like that you must clense others of their sins before you remove your own. If that Sin you fight against is so gross so palpable. Strange our fathers who were christians ay and men of sounder judgment than any we now possess, should have failed to see it. A sin: nonsense you never saw it as such, until it became unprofitable, And you would even now share in that sin, And you would even now share in that sin, if it was necessary to you and could be made to pay. We have said enough upon that head. Now for another corn. Skillful doctors will always find the source of the disease before they attempt a cure. The Revd: Mr. Beecher[29] generaly when he speaks, commences his sermon or what ever you may call it! By lauding you to the skys with praise. He speaks of your free press. Your great liberty of speech, while he takes shelter behind this and his white cravat! to belie his profession. And speak his treason.

What Sir is the object of a free press. Should it not be a type of truth & justice. Is it not its duty to enlighten the world, to promote concilation, to drag hidden guilt to light, to reward merit, to encourage industry, art, sciences & literature. ~~Can it do all this without truth for its motto. Can a paper be just that exaggerates the evils of mankind. And~~ Is it not (what Shakespeare says of the drama) to hold as it were the Mirror up to Nature, to show virtue her own feature.[30] Scorn her own image & the very age and body of the time its form & presence. Can it do all this without truth and justice for its motto. Can a paper be just that exaggerates the evils of man, and turns his good into crime. Can a paper be just which shows only one side of a question, leading its readers into darkness and despare. Show me a paper and for one word of truth you can find a hundred lies. Calculated to lead mankind into folly & ^into^ vice Ay false master which has brought on all these troubles by which we are surrounded instead of binding us closer in a loving brotherhood. It belies its calling: that is my view of it as a northern man. I am not a southerner, but viewing it as a southern man I will speak of it thus, It belies its calling. It makes me hate my brothers in the north. It severs all our bonds of friendship. It induces our brothers in the north to deny us our rights, to plunder us, to rob us! But he who steals my purse steals trash.[31] It does more than that. It filches from me my good name which not enriches him, but makes me poor indeed. It ~~induces~~ misrepresents me to the whole world. It induces all without our circle to look upon me as a hethen. It does more that all that; it induces my ^very^ servant to poison me at my meals, to murder me in my sleep.[32] It induces our very government to deny us the rights of man. It is unjust, untruthfull. It should be looked to. As there be a limit to every power, I ground this not upon individual cases, but upon rights of states and institutions.

What right have you to exclude southern rights from the teritory Because you are the strongest? I have as much right to carry my slave into the teritory as you have to carry your paid servant or your children.

The fugitive slave law. Gentlemen, when I was a school boy, my bossom friend was a boy 3 years my senior named Gorruge [Thomas Gorsuch],[33] he was as noble a youth as any living. He had two brothers grown to be men. And and an old father who loved and was beloved by them. He was all that a man of honour should be. Two of his negros committed a robbery, they were informed upon. They nearly beat the informer to death. they ran away from Maryland, came to this state [Pennsylvania]. The father, the two sons, and the boy my playmate, came to this state under the protection of the fugitive slave law (not only to recover their property, but to arrest the thieves who belonged to them)[34] [. . .][35]

Autograph manuscript, the Hampden-Booth Theatre Library at The Players, New York City.

1. A note in the hand of Edwin Booth on the first page of the manuscript reads: "This was found long after his death, among some old playbooks, & clothes, kept by John Wilkes Booth in my house."

2. JWB addressed his speech to an audience of Philadelphians. There was considerable sympathy for the South in Philadelphia before the outbreak of the Civil War. Many Philadelphians opposed abolitionism and feared that secession would ruin the economy of their city. See Russell F. Weigley, ed., *Philadelphia: A Three-Hundred-Year History* (New York: W. W. Norton, 1982), 392. Booth believed that most Philadelphians were "conservatives" who agreed with him in blaming the secession crisis on Northern extremists.

3. Hoping to sway his intended audience of Pennsylvanians, JWB was more than a little disingenuous in declaring himself "a northern man." As this speech shows, his sympathies were firmly with the South. It is impossible to know what he meant in the preceding sentence by "vindicat[ing] myself in the steps I intend to take" or by "what I intend to do" a few lines down. A friend of JWB claimed that a few months later, as the Civil War was beginning in the spring of 1861, Booth planned to go to his native Harford County, Maryland, to raise a company of men to fight for the Confederacy. It is possible that he already had ideas of actively helping the South at the time he drafted this speech.

4. South Carolina became the first state to secede from the Union on 20 Decem-

ber 1860, shortly before JWB drafted this speech. The next state to secede, Mississippi, did not do so until 9 January 1861.

5. By his repeated demand for equal rights for the South, Booth seems to be implicitly invoking the proposition, advanced by many Southern statesmen, that the Union was in effect a partnership between two different but equal societies—one slave and one free—which had agreed to unite under the Constitution of 1787. Although the North had outstripped the South in population, wealth, and power, the South was still entitled to its rights to political equality with the North.

6. Here JWB deleted a paragraph concerning his views on slavery. He later incorporated the passage, almost verbatim, on page eighteen of the manuscript. The deleted paragraph reads: "Much, too much has been said of slavery. Il touch it lightly, yet enough to show my views. Now as to Slavery being right or wrong. My opinion (which Ill die by) is this. First in accordance with the Constitution the South has a right to keep and hold them. And we have no right Constitutionally to interfear with her or her's. And instead of looking upon Slavery as a sin, (^mearly^ because I have none) I hold it to be a happiness for themselves, *And a social* & political blessing for us. Skillful doctors will always find the source of the disease before they attempt a cure."

7. Theodore Cuyler was a prominent Philadelphia lawyer who spoke at the "Grand Union meeting" on 13 December 1860 in Independence Square. Like many of the speakers at the great rally, Cuyler sought to conciliate the South, blaming the crisis on abolitionist agitation. Despite his distaste for abolitionism, in 1851 Cuyler had helped to defend successfully those accused of treason in violating the federal fugitive slave law by violently resisting slave-catchers in the Christiana riot. See Jonathan Katz, *Resistance at Christiana: The Fugitive Slave Rebellion, Christiana, Pennsylvania, September 11, 1851* (New York: Thomas Y. Crowell, 1974). JWB, who knew the slave-catchers, would allude to this episode at the end of the draft of his speech.

8. JWB would tell his sister in the summer of 1864 that he believed Abraham Lincoln would become an American king: "*He* is Bonaparte in one great move, that is, by overturning this blind Republic and making himself a king. This man's re-election which will follow his success, I tell you—will be a reign!" Asia Booth Clarke, *The Unlocked Book: A Memoir of John Wilkes Booth by His Sister* (New York: G. P. Putnam's Sons, 1938), 124.

9. Appeals to the heroes of 1776 were common during the secession crisis. One of the more notable examples was the peroration of the inaugural address Lincoln delivered on 4 March 1861.

10. At the 13 December rally JWB may have heard Mayor Henry condemn Americans who attacked slavery when he said, "We must restore public sentiment to the old stand-point, and the misplaced appeals from our pulpits, lecture-rooms, [and] presses against a section of our common country, must be frowned on. [Immense applause.]." *New York Times*, 14 December 1860, 1.

11. Here, William Lowndes Yancey's powerful oratory was echoed by JWB's demands for "equal rights and justice for the South." Yancey's political platform was founded on the principles that the Constitution was an agreement between sovereign states; that the federal government was obligated to protect the rights of a minority of Southern slaveowners from the free-state majority; that the government

must also protect property rights by enforcing the fugitive slave laws; and that slave-holders could not be denied their right to take their slave property into the territories. Yancey (1814–63) believed no governmental power could justly outlaw slavery in any U.S. territory. In sketching Yancey's career, *The Dictionary of American Biography* ventures that "without him there would have been no Confederate States of America."

12. Years later, John A. Ellsler, an actor friend and business associate of JWB, claimed that Booth's appeals for the preservation of the Union had gotten him into trouble during his tour through Alabama: "At the time the war broke out, previous to the bombardment of Fort Sumter, Wilkes was leading man in the stock company at Montgomery, Alabama, and his sympathy for, and utterances on behalf of the Union were so unguarded in their expression that his life was in jeopardy, and it became necessary for the manager of the theater to resort to strategy and spirit Wilkes Booth out of the city to save his life." *The Stage Memories of John A. Ellsler,* ed. Effie Ellsler Weston (Cleveland: The Rowfant Club, 1950), 129–30.

13. JWB refers to the Fugitive Slave Act of 1850, the federal law enacted to aid slave-holders in recovering slaves who had escaped into the free states. The power to recover such fugitives had been written into the U.S. Constitution in 1787; Congress passed the first fugitive slave law in 1793, during the presidency of George Washington. The 1850 act was a tougher version of the old law. The fugitive slave laws were highly controversial. In the North, many worked to thwart the capture (or "kidnapping") of runaways, whereas Southerners saw such interference as not only a blow against the central institution of their society but also as a deliberate and galling insult to Southern honor. "Others . . . passed to infringe those rights" refers to the so-called "personal liberty laws" passed by many of the free states. Personal liberty laws made the Fugitive Slave Act harder to enforce and were regarded by Southerners as both unconstitutional and dishonest because they tended to legitimize the theft of slave "property."

14. JWB may have meant the attempts made to "reconcile" the South at the 13 December rally. Resolutions condemning abolitionism, promising noninterference with slavery, calling for the enforcement of the fugitive slave laws, and acknowledging the right of slaveowners to carry their slaves into the federal territories were passed at the meeting. Ellis P. Oberholtzer, *Philadelphia: A History of the City and Its People* (Philadelphia: S. J. Clarke, 1912), 2:357.

15. This is JWB's only direct reference to the Republican Party; he never names President-elect Lincoln. Like many in the South, JWB incorrectly identifies the party of Lincoln with abolitionism.

16. At the 13 December demonstration, JWB may have heard one of the speakers, Philadelphia lawyer Joseph R. Ingersoll (1786–1868), declare that "we must show [the South] our good feeling by action, and not only by words. We must show the South that we will do nothing to interfere with their rights, but everything to protect them." *New York Times,* 14 December 1860, 1.

17. Senators Henry Clay (1777–1852) of Kentucky and Daniel Webster (1782–1852) of Massachusetts were revered as architects of compromises that held the Union together.

18. Compare this with a passage from President Buchanan's annual message of 3

December 1860, in which Buchanan also blamed the North for the crisis: "The long-continued and intemperate interference of the Northern people with the question of Slavery in the Southern States has at length produced its natural effects. The different sections of the Union are now arrayed against each other." Buchanan, *The Works of James Buchanan*, ed. John B. Moore (Philadelphia: J. P. Lippincott, 1910), 9:7.

19. Cardinal Richelieu (1585–1642) was a French statesman and chief minister of King Louis XIII. JWB frequently appeared in Edward Bulwer-Lytton's play *Richelieu*, from which this quotation is taken.

20. The secession crisis had prompted President Buchanan to proclaim 17 December 1860 a national day of fast and prayer.

21. Here Booth echoes President Andrew Jackson's famous declaration that "the Union must and shall be preserved."

22. Many years later, a veteran recalled the events of 24 November 1859, when "we were ordered to entrain at Seventh and Broad Streets, opposite the Marshall Theater. . . . J. Wilkes Booth was then playing in the theatre as a stock actor, under the stage name of J. Booth Wilkes. . . . Booth appeared at the door of the car and asked if he could go with us to Harpers Ferry. We informed him no one was allowed on the train but men in uniform. He expressed a desire to buy a uniform, since he was very anxious to go. So, after some consultation with him, [Louis F.] Bossieux and I each gave him a portion of our uniforms, took him in the car, and carried him with us. . . . Booth remained with us until after Brown's execution. He was a remarkably handsome man, with a winning personality and would regale us around the camp fire with recitations from Shakespeare." George W. Libby, "John Brown and John Wilkes Booth," *The Confederate Veteran* 37 (April 1930): 138–39.

23. The Richmond *Enquirer*, 28 November 1859, reported: "The Richmond Grays and Company F . . . which seem to vie with each other in the handsome appearance they present, remind one of caged birds, so wild and gleesome they appear. . . . Amongst them I notice Mr. J. Wilkes Booth, a son of Junius Brutus Booth, who, though not a member, as soon as he heard the tap of the drum, threw down the sock and buskin, and shouldered his musket with the Grays to the scene of deadly conflict." JWB's Southern patriotism was heartily applauded by the people of Virginia. At the time of his brief militia enlistment, his family was worried that he might actually throw over his acting career to become a professional soldier. His sister wrote a friend that "John is crazy or enthusiastic about going for a soldier. I think he will get off. It has been his dearest ambition, or perhaps it is his true vocation" (Asia Booth Clarke to Jean Anderson, no date, Peale Museum, Baltimore).

24. Demosthenes was an Athenian orator and statesman, and Cicero a statesman and orator of republican Rome.

25. At the Union demonstration JWB may have heard Joseph R. Ingersoll warn that "it is folly to suppose this country can be divided. It must be a Union in peace, or a Union in war." *New York Times*, 14 December 1860, 1.

26. In his famous speech in the Senate on 7 March 1850, Daniel Webster, who said that he spoke "not as a Massachusetts man, nor as a Northern man, but as an American," declared that disunion was a greater evil than slavery and warned the South that a peaceful secession was not possible.

27. John J. Crittenden (1787–1863), senator from Kentucky, chaired a committee

that tried to resolve the secession crisis after Lincoln's election with a proposed constitutional amendment that would reassure Southerners by explicitly protecting slavery in the states in which it already existed and by making possible the admission
of new slave states by extending the Missouri Compromise line all the way to the
Pacific. Lincoln, who believed at the time that secession was a hollow threat, opposed
the measure because it would have permitted the extension of slavery into new territories, something the Republican Party had been founded to oppose. The proposed
amendment died in committee on 22 December 1860. All the Republicans on the
committee voted against it.

28. Although Booth grew up in the slave state of Maryland, his family never
owned slaves. JWB's father, Junius Brutus Booth, had thought slavery immoral. Slaves
rented from neighbors served the Booth family.

29. Henry Ward Beecher (1813–87), a flamboyant clergyman and opponent of
slavery, was pastor of Brooklyn's Plymouth Church. Although not an outright abolitionist, he believed that all means must be used to fight the extension of slavery into
new territories. He was actively involved in supporting antislavery forces in Kansas.
Beecher's sister, Harriet Beecher Stowe, had published *Uncle Tom's Cabin* in 1851.

30. "To hold, as t'were, the mirror up to nature; / To show virtue her own feature, scorn her own image, / And the very age and body of the time his own form
and pressure" (*Hamlet,* III, ii, 20).

31. "Who steals my purse steals trash; . . . / But he that filches from me my good
name / Robs me of that which enriches not him, / And makes me poor indeed" (*Othello,* III, iii, 155).

32. JWB alludes to the South's widespread fear of slave rebellion. Many Southern whites believed that even though the new Lincoln administration might not directly attack the institution of slavery, Lincoln's election itself had given slaves sub-
versive ideas about their impending liberation and that this might be enough to impel
them to violent rebellion against their masters. President Buchanan, in his annual
message on 3 December 1860, had said that "the incessant and violent agitation of
the Slavery question throughout the North for the last quarter century has at length
produced its malign influence on the slaves and. . . . has given place to apprehension
of servile insurrection. Many a matron throughout the South retires at night in dread
of what may befall herself and her children before the morning. Should this apprehension of domestic danger, whether real or imaginary, extend, and intensify
itself . . . then disunion will become inevitable." Buchanan, *Works,* 9:7–8.

33. Even though he could not spell their name, John Wilkes Booth remembered
his friends, schoolmates, and neighbors, the Gorsuches. The Gorsuch place, "Retreat
Farm," was a plantation of several hundred acres and a number of slaves located in
Baltimore County, Maryland, not far from the Booths' Tudor Hall. The master of
Retreat Farm, the square-jawed Edward Gorsuch (1795–1851), was a prosperous, re-
spected community leader and "a man of forceful and determined temperament."
W. U. Hensel, *The Christiana Riot and the Treason Trials of 1851* (Lancaster: New Era
Printing, 1911), 21. Farmer Gorsuch had three sons. Two of them, Dickinson and John
S. Gorsuch, were, as Booth wrote, "grown to be men." The third son, Thomas, was
Booth's "bossom friend" at Milton Academy. The *Circular of the Milton Boarding
School, Situated in Baltimore County, MD* (Baltimore, 1859) lists in its "Catalogue of

Students" the names of John Booth, Joseph Booth, and four boys of the Gorsuch family: Joshua L., Noah F., Joshua, and Thomas.

34. Four, not two, of Edward Gorsuch's slaves stole wheat from the plantation granary, sold it to a local miller, and used the money to escape across the border into Pennsylvania. Two years later, when Gorsuch learned where his runaways were hiding, he found a U.S. marshall and got up a posse to go to Pennsylvania, arrest his slaves, and carry them back to Maryland. Included in the party were Dickinson Gorsuch and a nephew, Joshua Gorsuch. He did not bring along Thomas, as Booth mistakenly reports. Instead of four fearful runaways, the posse found a band of men determined to be free. Warned to leave before blood was shed, Gorsuch stubbornly stood his ground, insisting, "I want my property and I will have it." No one knows who fired the first shot, but it is certain that the slave-catchers got the worst of the gunfight that followed. Edward Gorsuch was killed, and Dickinson Gorsuch gravely wounded.

35. The manuscript ends here, at the bottom of a page. It is impossible to know if Booth simply stopped writing or whether there were additional pages of text that have been lost.

"A Star of the First Magnitude": John Wilkes Booth on Stage, 1861–64

It is hardly surprising that most of the surviving letters of John Wilkes Booth concern his theatrical career. Success had come quickly for the young actor. He was just twenty-two, with three seasons as a stock actor behind him, when he made his first star tour in 1860.[1] Although that tour had been marred by the accident that left a bullet in him, Booth had emerged as a star. In February 1861, the month that Jefferson Davis was inaugurated president of the Confederate States of America and Abraham Lincoln made the journey from Springfield to Washington for his own inauguration, Booth was starring in Albany, New York. As a stock actor in Richmond, "Mr. J. Wilkes" had earned $20 a week. As a star, J. Wilkes Booth could command hundreds, sometimes thousands, of dollars a night.

The star system dominated the American theater at midcentury. In cities large enough to support a theater with a stock company, theater-owners brought in famous performers for limited engagements, performances backed by the stock company. The star actor was given billing at the top of the playbill, above the name of the playwright and the title of the play itself. And, of course, a good portion of the box office went to the star. If the engagements lasted more than a few days, the star could usually count on a benefit.

Some have condemned the star system. As a twentieth-century theatrical dictionary defines the term, it is "the custom of selling a play by exploiting a prominent actor whose name is a guarantee of good box-office business. The play is diminished in importance and less care is exercised in selecting and producing it. In production, the consideration of the star takes precedence over dramatic considerations. As a system it is an evil, deleterious to the drama."[2] One cynical journalist described a star as "an actor who belongs to no one theatre, but travels from each to all, playing a few weeks at a time, and is sustained in his chief character by the regular or stock actors. A stock actor is a good actor and a poor fool. A Star is an advertisement in tights, who grows rich and corrupts the public taste."[3]

After he broke with Matthew Canning, Booth acted as his own agent. Most of the letters that follow are devoted to the actor's management of his flourishing career. Booth negotiated with theater-owners for his share of the profits; he also set the dates of his engagements and picked the plays to be performed. A typical theater of the period might seat 1,500, but some were large enough to accommodate an audience of two or three thousand; Ford's Theatre in Washington, D.C., for instance, sat 2,400. With admission ranging from 25 to 75 cents or more, a popular favorite could bring in hundreds of dollars a performance.

Actors worked for their money, however. An evening's performances—usually a five-act tragedy followed by a shorter comedy—began at seven and rarely ended before midnight.[4] A different program was usually presented each night. When not playing to an audience, actors were probably in rehearsal. The plays presented during a star engagement were drawn from the visiting star's repertoire. And the star might also assume the role of stage director; after all, the play was being performed chiefly as a vehicle for the star. Rehearsals gave the stock company a chance to learn how best to support the star.

Booth's 8 December 1862 letter to Edwin Keach, manager of the Boston Museum, about the staging of *Richard III* shows how much artistic control a star might exercise. The young actor was said to have possessed considerable talent as a director and by most accounts was considerate and helpful in working with supporting players, something that could not be said of many other stars. In other letters, Booth devises stratagems to extract more money from managers, reveals his intense interest in the success of other actors and rival theaters, urges that a *"big thing* may be made of" one of his engagements, and exults in his success: "My goose does indeed hang high (long may she wave)." By the beginning of 1863 the letters contain the hard proof of that success: Booth had more money than he knew what to do with, and he sought to invest substantial sums in real estate and stocks.

But a star's lot was not all applause. Booth's letters also reveal something of the grinding hardship and monotony of an actor's life on the road. There was danger as well. Booth nearly lost his life in a midwestern blizzard in January 1864. The United States was an enormous country in an era when the hundred-mile journey between two neighboring cities such as Washington and Richmond could take all day. (Booth once spent fifty-one hours on a train trip from Boston to Chicago.) Actors had to endure harsh weather, primitive railroads, shabby hotels, slow steamboats, rough roads, and cold theaters.

During his four years as a star—from 1861 to 1864—Booth played New York City; Rochester, Albany, and Buffalo, New York; Portland, Maine; Boston, Springfield, and Worcester, Massachusetts; Providence, Rhode Island; Hartford and New Haven, Connecticut; Philadelphia; Baltimore; Washington, D.C.; St. Louis and St. Joseph, Missouri; Chicago; Detroit; Indianapolis; Cleveland; Cincinnati; Leavenworth, Kansas; Louisville and Lexington, Kentucky; New Orleans; and Nashville, Tennessee. Some of his appearances were as short as a night or two. The longest—at the Boston Museum in the spring of 1864—ran for two months.[5] Although some biographers have charged that Booth played so many western towns because of poor reviews in the big cities of the East, touring the provinces was good business. "The star system," one theater historian has written, "was unequivocally aided by this western expansion, for western managers paid higher salaries than in the East to attract the best talent available."[6]

The picture that emerges from Booth's letters is of an ambitious, highly successful young actor. The contrast was all the greater when, at the height of his power in the summer of 1864, he abruptly abandoned acting to devote all his energies to the scheme to capture Abraham Lincoln.

----

1. The *Oxford English Dictionary* advises that as early as 1779 the term *star* had been used to mean "an actor, singer, etc., of exceptional celebrity."

2. Bernard Sobel, ed., *The Theatre Handbook and Digest of Plays* (New York: Crown, 1940), 734.

3. George Alfred Townsend, *Life, Crime, and Capture of John Wilkes Booth* (New York: Dick and Fitzgerald, 1865), quoted in Stanley Kimmel, *The Mad Booths of Maryland* (Indianapolis: Bobbs-Merrill, 1940), 157.

4. Gordon Samples, *Lust for Fame: The Stage Career of John Wilkes Booth* (Jefferson, N.C.: McFarland, 1982), 52–53.

5. "A Chronology of the Theatrical Performances of John Wilkes Booth" in Samples, *Lust for Fame*, 196–224, is marred by errors and omissions. The best listing of JWB's performances appears in Arthur F. Loux's unpublished study "John Wilkes Booth Day by Day," copy in the possession of Louise Taper.

6. Don B. Wilmeth, "The American Theatre in Transition," in *John Wilkes Booth, Actor: The Proceedings of a Conference Weekend in Bel Air, Maryland May 1988*, ed. Arthur Kincaid (North Leigh, Oxfordshire: Published privately, 1989), 20.

To Joseph H. Simonds
Philadelphia, 9 October 1861

No. 1004 Chesnut St:
Philada:

Oct 9th:/61

Dear Joe[1]

I know you will forgive me for not answering yours of Sept: 13th:—till this distant date, but I am, at the best of times, the worst letter writer in the world, And for the last month I have been so closely occupied, with so meny business letters to answer, that I really had to forgo the pleasure (and I assure you it is one,) of writing to you, How-ever, my pen is now in hand to assure you, that I have not forgotten you or any of my good friends in Boston, Remember me kindly to them all, the Bugbee's[2] in particular, not forgetting our old friend *Carruth.*

I had a letter from Davenport,[3] he wants me some time in November, but I am sure we shall not be able to agree about terms, whereupon, I am about to ask of you to render me a service, if any more of those *curious* members of *society* should trouble you about the possibility of my playing in Boston, let all those who are connected or ^who^ patronize the *Museum*[4] understand that Davenport wants me *bad,* but that the engagement is not satisfied yet, and that its doubtful whether it will be, and *others,*—if they should ask,— that I *want* to come to the *Howard,*[5] &c: which is all true. It will be a little move to bring our Friend D—[6] to terms, He thinks me a novice crazy to play in Boston and that he will get me for nothing. which to tell you the truth is nearly as much as he has offered me, More hereafter. Once more remember me to my friends, accepting for yourself the best wishes of, Yours Truly

John Wilkes Booth.

Autograph letter signed, offered by Federal Hill Autographs, Baltimore, 1981.

1. Joseph H. Simonds (1839–88) was a cashier at the Merchants Bank, Boston, and a close friend of JWB. They may have met in the summer of 1861 when JWB was in Boston visiting his brother Edwin. Simonds served as JWB's business manager. In 1864 Simonds gave up his bank job and moved to Franklin, Pennsylvania, to manage Booth's oil investments. Simonds had no knowledge of the conspiracy against Abraham Lincoln. In early 1865, when Booth was preoccupied with the plot, Simonds criticized him for neglecting his acting and investments. He described JWB's activities in the Pennsylvania oil fields in testimony at the trial of the Lincoln assassina-

tion conspirators in May 1865. At the time he knew Booth, Simonds was "a well-built man of about thirty-three. He was an immaculate dresser, had sandy hair, a mustache, and was a little austere in appearance. He had a deep interest in the stage as well as an intense desire to advance to a position more affluent than that of a bank teller." Ernest C. Miller, *John Wilkes Booth in the Pennsylvania Oil Region* (Meadville, Pa.: Crawford County Historical Society, 1987), 10.

2. Possibly John Stephenson Bugbee. A family named Bugbee lived in Maryland before moving to Boston. JWB was acquainted with them in both places. The Bugbees moved to California around 1861 (JWB to Joseph H. Simonds, 23 November 1861). Joseph A. Booth, JWB's brother, reported visiting the Bugbees in San Francisco in 1865. John Stephenson Bugbee was living in San Francisco in that year.

3. In 1861 actor Edward Loomis Davenport (1814–77) was the manager of one of Boston's principal theaters, the Howard Athenaeum. A respected heroic actor, Davenport had made his stage debut in a play with JWB's father in 1836. JWB's sister Asia remembered that as a novice actor Booth had admired Davenport for his "finish and correctness." Asia Booth Clarke, *The Unlocked Book: A Memoir of John Wilkes Booth by His Sister* (New York: G. P. Putnam's Sons, 1938), 111.

4. The Boston Museum, founded in 1841 by Moses Kimball, was Boston's most important theater. It was located on Tremont Street not far from the Boston Common. The Boston Museum and Gallery of Fine Arts was so named because "there were many people in Boston who looked with downright disapproval on theatres and theatre-goers. . . . The museum was at first a theatre that *wasn't* a theatre; it grew up in a kind of disguise, and therefore it drew the people who on principles disapproved of theatres as such." Claire McGlinchee, *The First Decade of the Boston Museum* (Boston: Bruce Humphries, 1940), 20–21. JWB played the Museum in 1862, 1863, and 1864.

5. The Howard Athenaeum was the Boston Museum's main rival. Like the Museum, the Athenaeum went by a name that was calculated to make its theatrical character more acceptable to proper Bostonians.

6. Edward Loomis Davenport.

To Fanny
Detroit, 20 November 1861

In the following initials you will

Find a soul made up of truth
And yet in mortal form.
Not clouded by the vanities of youth
Nor shaded by pride's fitful storm
Yes, she's one to serve, as, *instar omnium*

Yours with all respect,

J. Wilkes Booth

Detroit, Nov 20th:/61[1]

Autograph manuscript signed, offered by the Gallery of History, Las Vegas, Nevada, 1991.

1. On 18 November 1861, JWB made the last appearance of his Detroit star engagement. On 16 November the Detroit *Free Press* had declared that "Mr. Booth during his short appearance has won a host of friends who will heartily welcome him to the boards of the Metropolitan again." But Booth would never return to Detroit as a performer. Fanny, the subject of this acrostic, is unidentified.

To Joseph H. Simonds
Cincinnati, 23 November 1861

Cincinnati, Nov. 23d:

Dear Joe

I know you will forgive me, this long delay in answering your letters; if you knew me better you would not wonder at it, as I avail myself of any excuse to get rid of writing. No matter how I may long to hear from the person to whom I have to write, and I confess I should like to hear from you every day. I received your photograph, a thousand thanks, I think ^it^ very good, I believe you have mine. My second week in Buffalo[1] was so, so. I played 7 nights in Detroit[2] to a good Bus:[iness]—, Open here[3] Monday night, 25th:, they count high on me but I am doubtful as to my success, Maggyie Mitchel[4] is playing a good engagement here, I should ^have^ said has been; as she finished last night. my dear Joe excuse this as I am standing in the Office with about a hundred people about me blowing at a fearful rate, I am not fixed yet, so I cannot go to my room, Yours of the 16th:, also reached me, in Detroit, It seems that Forrest[5] is always in trouble. I am sorry his bus:[iness] is not better, for it is rough to see such trash (as Barney Williams[6] produces on the stage) get the best of the legitimate, but *sich* is life.

Give my kindest regards to the Bugbe's Has Mr. B-[7] gone to Calna [California] yet. I addressed a letter to him in your care did you get it.[8] I will write to you more intelligibly the next time. So asking you to excuse this again I am your true friend

J. Wilkes. Booth.[9]

Autograph letter signed, published in auction catalog: Christie's, 19 December 1986.

1. JWB appeared at the Metropolitan Theatre in Buffalo from 28 October through 9 November 1861, starring in *Hamlet, Othello, Richard III, Macbeth,* and *Romeo and Juliet,* among other roles. Although box office receipts were apparently disappointing, on 4 November the Buffalo *Courier* praised JWB's acting: "His engagement has fallen upon an unfortunate time, when war and politics so completely absorb the public attention, but we wish to have our readers realize, nevertheless, that they now have the opportunity . . . for seeing great Shakespearean parts rendered by one who has the manner of the great actors, and who has shown himself a worthy scion of the house of Booth."

2. JWB played at Mrs. Harry A. Perry's Metropolitan Theatre in Detroit from 11 through 18 November 1861, starring in *Hamlet, Othello, Richard III,* and *Macbeth.* His acting won praise, and he earned about $120 for performing on seven evenings. Mrs. Perry would later become the third wife of JWB's eldest brother, Junius Brutus Booth, Jr.

3. JWB starred at Wood's Theatre in Cincinnati, Ohio, from 25 November through 7 December 1861. Again, he played *Richard III, Othello, Macbeth,* and *Hamlet* as well as *The Merchant of Venice* and *The Marble Heart.* The Cincinnati *Commercial* declared on 29 November that "it is plain that Mr. Booth has caught some of the fire that animated his great father."

4. Miss Mitchell concluded a successful star engagement at Wood's Theatre on 23 November. JWB told Simonds that "they count high on me." The Cincinnati *Commercial* had reported on 23 November that "Miss Mitchell will be followed by J. Wilkes Booth, who appears on Monday evening. The genuine furor he has everywhere excited, leads us to anticipate another theatrical triumph at Wood's."

5. Edwin Forrest (1806–72) was a brilliant American tragedian and a friend of Junius Brutus Booth, JWB's father. Edwin Booth had been named for Forrest. Forrest's professional rivalry with the English actor William C. Macready resulted in the New York Astor Place riot in 1849. Supporters of the two rival actors battled each other, and twenty-two were killed. The Astor Place controversy and a bitter divorce wounded Forrest enough to make him give up acting for almost a decade. He made a comeback in 1860.

6. Barney Williams was the stage name adopted by the Irish actor Bernard Fla-herty (1823–76), who came to America in 1836. He was a popular comedian who portrayed farcical Irish characters.

7. Perhaps John Stephenson Bugbee.

8. This letter to Bugbee does not survive.

9. The letter is accompanied by an autograph envelope addressed by JWB: "J. H. Simonds, Esq Mechanic's Bank Boston, Mass." The envelope is postmarked "Nov. 24, Cincinnati" and endorsed "Recd Nov 27 61 Ans Nov 27 61."

To Joseph H. Simonds
St. Louis, 10 January 1862

St Louis/, Dec 10th:[1]

Dear Joe

Both your letters Recd. You must not flatter yourself that your letters are too long, or that you write too often, for although I hate writing myself, I can read your letters, if you send three or four a-day. My bus[iness] here so far has been fair As you may see by the papers[2] I play here all next week and then *may* go to Chicago,[3] but not sure of it. I think I have one of those pictures you allude to, Nevertheless you can take *two* for me I can get nothing but St Louis money here, and they wont take that East, or I would enclose the funds. The first Eastern note I get I will send it then you can send the pictures—Let me hear from you often Joe, Always delighted Excuse this as I write it in a hurry, as I always do it seems, Remember me to all my friends

I will write again soon

God bless you, Your True Friend

J. Wilkes Booth

I wrote this in the dark. Excuse mistakes, & et.[4]

Autograph letter signed, Andre de Coppet Collection, Princeton University Library.

1. JWB misdated the letter.

2. JWB's starring engagement at Ben DeBar's St. Louis Theatre ran from 6 through 18 January 1862. He repeated his popular Shakespearean roles of *Hamlet, Macbeth, Richard III*, and *Othello* in addition to several other plays. JWB's sword fighting in the last act of *Richard III* electrified St. Louis audiences. Local newspapers praised him as a genius.

3. JWB starred in a successful engagement at McVicker's Theatre in Chicago from 20 January through 1 February 1862.

4. The letter is accompanied by an autograph envelope with a printed address: "Planter's House Stickney & Scollay St. Louis, Mo." It is addressed by JWB to "Joseph Simonds, Esq. Mechanics Bank Boston Mass—"; the envelope is endorsed "Recd Jan 15/62 Ans Jan 23/62."

To Joseph H. Simonds
Baltimore, 18 February 1862

Baltimore, Feb. 18th.[1]

Dear Joe

As usual, I begin with excuses forgive me for not writing sooner, but as you say better late than never. Opened here last night a big house in spite of rain snow & outside show shops. But I do not think my success here will be very great as one's native place is the last place in the world to look for such a thing.[2] Yours Recd- this morning, I have made no engagement for Boston, but have time open after here, three weeks from now. I will write Fleming[3] today or tomorrow about time that is if he can keep open, three weeks, which I doubt would it be a good time for me March 10th: or 18th: do you know when do the Comb[inatio]n:[4] get through there? Write to me Joe and give me your advice about the whole thing.[5] I will then answer at greater length. Little or no new. so excuse the shortness of this Yours Truly

J. Wilkes Booth

I enclose $5. in this. What were those pictures; this may not be enough.
Yours
John

Autograph letter signed, published in auction catalog: Sotheby-Parke-Bernet, Sang sale, part 4, 3 June 1980.

1. JWB returned as a star to Baltimore's Holliday Street Theatre, where he had made his stage debut less than five years earlier. His lengthy engagement ran from 17 February to 8 March 1862. He starred in the characters of Hamlet, Macbeth, Othello, Romeo, and Richard III and also performed *The Robbers, The Apostate,* and *The Lady of Lyons.*

2. JWB was modest or mistaken—his Baltimore engagement was quite successful. The Baltimore *Sun* declared on 15 February that "we have in [Edwin Booth's] younger brother an actor that with the suddenness of a meteor now illuminates the dramatic horizon." Continuing the astronomical metaphor, the *Sun* reported that "'mid the galaxy of stars that have illuminated our theatrical firmament . . . none has shown with greater brilliancy than our young artist." In an apparent allusion to the

popular notion that he was engaged in an artistic rivalry with Edwin, JWB had boldly included a line from *Richard III* on the playbill heralding his Baltimore appearance: "I have no brother, I am no brother, . . . I am myself alone." It was a kind of declaration of theatrical independence.

3. The actor William Maybury Fleming (1817–66) was manager of the National Theatre in Boston. He was to die of wounds sustained as an officer with Sherman's army in 1865.

4. "The Combination" probably refers to a company of actors brought from New York's Winter Garden by Henry C. Jarrett to perform at the Boston Theatre. The company opened there on 17 February for a two-week run, presenting some of the Shakespearean plays JWB had made a regular feature of his star engagements. He may not have wanted to appear in Boston at the same time as the other company. Eugene Tompkins, *The History of the Boston Theatre: 1854–1901* (Boston: Houghton Mifflin, 1908), 96–110.

5. JWB did not appear in Boston until May 1862.

To Joseph H. Simonds
New York City, 22 March 1862

St: Nicholas[1]
March 22*d:*

Dear Joe

Telegraphed you yesterday that Debar[2] wont let me off, so if I come to Boston it must be for the two weeks commencing May 12th: So tell Keach[3] to write at once that I may answer Milwaukee and Cincinnati.[4] Just recd: yours of 22d:.

No news yet of Joe have hunted every place I can think of. I cant tell what to do poor Mother will take it so hard.[5] I will write you again in a few days excuse this hasty scrawl. Remember me with best wishes to the Bugbees. Your true Friend

J Wilkes Booth

Autograph letter signed, Andre de Coppet Collection, Princeton University Library.

1. The St. Nicholas Hotel, New York City. JWB opened at Mary Provost's Theatre in New York on 17 March 1862 for an engagement that extended through 5 April. He opened the theater itself, being the first star to appear there after Miss Provost assumed management. The New York *World* reported on 17 March that Mary Provost had "signalized her opening attempt at New York management by engaging a star of real magnitude, and singular through fitful brilliancy." Booth was her brilliant star. He opened with *Richard III.*

2. JWB opened at Ben DeBar's St. Louis Theatre on 21 April 1862. He apparently tried unsuccessfully to get out of the St. Louis engagement in order to play Boston again.

3. Edwin Frank Keach (1824–64) was an actor and the stage manager of the Boston Museum.

4. JWB opened at the National Theatre in Cincinnati on 10 November 1862. He did not appear in Milwaukee.

5. In March 1862 Joseph Adrian Booth (1840–1902), youngest of the six Booth children, disappeared for a time, greatly alarming his mother. JWB feared that his younger brother might kill himself. The family eventually learned that Joseph, who had been living in New York City, had traveled to England. From there, in July 1862, he took passage to Australia, returning to the United States in 1865. The episode prompted Junius Brutus Booth, Jr., to write to Edwin Booth on 20 October 1862, in a letter preserved in the Hampden-Booth Theatre Library, The Players, New York City, that "Joe seems an enigma, but I think I can guess him. . . . I am afraid his is not a sound mind. . . . Mind I do not say positive insanity but a crack that way. Which father in his highest had and which I fear runs more or less thro' the male portion of our family."

To Joseph H. Simonds
Philadelphia, 13 April 1862

No. 923 Chestnut St.[1]
April 13th

Dear Joe

My success in New York continued fair.[2] I will start in a few days for St Louis.[3] Don't you pity me? no news yet from the runaway.[4] Expect we shall get a letter in a few weeks, he is doubtless at sea.

Wrote to Keach yesterday.[5] Hope to see you in May as lively as ever, for you seem to be the only happy man I have ever met, hope it may last your life-time. God bless you Joe, have nothing to write about except that I am well and still remain your
    True Friend

    J. Wilkes Booth

Excuse this brief scrawl.

―――――――――――

Autograph letter signed, published in auction catalog: Sotheby-Parke-Bernet, Roy P. Crocker sale, 28 November 1979.

1. The address of Edwin Booth's house in Philadelphia.
2. JWB played to good houses during his first and only starring engagement in

New York City. His reviews were generally favorable. He would appear on a New York stage only one more time—in the celebrated November 1864 benefit performance of *Julius Caesar* with his brothers Edwin and Junius Brutus Booth, Jr.

3. JWB appeared at Ben DeBar's St. Louis Theatre from 21 April to 3 May 1862. During the engagement one St. Louis paper, the *Daily Missouri Democrat*, on 23 April went so far as to call JWB "the greatest tragedian in the country" and "undoubtedly the best and most original tragedian now on the American stage."

4. JWB's brother, Joseph A. Booth.

5. Edwin Frank Keach was manager of the Boston Museum, where JWB would open on 12 May 1862. Booth's April 1863 letter to Keach does not survive.

To Edwin Frank Keach
Philadelphia, 25 July 1862

Philad*a:*
July 25th:/62

E. F. Keach, Esq.

Dear Keach.

Yours recd:—, And as mercy is one of the *many* virtues in my composition, I will display it, for once in my life, by instantly releasing you from The tenter-hooks, upon which I have unwittingly placed you, So, be no longer at variance with those who are anxious as myself to fill up time, but be merciful like me, And answer their impatience. by yea, or, nay. Your humble servant accepts the time you propose, four weeks, beginning Janry: 19th: 1863,[1] And sincerely hopes that that *big thing* may be made of it, I am, afraid I shall not be able to visit Boston this summer, nevertheless, will try. Remember me to Simonds[2] and Warren[3] with best wishes. tell the former to write. Excuse this hasty scrawl. Hoping to be able to visit Boston in a few weeks. I remain [. . .][4]

Autograph letter, Herndon-Weik Collection, Library of Congress.

1. JWB played the Boston Museum from 19 January through 13 February 1863.
2. Joseph H. Simonds.
3. William Warren (1812–88) was a popular comedian whose troupe, the William Warren Comedy Company, played in Boston for many years.
4. Booth's signature has been clipped from this letter by some rapacious autograph collector.

To T. Valentine Butsch
Philadelphia, 3 August 1862

No 923 Chesnut St:
Philada:

Aug 3d:/62

V. Butsch, Esq[1]

Dear Butsch

In answer to yours of July 31*st:*, which has just come to hand. You must know that my time till after March, is all filled up with the exception of the two weeks mentioned in my last, (Nov 24th:/62 and Jan 5th:/63).[2] If Miss Thompson will not let you off, why then I will come for the one week beginning Jan 5*th:* Share after eighty dollars. and half clear benefit. I would like to come for two weeks. but you see its impossible on a/c[count] of other engagements. If this suits you. and she lets you off from Nov. 24th: Why you can book me for *both dates,*[3] if not, I will come Jan 5th:. Let me know as soon as she writes. Excuse this hasty scrawl

Yours Truly

J. Wilkes. Booth

Autograph letter signed, Huntington Library.

1. T. Valentine Butsch was owner of the Metropolitan Theatre in Indianapolis.

2. This letter does not survive.

3. The two men agreed on two dates. JWB played Indianapolis for six nights, 24 through 29 November 1862. He starred in *Macbeth, Hamlet, Othello, Richard III,* and *The Robbers.* The *Indianapolis Sentinel* reported on 25 November that the Metropolitan Theatre, which seated 1,500, "could not hold all the people who rushed to see and hear Mr. Booth." Two days later, the paper reported that "Mr. Booth's *Hamlet* was a masterpiece of acting and held the audience spellbound." The same critic, however, panned JWB's performance as Othello the next night. Booth returned to the Metropolitan on 5 January 1863 for another six-day engagement.

To Joseph H. Simonds
Chicago, 6 December 1862

Chicago Dec 6th:.

Dear Joe

Yours of 1st: recd:. Am much obliged to you my dear boy for attending to my bus:[iness] with so much punctuality. Have recd: dresses.[1] Am much pleased with them.

Poor Frank Hardenburgh[2] I have been wanting to write him every day, but know not how to do it. The more quiet we can keep in such sad afflictions.—I deem is better for the mourner. I do not like to write him, ~~him~~ for fear of opening his wounds afresh. Yet would not have him think me indifferent to his misery. For I am sure there is no one, *except himself,* who can appreciate his sad bereavement MORE than *I.*

I must now run to the Theatre Joe.[3] It seems always the case when I ^am about to^ write to you. My bus:[iness] here has been ~~excelen~~ ^great^ near $900. on my first week.[4] Remember me with best wishes to Monty Field, Keach Warren[5] and all my friends

Excuse this

Yours as Ever

J Wilkes Booth.[6]

Autograph letter signed, Andre de Coppet Collection, Princeton University Library.

1. "Dresses" were theatrical costumes.

2. Actor Frank Hardenberg was a member of the stock company of the Boston Theatre.

3. On the night of 6 December 1862 JWB played Pescara in *The Apostate* at McVicker's Theatre in Chicago.

4. JWB appeared at McVicker's Theatre in Chicago from 1 December through 20 December 1862. He starred in *Richard III, The Merchant of Venice, Hamlet, Othello, Macbeth,* and *Romeo and Juliet.* He also performed *The Apostate, The Marble Heart,* and *The Lady of Lyons.* Although Chicago critics faulted Booth for overacting, business was good, as JWB boasts. The *Chicago Journal* of 18 December reported that "during the entire season McVicker's theatre has been patronized in an unprecedented manner. Money has poured into the box office like rain."

5. Richard Montgomery Field, William Warren, and Edwin F. Keach. Field would succeed Keach as manager of the Boston Museum when Keach suddenly died on 1 February 1864.

6. The letter is accompanied by autograph envelope addressed to "J. H. Simonds, Esq. Mechanics Bank Boston Mass"; the envelope is endorsed "Recd Dec 9/62 Ans Dec 10/62."

To Edwin Frank Keach
Chicago, 8 December 1862

Chicago
Dec 8th:/62

Friend Keach

I will endeavour to write a few lines in answer to yours of the 1st:—so here goes. The dresses I recd: all right and am highly delighted with the Romeos'. I wrote Joyce the other day, telling him I would either send him the money now, or pay him when in Boston. I prefer the latter, as I do not fancy sending money by express. I have now been waiting (with all the patience in the world,) for over two weeks to hear of $800. I sent to my mother.

My goose does indeed hang high (long may she wave.) I have picked up on an average this season over $650 per week. My first week here paid me ~~over~~ ^near^ $900. And this week has opened better. I am glad the Museum[1] holds her own. But I fear *Trag*[edy] will be in the mud when I get there. If you will go to some trouble for Richard,[2] I think we can make it a strong card for three or four nights in the first and last week of the engagement. Viz—First of all, plenty of supernumeraries (*with one rehearsal.*) And then the Coronation scene, And the scene "Who saw the sun to day," could be made fine pictures, the latter by having the left *flat* painted camp running off in distance, Richard's tent (furnished as in his previous scene) Set L.U.E.[3] And on right flat Archers extending in line of battle. Carrying out that line I draw down right of stage. And the Lord Mayor's scene too (last of 3d: act) could be made something of. Think of it.

I am glad Ned[4] is doing so well. Give my love to him. Arrange bus:[iness] as you think best/. Excuse this hurried scrawl. Wishing you all thats good, I am to you now and ever the same

J. Wilkes. Booth.

P.S. Best wishes to *Monty,* Warren, Wally & Simonds.[5]
Yours

JWB[6]

Autograph letter signed, Gratz Collection, Historical Society of Pennsylvania.

1. The Boston Museum, of which Keach was stage manager.
2. Playing the villainous Richard III was JWB's most popular role, as it had been his father's before him.

3. Left upper entrance.

4. Edwin Booth, then appearing in Boston.

5. Richard Montgomery Field, William Warren, and Joseph H. Simonds.

6. The letter is endorsed "J. W. Booth\Dec 8th: 1862." with a note in another hand reading, "John Wilkes Booth - 1865 Distinguished tragedian Brother of Edwin Booth The Assassin of President Lincoln."

To Joseph H. Simonds
Philadelphia, 28 February 1863[1]

Philada: Feb. 28th:
J H Simonds Esq

Dear Joe

Yours of 26th: recd:. I think with you that the water power stock is a good investment and am only sorry I did not buy long ago When you get this we can not tell what it will be selling for. However I would invest at once. I send you by this a draft for Fifteen hundred dollars ($1500) ~~put~~ invest it for me at once dear Joe.[2] I think I will have to make you my banker and give you an interest in my speculations, so that if we are lucky you may be able in a few years to throw aside those musty Ledgers. I am anxious to hear from you about the Ogdensbergh mail road.[3] I can find the *town* but *no road* on the map. To where does it run. Find out all about it and let us invest at once if it is all you have heard it. I would like to risk about $2000. in it. Telegraph or write on the receipt of this, to No 1021 Race St:[4] Am anxious to hear from you. Your true friend

J Wilkes Booth

Autograph letter signed, Andre de Coppet Collection, Princeton University Library.

1. Writing to Edwin from Philadelphia on 17 February 1863, Mary Ann Booth had reported on her favorite son, "I expect John home some day this week, he tells me he has done well the last week in Boston was very good" (Mary Ann Booth, autograph letter signed to Edwin Booth, 17 February 1863, Taper Collection). JWB starred at the Boston Museum from 19 January through 14 February 1863. Reviews were mixed. On 19 January the *Transcript* called him "this Young American Actor, the rapidity of whose professional progress, and brilliance of whose success is almost without parallel in the records of the stage." But the *Advertiser* reported on 16 February that Booth "does not add that elegance to his energy which we could hope, and he cannot stand in the highest position of actors until he shall be willing to perfect his elocution as thoroughly as his sword play."

2. Simonds used JWB's money to purchase twenty-five shares of Boston Water Power Company on 6 March 1863. Booth sold the stock on 30 May 1864, probably to raise money to develop his lease in the Pennsylvania oil country. The original stock certificate, signed by Booth, is in the Taper Collection.

3. This particular investment opportunity is not further identified. There were towns named Ogdensburg in New York and New Jersey.

4. The address of the Philadelphia home of JWB's sister Asia and her husband, comedian John Sleeper Clarke.

To Joseph H. Simonds
Philadelphia, 1 March 1863

Philada:
March 1st:

Dear Joe

I open here tomorrow I dont expect to do much the Theatres here seem filled nightly with empty benches.[1]

I sent you a draft yesterday for $1500. I want you to be as careful of my money as if it were your own (but theres no good in saying that for I know you will, and in fact more so) but what I mean is to *"look before you leap"*. If we make any good speculations you can count on a good percentage of profits when I sell. For you should ^have^ something for the great trouble I put you to. And I am sure you need something to get you in time from that old desk of yours. How about the Ogdensbergh stock. Let me know too all about the water power. do they [declare?] their dividend in land or money and when and how is it paid. The draft I sent is on Spencer & [Viln?] & Co Boston from Drexel of Philada.

What did Henry say about his money was it enough. he wrote me about it (but I guess it was before I gave it you) telling me to send it. It raining here very hard. I have not struck your game yet, but I may. and be sure I will not let them slip.[2] I am in great haste. God bless you.

Your True Friend

J Wilkes Booth[3]

Autograph letter signed, Andre de Coppet Collection, Princeton University Library.

1. JWB appeared at Philadelphia's Arch Street Theatre from 2 to 14 March 1863. He starred in *Richard III, Hamlet, Macbeth, The Merchant of Venice* and *The Apostate, The Robbers,* and *The Marble Heart.* His reviews were generally good.

2. Probably a reference to an investment opportunity.

3. The letter is accompanied by an autograph envelope addressed to "J. H. Simonds, Esq. Mechanics Bank Boston Mass" and endorsed "Recd Mar 4th 63 Ans Mar 4th 63."

To Joseph H. Simonds
Philadelphia, 3 April 1863

April 3d:

Dear Joe

Did you or Orlando[1] send me that catalogue of Back Bay lands to be sold April 9th:?, However find out about them. For lots No. 5. 6. 7. 8. or 9 ^(any ONE of them)^ on the north side of Commonwealth Avenue.[2] I will bid as high as $2.70 ^cts^ per foot, (their minimum value is $2.25.) If you fail to get any *one* of the above I will bid on Corner lot (Commonwealth Avenue) No. 20. As high as $3.25 per foot. If you are out bid and fail to get ^any one of^ them, I will bid on any *one* (*single* lot) on south side of Marlborough street as high as 20 per cent above its minimum valuation (a Corner lot preferred.) Attend to this dear Joe. See Keach who said something about the auctioneer being sorry he did not know I wanted to buy last time. Let Orlando see this. Advise with him about it. He promised to buy for me or to let me know about it.

I dont care about the lots on Marlborough St: if I buy ^one of them^ it will only be on specula:[tion], So if you miss the Commonwealth Av—strike light on the first. When did you see Ned.[3] Love to him & Mother and remember me to Orlando Keach and Monty.[4]

I have written to my old Rector in behalf of Steffin[5] Will send it to day I hope you have pretty well got over your troubles. Bless you my dear boy keep your eye open a little wider.

Yours Truly

J Wilkes Booth

Autograph letter signed, Andre de Coppet Collection, Princeton University Library.

1. Orlando Tompkins was one of the original stockholders of the Boston Theatre and served as its manager from 1862 until 1878, when his son Eugene took over. He was a friend of Edwin and John Wilkes Booth. In 1865 JWB gave Tompkins a ring inscribed "JWB to OT."

2. Lot 115 Commonwealth Avenue was purchased for JWB at the auction on 9 April. He paid $8,192.10 for the land in Boston's Back Bay, with one-quarter due two weeks after the auction and the balance over the following eighteen months.

3. Edwin Booth.

4. Orlando Tompkins, Montgomery Field, and Edwin F. Keach.

5. From JWB's allusion in his 19 April 1863 letter to Simonds to "my letter to Van—", "my old Rector" can be identified as the Rev. Libertus Van Bokkelen, the Anglican clergyman who was headmaster of St. Timothy's Hall, the Catonsville, Maryland, boarding school Booth attended in 1852. Reverend Van Bokkelen was said to be abolitionist, a species of political conviction he would have been wise to keep to himself in Maryland in the 1850s. JWB's letter to Reverend Van Bokkelen does not survive.

To Benedict DeBar[1]
Washington, D.C., 17 April 1863

Dear Ben, Yours of 10th recd. All right. I open with you June 15 for two weeks.[2] For God's sake try for that time (2nd. June). I don't want to lay idle two weeks.

Autograph letter, private collection.

1. Benedict DeBar (1812–77) was a London-born actor, stage manager and theater-owner who came to the United States in 1834. His most celebrated role was Falstaff. DeBar owned or managed theaters in New York, New Orleans, and St. Louis. His sister Clementine DeBar had married JWB's eldest brother, Junius Brutus Booth, Jr. The marriage ended in divorce. The couple's daughter, Blanche DeBar Booth, became a moderately successful actress, appearing under the name Blanche DeBar. After her parents' divorce, Blanche Booth was brought up by her Uncle Ben. All the DeBars were strong Confederate sympathizers, and Ben DeBar and his theater were closely watched by federal military authorities in St. Louis. It was while playing there in 1862 that JWB was arrested for saying that he wished the "whole damn government would go to hell." After paying a fine and taking an oath of allegiance to the United States, the actor was released. William A. Tidwell, with James O. Hall and David Winfred Gaddy, *Come Retribution: The Confederate Secret Service and the Assassination of Lincoln* (Jackson: University Press of Mississippi, 1988), 258.

2. JWB opened at Ben DeBar's St. Louis Theatre on 15 June 1863. About a week before he sent this letter to DeBar, on 11 April, Booth had begun his first star engagement in the nation's capital. The Grover's Theatre playbill loudly proclaimed the "FIRST APPEARANCE IN WASHINGTON OF J. WILKES BOOTH THE PRIDE OF THE AMERICAN PEOPLE, THE YOUNGEST TRAGEDIAN IN THE WORLD! WHO IS ENTITLED TO BE DENOMINATED A Star of the First Magnitude! SON OF THE GREAT JUNIUS BRUTUS BOOTH. AND BROTHER AND ARTISTIC RIVAL OF EDWIN BOOTH."

To Joseph H. Simonds
Washington, D.C., 19 April 1863

Washington April 19th:

Dear Joe

I have just finished a fine engagement here.[1] I was idle this week but stay here in hopes to open the other Theatre next Monday for a week or two before going to Chicago.[2] I am glad to hear of your success in our different Spec[ulation]s: Try it again in anything you think will pay. I enclose a letter from my old Rector[3] which you can show our friend Stephen. in my letter to Van—I said I had met Mr. Stephen very often. Also that he was a fine linguist, he wishes him to write. Excuse this dear Joe. have a very bad pen. And am far from well. *have a hole in my neck you could run your fist in. The doctor had a hunt for my bullet.*[4] once more excuse this

Yours Truly

J Wilkes Booth

Rose[5] sent Orlando a draft from Phila: and I sent one from here[6] -Has-he enough

---

Autograph letter signed, Andre de Coppet Collection, Princeton University Library.

1. JWB played Washington from 11 April through 9 May 1863, appearing first at Grover's and then moving on to the Washington Theatre, which Booth leased for his own use for almost two weeks in a strong demonstration of the young actor's increasing success and confidence. In Washington, Booth starred in *Richard III, Hamlet, Macbeth, Romeo and Juliet, The Merchant of Venice, The Marble Heart, The Stranger, The Robbers,* and *The Lady of Lyons.* On 27 April the *National Intelligencer* reported that "we . . . believe he stands without a rival. Mr. Booth's acting in the fifth act of *Richard* is truly great. . . . In his battle scenes he is far ahead of any actor living."

2. JWB's plans to go to Chicago fell through. He was never to perform again in that city.

3. The Rev. Libertus Van Bokkelen. JWB was baptized at Reverend Van Bokkelen's St. Timothy's Church in Catonsville, Maryland, on 23 January 1853.

4. JWB had not been shot in the neck, despite his reckless boast. During his Washington engagement he sought out an eminent surgeon, Dr. John F. May, (1812–91), for treatment of what the doctor described as "quite a large fibroid tumour" on the left side of the actor's neck. Without agreeing to Booth's request that he report the injury to be the result of a bullet wound, Dr. May cut out the tumor. Although May carefully sutured the wound, JWB accidently pulled it open again during a performance, leaving "a *large and ugly scar.*" Two years later, Booth had a genuine—and mortal—bullet wound to the neck. When his corpse was brought to Washington for

identification, Dr. May was one of those called on to render an opinion. At first, May did not recognize the wretched cadaver as the "fashionably dressed, and remarkably handsome young man" he had treated two years before. But when he saw the scar on Booth's neck—"the mark of the scalpel"—he was able to make a positive identification. John F. May, "The Mark of the Scalpel," *Records of the Columbia Historical Society* 13 (1910): 49–68.

5. JWB's eldest sister, Rosalie Booth, (1823–89), was a reclusive woman the family delicately called an "invalid." She remained her mother's lifelong companion and was bereft when Mary Ann Booth finally died in 1885.

6. JWB and his sister sent funds to Orlando Tompkins to make the initial payments on the Boston Back Bay real estate purchased for them in an auction of 9 April 1863.

To R. J. Morgan
St. Louis, 22 June 1863

St. Louis[1]
June 22d:

Dr. Sir,[2]
    I will agree to give up Saturday Night 27th on condition you pay me fifty dollars $ 50—to be paid on or before Friday Morning 26th:.

    But it is understood I do not play myself these I consider very reasonable terms

    Yours respect[full]y

    J. Wilkes. Booth

    To Morgan Esq

Autograph letter signed, Illinois State Historical Library.

    1. JWB starred at DeBar's St. Louis Theatre from 15 to 26 June 1863. He performed his familiar roles in *Richard III, Hamlet, The Merchant of Venice, The Apostate,* and *The Marble Heart.* He moved on to a quick four-night engagement in Cleveland, Ohio, from 30 June through 3 July, followed by a week's engagement in Buffalo, before hot weather ended the theater season.

    2. The recipient of this letter, R. J. Morgan, was a St. Louis businessman who fancied himself an actor. He had asked JWB to cancel his performance at Ben DeBar's St. Louis Theatre on the night of 27 June 1863 so that Morgan might appear as leading player that night.

To John T. Ford
New York City, 17 September 1863

No 107 East 17th: St:[1]
Sept 17th:

John. T. Ford Esq[2]

Dear John

Your telegraph just recd:. Now that I understand it. *All right Book me for Nov 2d: for two weeks.*[3] I *will be there* and I will keep the two following weeks *open* a time longer. there may be a chance for Baltimore then, or you may want me to keep on in Washington. But consider the two weeks from Nov 2d: settled. With best wishes I am yours Truly

J. Wilkes Booth

Autograph letter signed, John T. Ford Papers, Library of Congress.

1. The address of the house Edwin Booth had rented in New York City. JWB often stayed there when in New York, but only because his mother lived with Edwin. "If it weren't for mother I wouldn't enter Edwin's house," JWB told his sister. The two brothers disagreed on politics. After playing Buffalo in early July 1863, JWB had visited Edwin and soon found himself in the midst of the New York draft riots, the most deadly urban unrest in U.S. history. As violence ruled the city, JWB cared for a wounded Northern officer (author Adam Badeau), who was also staying with Edwin, and helped to conceal a black servant, whose safety was threatened by the rioters. Quotation from Asia Booth Clarke, *The Unlocked Book: A Memoir of John Wilkes Booth by His Sister* (New York: G. P. Putnam's Sons, 1938), 118.

2. John Thomson Ford (1829–94) owned and managed theaters in Baltimore, Richmond, and in Washington, D.C. Ford's Washington theater burned to the ground in December 1862. On the same site in 1863 he built the new Ford's Theatre, and it was there that John Wilkes Booth shot and mortally wounded Abraham Lincoln on 14 April 1865. Ford's imposing brick theater could accommodate an audience of 2,400. It was the finest theater in the nation's capital, with the best acoustics and a stage engineered for spectacular productions. Although he knew nothing of Booth's conspiracy, John T. Ford was imprisoned for thirty-nine days after the assassination.

3. JWB starred at Ford's Theatre from 2 through 15 November 1863, giving three performances of *Richard III* and also playing *Hamlet, Romeo and Juliet,* and *The Merchant of Venice,* as well as *The Apostate, The Robbers,* and *The Lady of Lyon.* On 9 November 1863 President Lincoln saw Booth star in *The Marble Heart* at Ford's. The president watched from the same box he would occupy on 14 April 1865. Lincoln's secretary John Hay, who accompanied the president that night, called Booth's performance "rather tame than otherwise." William A. Tidwell, with James O. Hall and David Winfred Gaddy, *Come Retribution: The Confederate Secret Service and the As-*

sassination of Lincoln (Jackson: University Press of Mississippi, 1988), 259. JWB appeared as an actor at Ford's Theatre on only one other night. He starred in *The Apostate,* the last performance of his career, on 18 March 1865.

To Benedict DeBar
Boston, 22 September 1863

Sept. 22'/63

B DeBar Esq

Dear Ben
    Yours of 20th recd: All right book me for the two weeks to begin Jan. 4th:/ 64.[1] Share after $140 per night, and benefit each week.[2]
    With regards to all.
    I am Truly Yours,

    J. Wilkes Booth.

PS Answer[3]

Autograph letter signed, National Archives.

    1. Although he here contracted to appear at DeBar's St. Louis Theatre for two weeks beginning 4 January 1864, bad weather caused the actor to miss the first week. He didn't open in St. Louis until 12 January (JWB to Moses Kimball, 2 January 1864, and JWB to John A. Ellsler, 23 January 1864).

    2. Compare these figures to the fee JWB stipulated in his letter to T. Valentine Butsch a year earlier. On 3 August 1862 Booth had set the terms for his appearance at Butsch's theater in Indianapolis as "share after eighty dollars. and half clear benefit."

    3. JWB's 22 September 1863 letter to DeBar was seized by the government after the assassination. On 21 April 1865 the War Department ordered the provost marshal general of St. Louis to "make a thorough search of the premises and effects of Mrs. Blanche Booth alias DeBar, and Ben DeBar, St. Louis Theater, for any correspondence of J. Wilkes Booth, or any other evidences of his conspiracy to murder the President. Send any secret ciphers or other suspicious papers you may find." Stanley Kimmel, *The Mad Booths of Maryland* (Indianapolis: Bobbs-Merrill, 1940), 373.

To John Adam Ellsler
New York City, 18 October 1863

New York, Oct. 18[1]

Dear John:[2]

Have not heard from you of late. November 23d and 30th is the only time I have for Cleveland.[3] I asked for Feb. 1st and 8th in Columbus.[4] I can still give you that time I guess, but let me hear from you at once, as I must answer Nashville.[5] If you can not arrange that time for Columbus I may be able to give you Feb. 29th and March 7th for Columbus, but you must answer at once by telegraph. I play tomorrow, Monday 19th here in Providence and the next night in Hartford.[6]

Yours truly,

J. Wilkes Booth.

Autograph letter signed, Harvard Theatre Collection, Houghton Library, Harvard University.

1. JWB apparently misdated this letter; he was almost certainly in Providence, Rhode Island, not New York City, on 18 October 1863. He appeared at Providence's Academy of Music from 16 through 19 October 1863, starring in *The Lady of Lyons, Richard III,* and *Hamlet;* 18 October was a Sunday. The theater was closed, but JWB may have been rehearsing with the stock company of the Academy of Music.

2. JWB's friend John Adam Ellsler (1822–1903) was an actor and the owner and manager of the Academy of Music in Cleveland, Ohio. He had first met Booth when Wilkes was a schoolboy in Baltimore. Ellsler was also Booth's partner in the oil business and visited the oil fields with Booth in December 1863, immediately after JWB's engagement at the Cleveland Academy of Music. The two men returned to the oil region in the summer of 1864. See John A. Ellsler, *The Stage Memories of John A. Ellsler,* ed. Effie Ellsler Weston (Cleveland: The Rowfant Club, 1950), 122–30. Ellsler acted with Booth on several occasions. Of JWB, Ellsler predicted: "John has more of the old man's [Junius Brutus Booth] power in one performance than Edwin can show in a year. He has the fire, the dash, the touch of *strangeness.* . . . Full of impulse just now, like a colt, his heels are in the air nearly as often as his head, but wait a year or two till he gets used to the harness and quiets down a bit, and you will see as great an actor as America can produce." Clara Morris, *Life on the Stage: My Personal Experiences and Recollections* (New York: McClure, 1901), 103.

3. JWB opened at Cleveland's Academy of Music on 25 November 1863. He played for ten nights in all, finishing on 5 December. Booth starred in *Richard III, Othello, Hamlet, The Lady of Lyons,* and *The Marble Heart.* In one of his performances of *Richard III,* Booth was badly cut on the forehead in violent swordplay of the last act. Although bleeding heavily, the actor played the scene to its end, thrilling the audience. After the engagement ended, Booth stayed in Cleveland, boarding at the Amer-

ican House, until about 11 December before visiting the Pennsylvania oil fields in the company of John A. Ellsler.

4. JWB did not appear in Columbus, nor did he return to Cleveland after his 1863 engagement.

5. JWB played Wood's Theater in Nashville, Tennessee, from 1 through 13 February 1864.

6. JWB appeared in Hartford, Connecticut, for three nights—20 through 22 October 1863. He starred in *Richard III, The Lady of Lyons,* and *Hamlet.* The *Hartford Daily Republican* on 22 October observed that "there is scarcely another instance . . . where an actor has arisen to the position now held by Mr. Booth, at so young an age and in so short a time." After Hartford, JWB played Springfield, Massachusetts, Brooklyn, and New Haven before beginning his extended engagement at Ford's Theatre in Washington, D.C.

To Moses Kimball
St. Joseph, Missouri, 2 January 1864

St: Joseph[1]
Jan. 2d: 1864
10 PM

Dear *Kim*[2]

Here I am snowed in again. And God knows when I shall be able to get away. I have telegraphed St: Louis for them not to expect me.[3] It seems to me that some of my *old luck* has returned to hunt me down. I hope you passed a delightful New Years you and your kind lady. but I fear not. I will give you a slight glimpse of mine. I arrived at Fort[4] with an ear frost bitten. I saw our friends there had a——, well I wont say what then after giving my boy[5] my flask to keep for me, I started for a *run* and made the river (four miles) on foot. I RUN without a stop all the way. I then found my boy had lost that treasured flask. I had to pay five dollars for a *bare-backed* horse to hunt for it. I returned within sight of the Fort and judge my dismay upon arriving to see a waggon just crushing my best friend. But I kissed him in his last moments by pressing the snow to my lips *over* which he had spilled his noble blood. I got back to the river in time to help and cut the ice that the boat might come to the shore. And after a "sea of troubles" reached this Hotel[6] a *dead man.* Got to bed as soon as I could where I have been ever scince. am better now and will I expect get up tomorrow. You must excuse this scrawl. I am the worst letter writer alive. and am trying to get through this on a cold bed. Give my best wishes to Mrs Kimbal. And ask her to forgive me for keeping her husband out so late at night. I guess she is glad I am gone. We may get away from here Monday or tomorrow. we can-not tell. Hoping you will remember me to all my friends. And that you will look over this poorly written letter.

I remain

Yours truly

J. Wilkes Booth[7]

Autograph letter signed, Taper Collection.

1. JWB had opened at the Union Theatre in Leavenworth, Kansas, on 22 December 1863. He played nine evenings in all, giving his last performance on the last night of 1863. JWB starred in *Richard III, Hamlet, Othello, The Taming of the Shrew* and *Richelieu, The Marble Heart,* and *The Lady of Lyons.* The Leavenworth *Conservative* declared on 1 January 1864 that "we have enjoyed the performances of this brilliant and intellectual young artist as we have done that of no other actor who has visited our city." While in Leavenworth, Booth roomed at the Planters House, the same hotel in which Abraham Lincoln had stayed on his western speaking tour in 1859. Booth seems to have been traveling with Moses Kimball, owner of the Boston Museum, and Kimball's wife. This letter is addressed to Kimball at the Planters House, and in it Booth mentions having left the Kimballs there.

2. Moses Kimball was the founder, in 1841, of the Boston Museum and Gallery of Fine Arts, better known as the Boston Museum. The Museum was Boston's leading theater. Kimball and his wife were on friendly terms with John Wilkes Booth; the rising young actor played the Museum in 1862, 1863, and 1864.

3. JWB was to have opened at Ben DeBar's St. Louis Theatre on 4 January 1864 (JWB to Benjamin DeBar, 22 September 1863). He could not begin his St. Louis engagement until 12 January.

4. Fort Leavenworth, Kansas. Concluding his Leavenworth engagement with a performance of *Othello* on 31 December, JWB had given himself four days to make the journey to St. Louis for his opening night at DeBar's theater. It would have been enough time had severe winter weather not frozen the area and brought the railroads to a standstill. The first leg of the trip, on New Year's Day 1864, took Booth from Leavenworth to Fort Leavenworth, where he visited "friends." The fort was about four miles from the Missouri River. Booth boarded a riverboat that carried him to St. Joseph, Missouri. From St. Joseph he had hoped to continue on to St. Louis by rail. In the days ahead he would be subjected to more extreme cold and danger.

5. JWB's "boy" was a "trusted young black servant" named Leav who accompanied him on his travels in the winter of 1863 and 1864. Gordon Samples, *Lust for Fame: The Stage Career of John Wilkes Booth* (Jefferson, N.C.: McFarland, 1982), 138.

6. The Pacific House in St. Joseph, Missouri.

7. The letter is accompanied by an autograph envelope addressed by JWB to "Kimball Esq Planters House Leavenworth K[ansas] T[erritory]." The designation of Kansas as a territory is in error; Kansas became a state in 1861.

To Thomas Harbine, John L. Bittinger, and P. L. McLaughlin
St. Joseph, Missouri, 4 January 1864

Thomas Harbine, John L. Bittinger, P. L. McLaughlin:[1]

Gentlemen:—Your flattering request has just been received, and I endeavour to show my appreciation of it by the promptness of my compliance. I have gained some little reputation as an actor, but a dramatic reading I have never attempted.[2] I know there is a wide distinction, as in the latter case it is impossible to identify one's self with any single character. But as I live to please my friends, I will do all in my power to please the kind ones I have met in St. Joseph. I will, therefore, designate Tuesday evening at Corby's Hall.[3]

> I am, very respectfully,
>   John Wilkes Booth

Letter published in the St. Joseph Morning Herald, 4 January 1864; reprinted in Franklin Graham, Histrionic Montreal: Annals of the Montreal Stage (Montreal: J. Lovell and Son, 1902), 145–46.

1. This letter is described as JWB's response to a petition from the mayor and sixty-eight citizens of St. Joseph, Missouri, requesting that the actor give a public reading in their city (Graham, Histrionic Montreal, 145–46). Graham also cites a "programme" of JWB's St. Joseph public reading belonging at that time to "Mr. Fred Leclair, manager of the Theatre Royal" in Montreal. According to the program, JWB presented the trial scene from The Merchant of Venice, selections from Hamlet, and the poems "The Shannon Bells," "Beautiful Snow," and "The Charge of the Light Brigade." But it seems clear that the reading was planned by Booth himself. In the following letter (JWB to John Ellsler, 23 January 1864), Booth writes that "in St Joe, I was down to my last cent and had to give a reading to pay my way. It gave me $150."

2. JWB may not have been entirely accurate in his assertion that he had never before attempted a dramatic readings. Several printed tickets (at The Players, New York City; in the Harvard Theatre Collection; and in the Taper Collection) survive from a public reading the novice actor gave in early 1859, probably in Charleston, South Carolina.

3. The St. Joseph Morning Herald ran the following piece on 5 January: "J. Wilkes Booth . . . will appear at Corby's Hall tonight at half past seven, where our citizens will have an opportunity of hearing some of the finest dramatic reading ever. . . . Wherever he appears, Mr. Booth is greeted with unbounded favor . . . and we are confident our people will show their appreciation of splendid talent and acknowledged genius by turning out en masse tonight." The next day, the Herald reported that Booth's excellent performance had been marred by the extreme cold in Corby's Hall and by the noise the audience made by constantly shifting about in an attempt to keep warm.

To John Adam Ellsler
Louisville, Kentucky, 23 January 1864

Wood Theatre
Louisville[1]
Jan 23d:/64

Dear John

I know you will not believe me when I say that this is the only moment I have had in which I could sit down and write at my ease Every day I have thought of writing you, for I am as anxious for our bus:[iness] to go on, as you can be. I have written to Mears[2] several times. The last time I wrote him[3] I requested him to have the agreement drawn up and to send it to me and I would sign it. He said he wanted about $500. to begin with I told him if you could not spare it, that *I* would send it to him.[4]

I have had a rough time John scince I saw you. It was hard enough to get to Leavenworth but in coming back was a hundred times worse Lost all but *four nights* of my St. Louis engagement. In St Joe, I was down to my last *cent* and had to give a reading to pay my way. It gave me $150. with which I hired a sleigh and came 100 miles over the plains. *Four days and nights* in the largest snow drifts I ever saw[5] Its a long story which I want to tell you when I see you, but I will say this that I never knew what hardship was till then. Write to Tom,[6] John; and let us push this thing through. Give my love to all. Hows my little girl

Your friend

J Wilkes Booth

I am more than sorry to hear of the various troubles you have had I hope alls well now

P.S. I go from here to Nashville and then to Cincinnati at Woods in both places[7]

Yours

John

Autograph letter signed, Western Reserve Historical Society, Cleveland, Ohio.

1. JWB began a two-week engagement at Wood's Theatre in Louisville, Kentucky, on 18 January 1864. He opened with his most celebrated role, *Richard III*, and went on to star in *Othello*, *The Apostate*, *The Robbers*, and *Richelieu*. Booth concluded his engagement on Saturday, 30 January, with a benefit performance of

Macbeth. The Louisville *Journal* reported on 21 January that "our citizens appreciate the great talent of Mr. J. Wilkes Booth, the great tragedian, whose name has
become illustrious with the American people. . . . His praise is on every tongue, and
he richly deserves it." But an actress remembered, many years later, that during a
performance of *Richelieu,* Booth was so drunk that he briefly fell asleep on stage.
Gordon Samples, *Lust for Fame: The Stage Career of John Wilkes Booth* (Jefferson,
N.C.: McFarland, 1982), 139.

2. Thomas Y. Mears, a gambler and former prizefighter, was a partner with JWB
and John A. Ellsler in the Dramatic Oil Company, a speculative venture the men
undertook in 1864 in hopes of winning quick riches in the Pennsylvania oil country.
Mears was said to have been an abolitionist. Ernest C. Miller, *John Wilkes Booth in
the Pennsylvania Oil Region* (Meadville, Pa.: Crawford County Historical Society,
1987), 13ff.

3. No correspondence between Booth and Mears survives.

4. In December 1863, after finishing his engagement at the Cleveland Academy
of Music, the theater John Ellsler managed, JWB, Ellsler, and Thomas Mears made a
scouting trip to the oil fields near Franklin, Pennsylvania. Although his acting could
now command substantial fees of $300 to $900 a week in addition to the proceeds
of benefit performances, Booth was anxious to make even more money through
investments. One of the riskiest investments of the day was in oil—petroleum had
been discovered in western Pennsylvania in 1859. In the boom that followed, fortunes
were made and lost by investors who drilled wells or bought and sold oil stocks or
leases on likely drilling sites.

After their first visit, Booth and his friends agreed to form a partnership to buy
up leases. Although the partners came up with the name the Dramatic Oil Company, they never legally incorporated their venture. Mears was to do most of the work,
with Booth and Ellsler providing the capital. In this letter Booth offers to advance
some of the funds that should have come from Ellsler. Booth also brought his Boston friend and business agent Joseph H. Simonds into the oil venture.

Booth would return to the Pennsylvania oil country in the summer of 1864. Although the actor liked to boast that he had made a fortune in oil, he actually lost
heavily. At the trial of the Lincoln conspirators in May 1865, Simonds testified that
Booth had lost $6,000. Benn Pitman, comp., *The Assassination of President Lincoln
and the Trial of the Conspirators* (New York: Moore, Wilstach and Baldwin, 1865;
facsimile edition edited by Philip Van Doren Stern, New York: Funk and Wagnalls,
1954), 45.

5. JWB was stuck in St. Joseph, Missouri, until 9 January, four days after he presented his dramatic reading in Corby's Hall. Railroads were not running, and some
trains were reported to be buried on the tracks in snowdrifts thirty feet deep. The *St.
Joseph Morning Herald* recorded temperatures of 20 below zero and reported on 5
January that "the snow has effectively shut us out from the world and the rest of
mankind, and there is no prospect of relief." Booth, however, was determined to get
to St. Louis. With $100 of the money he had earned from his reading, the actor hired
a four-horse sleigh to travel sixty miles cross-country to Breckinridge, Missouri. He
had learned that trains to St. Louis were running from there. JWB later told a harrowing tale of making his way through deep snow and extreme cold. He even claimed

he had been attacked by wolves. His difficulties did not end when he finally boarded the train on 11 January. At one point he had to threaten a conductor with a pistol to force the train to continue through deep snowdrifts. Samples, *Lust for Fame*, 135. JWB's frigid ordeal may have had longlasting consequences—the exposure may have been the cause of bronchial problems and impaired speaking ability that troubled him from time to time for the rest of his acting career.

6. Thomas Y. Mears.

7. JWB had reportedly contracted, at a weekly salary of $300, to appear at the Wood's Theatres in Louisville, Nashville, and Cincinnati.

To Edwin Frank Keach
Louisville, Kentucky, 30 January 1864

Jan 30th:
Woods Theatre
Louisville

E. F. Keach, Esq.

Dear Frank

Just recd: a letter from Mr Blatchford in reply to my last to you.[1] ITS ALL RIGHT. But ~~but~~ be kind enough to write me naming exact Time Terms etc. which he did not do in his letter. Direct me Woods Theatre, *Nashville,* where I open Monday night for two weeks, then Cincinnati. I hope you are quite well by this. Excuse this

With best wishes for all
I remain Yours Truly

J Wilkes Booth

Autograph letter signed, Swift Collection, University of Tulsa, Tulsa, Oklahoma.

1. Blatchford, like Keach, was a manager at the Boston Museum.

To Moses Kimball
Nashville, Tennessee, 9 February 1864

Woods Theatre
Nashville[1]
Feb 9th:/64

Moses Kimball Esq

My Dear Sir
    Yours of the 4th: just recd:. Poor Keach.[2] I heard of his death by telegraph and sincerely mourn him, as will *all* his friends and brother professionals. I can easily enter into all your regrets.
    As for our engagement It was agreed between Mr Keach and myself, that I should open at the Museum[3] April 25th:/^64^ on old terms for ^a^ six week engagement, I have his answer closing *Time. Terms* etc In a way that there may be no misunderstanding. Then I receive yours to day naming other time etc.[4]
    My dear sir I hope you will excuse this as I write in great haste. I open Monday at Woods Theatre Cincinnati for two weeks. Write me there. I then go to New Orleans for a five week engagement. With best wishes for yourself and family, I remain Yours Truly

    J Wilkes Booth[5]

Autograph letter signed, the W. E. Hill Theatre Collection, Fine Arts Department, Dallas Public Library, Dallas, Texas.

    1. JWB played two weeks in Nashville, Tennessee. He opened 1 February as *Richard III* and starred in *Hamlet, Othello, The Merchant of Venice* and *The Apostate, The Robbers,* and *Money* and finished the engagement with a performance of *The Corsican Brothers* on 13 February. Although JWB played to a theater "crowded to a perfect jam," on 3 February the Nashville *Dispatch* criticized his bombastic, ranting acting. "It may be that we are so firmly wedded to that quiet school, which recognizes the right of an actor to speak and walk and act naturally, and which forbids the tearing of a passion to tatters, as to suppose nothing good can come from any other school, but if so, we cannot help it, and therefore cannot commend Mr. Booth as a finished *artiste;* he is too violent by half." Other observers suspected that Booth was drunk during some of his performances. Charles E. Holding, "John Wilkes Booth Stars in Nashville," *Tennessee Historical Quarterly* 23 (March 1964): 73–79.
    2. Edwin F. Keach, stage manager of the Boston Museum, died on 31 January or 1 February 1864 of "paralysis of the brain."
    3. The Boston Museum.
    4. Neither Keach's nor Kimball's letters to JWB survive, but see the following letter (JWB to Richard Montgomery Field, 9 February 1864).

5. While in Nashville in February 1864, JWB made the acquaintance of Andrew Johnson, whom Lincoln had appointed military governor of Tennessee, and his secretary, William A. Browning. William A. Tidwell, with James O. Hall and David Winfred Gaddy, *Come Retribution: The Confederate Secret Service and the Assassination of Lincoln* (Jackson: University Press of Mississippi, 1988), 261. Later that year, Johnson would be elected as Abraham Lincoln's vice president and, after the assassination, would become president. Booth would attempt to see Johnson or Browning in Washington on the day he killed Lincoln, leaving a calling card at their hotel (JWB to Andrew Johnson, 14 April 1865). Booth would also assign to one of his team of conspirators the mission of killing Johnson.

To Richard Montgomery Field[1]
Nashville, Tennessee, 9 February 1864

[. . .] it, but in the letter he said "Let us make the engagement for *two weeks*. Each of us keeping the *two* or *four* following weeks open that we may continue it, if paying us mutually

I answered "all right, but sup*pose we say for four* ^(4)^ weeks sure, (as I played there that long

P.S. My proposition was. Open April 25th: for six weeks on old terms, *four weeks sure* and for each of us to keep the two following (the 5th and 6th: Week) open to continue on, if it paid us mutually[2]

J Wilkes Booth[3]

Autograph letter signed, incomplete, Taper Collection.

1. Richard Montgomery Field, who had been a dramatic critic with the *Boston Post*, succeeded Edwin F. Keach as stage manager of the Boston Museum after Keach's sudden death.

2. In this incomplete letter, written from Nashville, JWB is trying to reestablish with Field the terms he had set with Keach for his engagement at the Boston Museum in April 1864. Here Booth is apparently quoting from Keach's letter and from his own response to Keach. He did in fact open at the Boston Museum on 25 April and played there through 27 May, in what was the longest single run of Booth's career as a star.

3. The letter is endorsed "J Wilkes Booth Ans. Feb 9/64 Feb. 17th—copie."

To Richard Montgomery Field
Cincinnati, 22 February 1864

Woods Theatre
Cincinnati[1]
Feb 22d:/64

Dear Monty

Its all right Yours I have just read and hasten to answer it. Depend on me for April 25th: I start from here (God willing) on Saturday for New Orleans, where I play a five weeks engagement. have two weeks to get from there to Boston. If you wish to write me direct. Care St. Charles Theatre. I have been very sick here, but am all right again.[2] Thank God.

Joe[3] told me I would be astonished when I found out my new Managers name.[4] And I am so. I wish you more success than you have ever hoped for. Excuse this

I wish to be remembered to all,

I am your true Friend

J Wilkes Booth

Autograph letter signed, Andre de Coppet Collection, Princeton University Library.

1. JWB appeared at Wood's Cincinnati theater from 15 to 26 February. He missed two of his scheduled performances because of sickness. He performed *Othello, The Merchant of Venice, Hamlet,* and *Richard III,* as well as *The Apostate, Money,* and *Richelieu.*

2. By the time he reached Cincinnati, JWB's hoarseness and the cold he had been suffering from ever since his frigid journey across the prairies had become serious impediments to his acting. The continuing cold weather during January and February certainly did not help; the theaters in which he appeared were poorly heated. Booth had intended to open in Cincinnati with his most successful role, *Richard III.* Audiences found Booth's rendering of this violent adaptation of Shakespeare's tragedy thrilling, particularly the final swordfight, which often brought the whole house to its feet. JWB liked to open his star engagements with *Richard* and to repeat the play, sometimes twice, during the course of a two-week run. He was forced to open in Cincinnati, however, in the less strenuous role of *Othello* on 15 February. (One lazy drama critic didn't bother to attend the opening; the next day his paper praised JWB's acting in *Richard III.*) Booth missed one night altogether, "his physician [having] positively forbidden him from leaving his room," and was hoarse and weak throughout his Cincinnati engagement. After his last performance he rested for a few days in his room at the Burnett House hotel, attended by a friend named H. C. Young. Young remembered that Booth's chest and arms were covered with scars from wounds

the actor had received in many stage fights. Constance Head, "John Wilkes Booth, 1864: Prologue to Assassination," *Lincoln Herald* 85 (Winter 1983): 256.

3. Joseph H. Simonds.

4. JWB refers to Field's having replaced Edwin F. Keach as stage manager of the Boston Museum.

To Richard Montgomery Field
New Orleans, 26 March 1864

March 26th, 1864[1]
St Charles Theatre[2]

Dear Monty

Yours recd: only four days ago Have been sick[3] or would have answered it before.

Besides I have been trying to find out the whereabouts of Harrington,[4] whom I have met lately but cannot tell where, and as for the other party I know nothing of him.

I will be with you in April, all right. God willing

Give my love to Joe and tell him I will write soon.

With best wishes to Warren[5] and the rest

I remain yours Truly

J Wilkes Booth[6]

Autograph letter signed, Massachusetts Historical Society.

1. The letter is written on stationary with the printed heading "Office of Cutler & Thomas Attorneys and Counselors at Law 5 Commercial Place New Orleans, La." JWB has crossed out the heading.

2. JWB traveled from Cairo, Illinois, to Memphis, Tennessee, aboard a riverboat named the *C. W. Hillman.* The boat reached Memphis about 2 March. From there, Booth continued his journey to New Orleans on the *J. C. Swon,* probably departing on 5 March. He arrived in New Orleans a few days later. He did not open at the St. Charles Theatre until 14 March, a week late, likely because he was still too sick to perform. His engagement in New Orleans lasted until 3 April but was interrupted by illness. Three scheduled performances were canceled. Still, JWB played eighteen nights in New Orleans, one of his longer star engagements. He presented his usual battery of plays, including *Richard III, Hamlet, Othello, Macbeth, Romeo and Juliet,* and *The Merchant of Venice,* as well as *The Apostate, Richelieu, The Marble Heart,* and *The Lady of Lyons.*

3. On the evenings that JWB did go on stage, his acting was marred by hoarse-

ness and an indistinctness of speech that both audiences and critics remarked on. The New Orleans *Picayune* reported that "his [first] performance . . . disappointed us. His elocution appeared to us to be deficient in clearness and very labored." Other reviewers were more charitable, but although many praised Booth's talent, even his "genius," nearly all noted a "severe hoarseness." When he concluded the New Orleans run on 3 April with *Richard III*, the *Picayune* declared, "It is a matter of regret that a physical disability, we trust temporary, prevented his engagement from being so gratifying to himself or his friends as was desirable, and we look for his return here next season under more favorable auspices." But Booth never returned to the Crescent City. He made only one more star engagement, in Boston in April and May 1864. John S. Kendall, *The Golden Age of the New Orleans Theater* (Baton Rouge: Louisiana State University Press, 1952), 497–502.

4. Possibly "Professor" Jonathan Harrington, a celebrated ventriloquist.

5. Joseph H. Simonds and William Warren.

6. The letter is endorsed "J. Wilkes Booth New Orleans Recd. April 11 64."

To Richard M. Johnson
New Orleans, 28 March 1864

St: Charles Theatre[1]
New Orleans
March 28th:/64

R. M. Johnson Esq[2]

Dear Johnson

Yours of 12th: recd:. I am glad to find that you have not forgotten me, and hope I may ever live in your generous remembrance. I enclose in this a picture of myself, *better* (I think) than the one I gave you.

This of you[3] I will ever keep among my *very few* and chosen friends. Excuse the shortness of this, ^am in haste.^ I am your's

J. Wilkes Booth[4]

Autograph letter signed, Huntington Library.

1. JWB's father, the "mad tragedian" Junius Brutus Booth, had given the last performance of his career in New Orleans's ornate St. Charles Theatre in November 1852. On his way home from a tour of California, the elder Booth staged several lucrative performances before heading north on a Mississippi River steamboat. While on board, Booth incautiously drank of the great river's murky, pathogenic waters and was soon overtaken by fatal sickness. Unable to move and almost unable to speak, he died in his cabin, attended only by a compassionate stranger.

2. While aboard the riverboat that took him to Memphis on his way to New Orleans, JWB met Union Col. Richard M. Johnson, a native of St. Louis, who had served for a time on Grant's staff. Johnson remembered that he had been drinking, distraught over the loss of a friend. Despite his Southern sympathies, Booth became friendly with the federal officer; he consoled Johnson and told him about his investments in the oil business. Johnson's letter to Booth reads in part: "I may be vain in presuming our brief Memphis acquaintance has made us friends, but on my part it has—we met that day, when I was plunged into the deepest grief from the loss of a dear friend. I had tried to drown my sad thoughts in the cup to no avail, when on the [illegible] I came across you—your thoughts were so fresh and original and your heart seemed to commune with my own, I half forgot my sorrows" (R. M. Johnson to JWB, 12 March 1864, Lincoln Assassination File, National Archives).

3. A photograph of a young man by a St. Louis photographer, seized with JWB's personal effects, may be the one Johnson had sent Booth in his letter of 12 March 1864. That photograph is reproduced, as photograph number 1, in Richard J. S. Gutman and Kellie O. Gutman, *John Wilkes Booth Himself* (Dover, Mass.: Hired Hand Press, 1979), 37.

4. Despite JWB's professions of friendship to a Northern officer, it was recalled that, on a dare, the actor sang "The Bonnie Blue Flag" on a New Orleans street, a Confederate anthem banned by the federal military authorities who ruled the occupied city. Quickly surrounded by angry soldiers, Booth just as quickly talked his way out of trouble. John S. Kendall, *The Golden Age of the New Orleans Theater* (Baton Rouge: Louisiana State University Press, 1952), 498.

To "My Dear Miss"
New Orleans, 4 April 1864

St: Charles Theatre
April 4th:

My Dear Miss

I recd: yours yesterday, but was kept (by business) from answering till now.

I have come to the conclusion that a noncompliance with your request would be a crime, especially if my *not refusing* will afford you the pleasure you mention. I therefore enclose, (with my best wishes for your future) A picture of my humble self. I start next Saturday for Boston[1]

With all respect
I remain yours
to command

J.W.B.[2]

Autograph letter signed, Taper Collection.

1. JWB left for Boston on 9 April. He probably traveled by boat up the Mississippi to Cairo, Illinois, or St. Louis, Missouri, to make a rail connection to the East.

2. Despite his recurring illness and the burden of nightly performances—the New Orleans theaters were open Sundays—JWB kept up an active social life during his five-week stay in New Orleans. "Booth made many friends during his brief residence in New Orleans," John S. Kendall has written. "He was the sort of man who forms acquaintances easily, and his talent was already recognized sufficiently to make people anxious to know him. He was interested in all kinds of diversions. He played billiards and tenpins, rode horseback—and did these things with considerable skill. Into everything he projected the full force of his exuberant personality. He was never content unless he occupied a conspicuous position, even in his amusements." *The Golden Age of the New Orleans Theater* (Baton Rouge: Louisiana State University Press, 1952), 497. An acquaintance of Booth's during his New Orleans days remembered that "Booth drank a great deal in those days, although he was never so entirely under the influence of intoxicants as to be unable to fulfill his duties at the theater. Usually, even in his cups, he was an affable, considerate, courteous companion; but sometimes, when he had imbibed more than his custom his mind was haunted by strange ideas— particularly, the notion that he was the victim of conspiracies" (ibid., 499).

To Junius Brutus Booth, Jr.
[ca. April 1864][1]

[. . .] Heard from Mother yesterday. God Bless her, she complained at your silence. She and the rest are well. How is dear little Mary[2] Have you ever told her she has an Uncle John? However, she will know it before [. . .]
[. . .] you a thousand [. . .]
Your Loving Brother

    J. Wilkes Booth

Autograph letter signed, incomplete, private collection.

1. Junius Brutus Booth, Jr., left San Francisco for New York City, where he was to help Edwin Booth manage the Winter Garden Theatre, on about 23 April 1864. On that basis, this fragmentary letter to Junius is tentatively dated early April. Stanley Kimmel, *The Mad Booths of Maryland* (Indianapolis: Bobbs-Merrill, 1940), 183.

2. Daughter of Junius Brutus Booth, Jr.

Document signed
31 May 1864

This is to certify that the undersigned has purchased the dressing gown from Mrs. Wilson for seventy-five dollars and which is paid this date. 31 May 1864, J. Wilkes Booth.[1]

Document signed, published in auction catalog: Charles Hamilton Galleries, New York, 25 May 1972.

1. The Charles Hamilton Galleries catalog description of document reads, in part, "Manuscript D.S., five lines on an oblong narrow 8vo. sheet (about 4" x 7½"), May 31, 1864. Certification, penned by a clerk. . . . Booth has affixed a bold signature (almost four inches long) and M. A. Wilson has also signed." Neither the identity of Mrs. Wilson nor the circumstances of this transaction are known.

Isabel Sumner

In the spring of 1864, during his triumphant starring engagement at the Boston Museum, John Wilkes Booth met a sixteen-year-old Boston girl named Isabel Sumner. She was by all accounts a beautiful young woman. Booth had known many women; it is not likely that Isabel Sumner had known many matinee idols. Yet the only evidence of the romance that does survive—the six letters that follow—suggests that Booth was the one most smitten, that the man who had been pursued by so many women devoted considerable energy to the pursuit of this particular girl. The circumstances of their meeting can probably never be recovered, but it is likely the actor met Isabel at the theater, where crowds of admirers eagerly awaited him at the end of each performance. Booth had opened at the Boston Museum on 25 April and played there through 28 May. It was the longest appearance of his career as a star. In 1881 John T. Ford described Booth's 1864 conquest of Boston: "Doubtless he would have been the greatest actor of his time if he had lived. Beside being the handsomest man I ever saw, he was an athlete. He put into all his impersonations the vitality of perfect manhood. . . . When he was playing in Boston he doubtless made the greatest success of an actor of his day. People waited in crowds after the performance to catch a glimpse of him as he left the theater."[1] An actress who supported Booth in some of his roles at the Boston Museum that summer remembered that "the stage door was always blocked with silly women waiting to catch a glimpse, as he passed, of his superb face and figure."[2] A quarter century after his death, Clara Morris

Booth gave this copy of his *cartes de visite* portrait to Isabel Sumner in Boston in the spring of 1864. (Taper Collection)

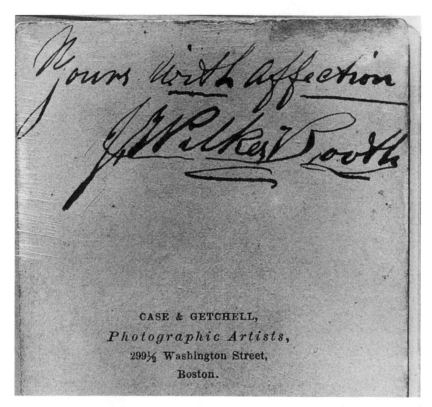

CASE & GETCHELL,
Photographic Artists,
299½ Washington Street,
Boston.

Booth's inscription to Isabel on the verso of the photograph. (Taper Collection)

Detail of the inscription ("J.W.B. to I.S.") within the band of the ring given by Booth to Isabel. (Taper Collection)

No 28 East 19th St.
June 7th /64

Dear Miss Isabel.

How, shall I
write you; as lover, friend,
or brother, I think so much
of you, that (at your bid-
-ding) I would even try to
school my heart, to beat
as the latter. The first and
second, would require no
exertion, for the first
(forgive me) I cannot help
being, and the second, I
am, and hope I ever shall
be, Then, until I hear
from you, I will act upon

The first page of Booth's first letter to Isabel Sumner, 7 June 1864. (Taper Collection)

"The handsomest man in America": An elegant John Wilkes Booth leans against a studio prop in this photograph taken by the Boston firm of Silsbee, Case and Company, probably in 1862. (Taper Collection)

Isabel Sumner. (Taper Collection)

Cased photograph of Booth with strands of hair cut from his head by a Virginia girl a few moments after his death. (Taper Collection)

Miss White.

May all good angels guard & bless thee.
And from thy heart remove all care.
Remember you should ne're distrest be.
Youth & hope, can crush dispare.
+
Joy can be found, by all, who seek it.
Only be, right, the path, we move upon
Heaven has marked it; Find & keep it
Ne're forget the wish of John.

Richmond Feb 18th 1860

He who will ever be your friend
J. Wilkes Booth

The twenty-one-year-old actor wrote this acrostic poem in Mary White's autograph album two weeks before the inauguration of President Abraham Lincoln. The initial letters spell out the names Mary and John. (Taper Collection)

John Wilkes Booth's copy of *Julius Caesar,* owned by the novice actor in his days as a member of the stock company at Wheatley's Arch Street Theatre, Philadelphia, 1858. Booth memorized Shakespeare's story of political murder. (Taper Collection)

"Lincoln Drafting the Emancipation Proclamation," cartoon by Adalbert J. Volck (ca. 1864). Like many Americans, Booth believed that Abraham Lincoln was a tyrant who had betrayed the white race by turning the Civil War into a crusade against slavery. In Volck's savage cartoon, a president inspired by demons and images celebrating bloody race war tramples the Constitution underfoot as he composes the Emancipation Proclamation. (Huntington Library)

"The Assassination of President Lincoln in His Private Box at Ford's Theatre," *Frank Leslie's Illustrated Newspaper,* 29 April 1865. This contemporary woodcut probably provides a reasonably accurate depiction of the fatal instant. (Huntington Library)

$30,000 REWARD

DESCRIPTION

OF

JOHN WILKES BOOTH!

Who Assassinated the PRESIDENT on the Evening of April 14th, 1865.

Height 5 feet 8 inches; weight 160 pounds; compact built; hair jet black, inclined to curl, medium length, parted behind; eyes black, and heavy dark eye-brows; wears a large seal ring on little finger; when talking inclines his head forward; looks down.

Description of the Person who Attempted to Assassinate Hon. W. H. Seward, Secretary of State.

Height 6 feet 1 inch; hair black, thick, full and straight; no beard, nor appearance of beard; cheeks red on the jaws; face moderately full; 22 or 23 years of age; eyes, color not known—large eyes, not prominent; brows not heavy, but dark; face not large, but rather round; complexion healthy; nose straight and well formed, medium size; mouth small; lips thin; upper lip protruded when he talked; chin pointed and prominent; head medium size; neck short, and of medium length; hands soft and small; fingers tapering; shows no signs of hard labor; broad shoulders; taper waist; straight figure; strong looking man; manner not gentlemanly, but vulgar; Overcoat double-breasted, color mixed of pink and grey spots, small —was a sack overcoat, pockets in side and one on the breast, with lappells or flaps; pants black, common stuff; new heavy boots; voice small and thin, inclined to tenor.

The Common Council of Washington, D. C., have offered a reward of $20,000 for the arrest and conviction of these Assassins, in addition to which I will pay $10,000.

L. C. BAKER,
Colonel and Agent War Department.

A rare example of the earliest reward poster naming Booth as Lincoln's killer. (Taper Collection)

(Opposite page) Despite the prodigious rewards offered for his capture, Booth remained free for almost two weeks. (Huntington Library)

War Department Washington, April 20, 1865,

$100,000 REWARD

THE MURDERER

Of our late beloved President, Abraham Lincoln,

IS STILL AT LARGE.

$50,000 REWARD

Will be paid by this Department for his apprehension, in addition to any reward offered by Municipal Authorities or State Executives.

$25,000 REWARD

Will be paid for the apprehension of JOHN H. SURRATT, one of Booth's Accomplices.

$25,000 REWARD

Will be paid for the apprehension of David C. Harold, another of Booth's accomplices.

LIBERAL REWARDS will be paid for any information that shall conduce to the arrest of either of the above-named criminals, or their accomplices.

All persons harboring or secreting the said persons, or either of them, or aiding or assisting their concealment or escape, will be treated as accomplices in the murder of the President and the attempted assassination of the Secretary of State, and shall be subject to trial before a Military Commission and the punishment of DEATH.

Let the stain of innocent blood be removed from the land by the arrest and punishment of the murderers.

All good citizens are exhorted to aid public justice on this occasion. Every man should consider his own conscience charged with this solemn duty, and rest neither night nor day until it be accomplished.

EDWIN M. STANTON, Secretary of War.

DESCRIPTIONS.—BOOTH is Five Feet 7 or 8 inches high, slender build, high forehead, black hair, black eyes, and wears a heavy black moustache.

JOHN H. SURRAT is about 5 feet, 9 inches. Hair rather thin and dark; eyes rather light; no beard. Would weigh 145 or 150 pounds. Complexion rather pale and clear, with color in his cheeks. Wore light clothes of fine quality. Shoulders square; cheek bones rather prominent; chin narrow; ears projecting at the top; forehead rather low and square, but broad. Parts his hair on the right side; neck rather long. His lips are firmly set. A slim man.

HAROLD is a little chunky man, quite a youth, and wears a very thin moustache.

BOOTH'S CAPTURE—THE ASSASSIN BROUGHT TO BAY.

"Booth's Capture—The Assassin Brought to Bay," *Harper's Weekly,* 13 May 1865. The flames at Booth's feet flared like the footlights of the last act, and so lighted he was an easy target when, against orders, a veteran sergeant fired. (Huntington Library) recalled the indiscretions into which their fascination for John Wilkes Booth led some women:

> Let me tell you there were many handsome, well-bred and wealthy ladies in the land, married as well as unmarried, who would have done many foolish things for one of those kisses. Booth's striking beauty was something which thousands of silly women could not withstand. His mail each day brought him letters from women weak and frivolous, who periled their happiness and their reputations by committing to paper words of love and admiration which they could not, apparently, refrain from writing. He gave orders to have his letters sorted in the box office and often his pile of business letters would look small, indeed, beside that which contained epistles which bore anything but the imprint of business on their faces. These fond epistles were seldom read. He instructed his dresser to burn them. Many of them were signed with the real names of the foolish women who wrote them. The dresser one day boasted that a certain lady, moving in high social circles, had written a compromising letter to Mr. Booth. The statement was treated as an absurd lie and, to prove that he had not been boasting, the dresser displayed the letter, which he had not burned as he had been instructed to do. Mr. Booth's anger was terrible when he learned the facts, and the dresser was dismissed, and ever after the signatures to these letters were torn into tiny fragments by the actor.[3]

Whatever may have brought the two together, the romance of John Wilkes Booth and Isabel Sumner clearly went beyond a mere flirtatious correspondence. They exchanged photographs. Booth rhapsodized over Isabel's likeness in his first letter to her; Isabel kept the signed photo the actor gave her all her life. He also gave her a ring, set with a modest pearl and bearing within the band the inscription "J.W.B. to I.S." She sent him flowers when he lay sick at Edwin's house in New York City. It is unlikely that Isabel's family knew of her involvement with the actor; his letters had been directed to her at general delivery, the Boston Post Office. In August, the teenage girl, probably employing some subterfuge, managed to travel to New York, where she saw Booth at least once. (This was, of course, the period during which Booth was becoming increasingly involved with the Confederate secret service.) There is no evidence that Isabel and Booth met again after August 1864. But while others, out of fear or disgust, destroyed correspondence with or mementoes of John Wilkes Booth, Isabel Sumner preserved hers until the day she died, testament, perhaps, to the enduring importance of her memories of the brief liaison of the 1860s. Unfortunately, none of Isabel Sumner's letters to Booth are known to survive.

◇◇

Isabel Sumner was born in Boston on 31 May or 1 June 1847, the daughter of Charles Henry Sumner (1821–91) and Sally Tileston Sumner (ca. 1826–1909). Although later generations of the family remembered that Charles Henry Sumner had been cousin to Massachusetts Senator Charles Sumner, no evidence of such a connection has been uncovered. In 1864 the Sumners were living at 916 Beacon Street, not far from the Tremont Hotel where Booth usually lodged when he played in Boston. The 1865 Massachusetts State Census gave Charles H. Sumner's occupation as "Provisions"; he was apparently a grocer.[4] The 1865 census also provided these bare facts about the couple and their four daughters: Charles H. Sumner was forty-five; his wife was forty, her occupation was "married." "Isabella," at eighteen the eldest, was "single," her profession was "Scholar"; sister Josephine, sixteen, was also an unmarried student. The census-taker also recorded that little sisters Clara and Maria, twelve and four, respectively, were also "single." All the Sumners had been born in Massachusetts. Living with them in 1865 was an English servant named Mary Scott.

In Boston, on 31 January 1877, Isabel Sumner married David Albert Dunbar, Jr. (1847–95). They were married by the Rev. Edward Everett Hale, minister of Boston's South Congregational Church and remembered as author of the short story "The Man without a Country." Dunbar's occupation was given as "Trader" on the marriage license. Isabel was twenty-nine at the time of her marriage. More than twelve years had passed since her affair with John Wilkes Booth. In 1880 the U.S. Census recorded that the Dunbars and their two-year-old daughter, Laura, were then living with Isabel's parents. A second daughter, Sallie, was born to the couple in 1888. By the 1900 census, after both Isabel's father and husband had died, she and her two daughters were living in Boston with her mother. When David Albert Dunbar died at the end of 1895, his wife of nineteen years entered into a widowhood that lasted the rest of her life, more than three decades. They were not happy years. One of her daughters remembered that although the decade before Dunbar's death had been bright and prosperous, after he died Isabel Dunbar was plagued by financial worries, loneliness, and depression. She had to give up the house at 916 Beacon Street, where she had lived all her life, and move to a less expensive suburb of Boston. Her mother died in 1909. A small scandal, complete with some lurid coverage in the press, followed the 1911 wedding of Isabel's youngest daughter Sallie, then an attractive twenty-three-year-old, to a wealthy man of sixty-three. In 1919 Isabel Sumner Dunbar moved to New

York City. She died of stomach cancer at her apartment in the Fairfax Hotel, East 56th Street, on 23 February 1927, and was buried in Forest Hills Cemetery, Boston.

Isabel had an interest in the occult and commissioned at least two astrological charts. She was apparently much impressed by two passages from them. In the first, the stars revealed that "friendships before and after marriage are prone to die in a curious or unexpected manner . . . and ending the career of some person connected with [Isabel Sumner] in discredit and at a sacrifice of character." The second chart indicated that Isabel's "position of Venus does not argue well for domestic and love relations during the earlier part of life. The native born under such relations usually meets with disappointments—separation or some unhappy results." An enigmatic scrap of paper bearing a list of names that includes Booth's might be the record of a séance at which the presiding charlatan had convinced Isabel that the assassin's spirit was present.

The last living person who knew Isabel Sumner Dunbar is her granddaughter, Bobbie Makepiece, who was fourteen when the old woman died. Much of the information about Isabel given in these notes was provided by Bobbie Makepiece in an interview with Louise Taper on 2 June 1989. Makepiece is the daughter of Isabel Sumner's younger daughter, Sallie, and the older man she married in 1911, Edward Everett Richards. Richards died about 1918. Bobbie Makepiece remembers her grandmother as a small, pretty, blue-eyed old woman who had a good sense of humor and never spoke of John Wilkes Booth.

---

1. Gordon Samples, *Lust for Fame: The Stage Career of John Wilkes Booth* (Jefferson, N.C.: McFarland, 1982), 128.

2. George S. Bryan, *The Great American Myth* (New York: Carrick and Evans, 1940; repr., with an introduction by William Hanchett, Chicago: Americana House, 1990), 94.

3. *Boston Herald*, 10 January 1890.

4. A surviving business card or packaging label in the Taper Collection reads "C.H. SUMNER & CO, dealers in provisions, fruit, game—also canned goods of all descriptions."

To Isabel Sumner
New York City, 7 June 1864

No 28 East 19th: St:[1]
June 7th:/64

Dear Miss *Isabel.*

How, shall I write you; as *lover, friend,* or *brother.* I think *so much* of you, that (at your bidding) I would even try to school my heart to beat as the latter. The first and second, would require no exertion. for the *first* (forgive me) I cannot help being, and the second, *I am,* and hope I ever shall be, Then, until I hear from you, I will act upon what I think a certainty, and say DEAREST FRIEND. (Let me call you so) May God bless you. As I am wishing him to do with every breath, And protect you, from the *wiles* of this *bad world* of ours, *keeping you* EVER, GOOD *and* PURE as, *you are,* (in my eyes) *beautiful* I wish I could have seen more of you,—or not have seen, at all,—for our short acquaintance has set me thinking wildly. Bless you dear friend. O, how I wish I could understand you, Tell me (and from your heart) do you *think* the *least* LITTLE BIT ~~in the world~~ of *me;* Forgive me for asking such a question, but I know the *world,* and had begun to hate it. I saw you, Things seemed changed.

I believe you have MORE than *kind feelings* for *me,* but, *I* have been deceived a thousand times, May I not be so now; May you not be deceiving yourself, Reflect before you answer. Ask yourself if this attachment (If on your-side, any should exist), is not for the mere pastime of the hour, A Girls caprice, which even now, you find passing, from your mind. I fear it is. therefore write so. Forgive me dearest, but ask yourself these questions. Think well upon it. *Then Say:* Am I to be your brother, *friend,* or LOVER. Dearest Isabel never, never trifle with *anothers heart,* or try to *cheat your own.* Forgive me Isabel, I am such a *miserable letter* writer ^that^ I am always ashamed of them So I cannot tell what I have been writing *about,* for should I read it over, I am sure that ^that^ would be ^the^ end of it.

But, God bless this *sweet face* before me, *It* would *move me to* do *anything* (even to write a love letter, if I knew how) Will you believe me, when I tell you, I have—well no matter, God Bless *it* and the original say I. Isabel dear friend Will you grant me a little favor? It is *never* to show my letters even to your dearest friends. I have no fear that you will do so, but you might think *like others* that it would be no *harm.* But dear friend it would do you *no good* and to tell you a secret—(I was just about to say, *I love you.* Well perhaps I do.) but the *secret* is ^that^ I am ashamed to read my own letters, much less to have them seen by strangers. And in writing to you I may say some *foolish things* (for I think *love* and *folly* are synonymous terms,) which though *you might forgive,* others *would condemn.* Dear friend I will write no more, but I dare say you think I have written too much already.—

I start tomorrow for the mountains of *Penn.* where I remain about three weeks.[2] But should you be kind enough to write me *Direct to me* HERE, and I will get it. Write soon. and remember me to our friend Mrs D— (she said I might call her friend.) and say she shall have those lines on *my return.* As I will be unable to see pen, ink or paper where I am going. Write soon. God, *God bless you* Write soon. Write at once. to

John

Autograph letter signed, Taper Collection.

1. The address of Edwin Booth's home in the Gramercy Park section of New York City. JWB's mother, Mary Ann Holmes Booth, made her home with Edwin. In order to see his mother, JWB often stayed with Edwin when he was in New York, despite the brothers' disagreements over the war. "Knowing my sentiments," Edwin later explained, "he avoided me, rarely visiting my house, except to see his mother, when political topics were not touched on, at least not in my presence." Edwin Booth to Nahum Capen, 28 July 1881, in Edwina Booth Grossman, *Edwin Booth: Recollections by His Daughter* (New York: Century, 1894), 227–28.

2. An entry in the diary of Junius Brutus Booth dated 6 June 1864 notes that "John cut his nose against a clothes line" The entry for 9 June reads "John & Joe Simonds left for oil city." Junius Brutus Booth, Jr., diary, 1864, Folger Shakespeare Library, Washington, D.C.

To John Adam Ellsler
Franklin, Pennsylvania, 11 June 1864

Franklin[1]
June 11th:

Dear John
    just recd: your telgm:, we whent over the a/c[count]s: to day. I find them all right. Tom[2] will show the accounts, I have advanced $390.00 more than you have Now if we have $1500, ^now^ between us, (that is you paying the $390. up, to meet me.) Say I pay 555.00 and you pay 945.00 which will make the 1500. I am sure we will be *pumping oil in less than a month,* Tom goes to Cleveland to buy rope, [chambers?] &c., which we MUST *have* or we are at a stand still. we can do nothing without this money. So meet it John, It will be

the last BIG PULL, (except the sum we have to raise for the *purchase* of the lands, and you have paid half of your share already, and I have mine ~~ready~~ ^in hand.^)

Now I think you ought to meet me half way in this (if you intend to go through with it at all.) for I have as little ^money^ and as much *use for* that little as any man can have, If you can not pay all of it (ie 945.) get the rope and [chamber?] on *your* note. But John *come up* for we must have this money to go on with.

Tom says he has been trying to draw no more than $90. per month from us, and that he cannot live upon it. I said I was willing to let him have as much, as you would meet me half way with. I would like to see you here, if you can, come next week I write this letter from myself. Tom has said nothing about this affair, but I am sure he thinks you ought to meet me half way, and I hope and expect you to do so.

Love to all, In haste.

yours Truly

J Wilkes Booth

Autograph letter signed, Harvard Theatre Collection, Houghton Library, Harvard University.

1. In December 1863, Booth, Ellsler, and Thomas Y. Mears had visited the petroleum boomtown of Franklin. Agreeing to speculate in oil and oil leases, they named their partnership the Dramatic Oil Company (see JWB to John Adam Ellsler, 23 January 1864). The two men returned to the oil region in the summer of 1864. In the memoir published as *The Stage Memories of John A. Ellsler* (Cleveland: The Rowfant Club, 1950), Booth's partner recalled Booth in Franklin in June 1864: "[Booth's] engagement with us was at the time of the mania for oil territory in Pennsylvania. Through a mutual friend [probably Cleveland businessman George Paunell], we were persuaded to invest in a profitable piece of oil land, the understanding being that at the conclusion of the dramatic season [about the end of May 1864], John and myself would repair to our property, purchase the necessary machinery, and develop our investment. As arranged, Wilkes preceded me to the base of operations, and when I reached him, I found him hard at work, dressed in a slouched hat, flannel shirt, overalls, and boots. Who that had seen him as 'Hamlet,' 'Claude Melnotte,' 'Richard,' etc., would suppose that such a transformation was possible!" (127). On 29 October 1864, as he was preparing for the capture of Abraham Lincoln, JWB liquidated his oil investments, assigning the property to his brother Junius Brutus Booth, Jr., his unmarried sister Rosalie, and his friend Joe Simonds. Simonds later testified that the actor had lost about $6,000 in his oil speculations. Booth's activities in the oil fields are discussed in some detail in Ernest C. Miller, *John Wilkes Booth in the Pennsylvania Oil Region* (Meadville, Pa.: Crawford County Historical Society, 1987), and in Hildegarde Dolson, *The Great Oil Dorado* (New York: Random House, 1959).

2. Thomas Y. Mears had remained in Franklin to manage the affairs of the Dramatic Oil Company in which he was a partner with JWB and Ellsler. The partners' well was named the Wilemmena in honor of Mears's wife.

To John Ellsler
Franklin, Pennsylvania, 17 June 1864

June 17th:/64
Franklin

Dear John

I want to see you here bad. This may be a big thing for us or it may be *nothing*. The last sure if we do not give it our attention. Throw things overboard and come as soon as possible. I must see you. I have seen all the oil regions. I got back the other day from a two days *walk* of 48 miles.[1] And I know more about these things than anyone can tell me. Make it your bus:[iness] to come at once. Kiss Effe.[2] Kind regards to all. Yours Truly

JW Booth

Autograph letter signed, Illinois State Historical Library.

1. One acquaintance of JWB during his Franklin days recalled that he "used to take long walks with Booth in the hills. A young man here from New York, an amateur actor and friend of Booth's reluctantly accompanied them on these rambles. Booth was a good fast pedestrian and a great lover of nature and pure air and freedom of the country and hills. Used to talk on all sorts of subjects on these walks: poetry, theatrical profession, literature, and in fact anything that crossed their minds was talked on freely. Nothing was said on politics." Ernest C. Miller, *Booth in the Pennsylvania Oil Region* (Meadville, Pa.: Crawford County Historical Society, 1987), 69.
    2. Ellsler's daughter, Effie Ellsler (Mrs. Frank Weston).

To Isabel Sumner
Franklin, Pennsylvania, 17 June 1864

Franklin
June 17th:/64[1]

Dearest Isabel

Have you forgotten me so soon? I hope not. Yet why not write me. But perhaps you have already done so and it has not been forwarded to me. *If so it is safe.* God bless you dear friend. *Do not forget me.* And excuse my foolish letters. You know you promised to teach me how to write. I have been here over a week now, and may be here a week longer. I then go to New York again. This is a great country, Every-thing is Oil and smokes. I returned yesterday from a two days walk—through the mountains—of over 48 miles. and am still quite used up. God bless you

Do you think of me sometimes *do,* if only for a moment I should hate to be forgotten so soon. God bless you ever

Your friend.

J.W.B.

Autograph letter signed, Taper Collection.

1. On 17 June Edwin Booth wrote to Emma F. Cary that "My brother W—— is here for the summer, and we intend taking advantage of our thus being brought together, with nothing to do, and will, in the course of a week or two, give a performance of 'Julius Caesar' in which I will take the part of *Brutus* instead of *Cassius*— for the benefit of the statue we wish to erect in Central Park." See Edwina Booth Grossman, *Edwin Booth: Recollections by His Daughter* (New York: Century, 1894), 153–54. The celebrated performance of *Julius Caesar* by the three Booth brothers did not take place at the Winter Garden Theatre in New York City until 25 November 1864. Edwin played Brutus, Junius Brutus acted Cassius, and John Wilkes was Marc Anthony. The audience numbered more than two thousand. Nearly $4,000 in proceeds from the "Booth Benefit for the Shakespeare Statue Fund" went to the purchase of a statue that still stands in Central Park.

To Isabel Sumner
New York City, 14 July 1864

28 East 19th:
July 14th:

Dearest Friend

I have just returned from the mountains of Penn——. God bless you, I was sure you had forgotten me, As I had told my Mother *to forward* all letters. but she expecting my return every day, neglected to do so. *But I have recd:* them *at last.* Bless you, Only think of the pleasure I have *now* in reading them.[1]

Indeed, I thought you had forgotten me, and I had no idea how much I *cared* for you till the last week or so. Since my last to you I have been ever saying to myself. "Just my *luck now* that I truly . . . . I am laughed at" But it *is not* so, bless you. Is it? I would come on to B[oston]——if I thought I could see *you.* so I could talk to you without reserve.

But I am afraid you are not in the City now, And have some doubt of your getting *this.* And I will be kept busy *here,* for a week or two yet. But I will run the risk of not seeing you and come on as soon as I can.

Dearest Isabel, I can not write to you. I want to talk to you. I have just travelled over 600. miles. It is now 2½ A.M. I am tired and sick. Let that, be an excuse for this miserably written letter. But let the *style* or *manner* of my letters *be what it may. I LOVE YOU,* and I feel that in the fountain of my heart a *seal is set* to keep its waters, *pure* and *bright* for *thee alone.* God bless you. You see (to follow *your* wishes, NOT MY-OWN) I call myself your FRIEND *only* ^good night^ [. . .] JWB[2]

Autograph letter signed, Taper Collection.

    1. Isabel Sumner's letters to JWB do not survive.
    2. The letter is accompanied by an autograph envelope postmarked 15 July, New York, and addressed to Isabel Sumner at the Boston Post Office.

To Isabel Sumner
New York City, 24 July 1864

No 28 East 19th: St:
July 24th:

My dear Friend.

Have I, in any way, offended you? if so. it has been unwittingly. And God knows how full of repentance, and how anxious I would be to make every atonement.

I have been so uneasy, of late, thinking (by your silence) I may have said something in one of my letters to offend, that its impossible for me to rivet my mind to a single line of study, or in fact, to anything else.

Oh Isabel dear friend (you said I might call you so) *please* take no offence at anything I may—inadvertently—have ~~said~~ written for believe me I never look over my letters, to weigh their contents, for fear I should destroy them. As I am always—more or less—disgusted with my own bad writing etc. Therefore what I write is just what I may feel, at the moment, And may often say things to be sorry for. If it has been *this* forgive me. And tell me of it. *And* you will see (at *your* bidding) how quickly I shall mend.

Or is it—as I begin to fear it is—that you are *weary of reading my poor, poor letters.* If such is the case I am sorry. Sorry indeed, for having given *you a moments trouble.* Sorry for myself, that I have allowed my *fancy* to play so free.

I can write no more: The mere thought that. *It may be so,* seems to paralyze my hand.

God forever *bless* you Isabel, I will *trouble you no more,* if you say the word. but can never, *never cease* to *think* of *you* as something *pure and sacred,* A *bright* and *happy* dream, from *which* I have been awoke to *Sadness.* You will I hope give my best wishes and never-dieing friendship to Mrs D—. Strange but there is something about that lady that from the very first I felt I had *known* and *respected* all my life.

Remember, dear friend ~~to~~ not to let *anyone* see my letters. *I will come at once to Boston.*

Never.—MORE, till I hear from you.

Wishing once more for every blessing to be yours

I am your friend

    Forever

      John[1]

Autograph letter signed, Taper Collection.

1. The letter is accompanied by an autograph envelope postmarked 25 July, New York, and addressed to Isabel Sumner at the Boston Post Office.

To Isabel Sumner
New York City, 26 August 1864

Aug 26th:

Dearest Friend Isabel

I recd: your sweet flowers yesterday And you know how delighted I must have been in knowing that you sometimes thought of me. God bless you. When your message came this morning I was still in bed waiting for the doctor to come. He came at last; but did not cut my arm. he has put it off till tomorrow.[1]

You cannot imagine how sorry I was in not being able to see you. I have not been out of the house since I saw you. but will walk up with this to see it delivered. God bless you dearest friend

I am yours

John

Autograph letter signed, Taper Collection.

1. JWB had been stricken with a severe case of erysipelas on his right arm. It took him about three weeks to recover. Erysipelas is a brilliantly red, rapidly spreading streptococcus infection of the skin. In the nineteenth century the disease could be debilitating, even life-threatening. On 15 August 1864 Asia Booth Clarke reported "a delightful stay at the seaside and a pleasant time with Mother in NY. Wilkes is quite sick" (Asia Booth Clarke to Jean Anderson, Peale Museum, Baltimore). Later she recalled that JWB "was once stopping at Edwin's New York house, and, suffering from a diseased arm, he fainted from the acute pain, and Junius carried him and laid him upon his bed. As he lay there in his shirt-sleeves so pale and death-like, we all felt how wondrously beautiful he was. It was a picture that took hold deeply in all our hearts, for soon he was to lie dead among his foes, and not one of us should gaze upon his face. As we saw it then, pallid and death-like on his bed, we were to ponder it all our lives." Asia Booth Clarke, *The Unlocked Book: A Memoir of John Wilkes Booth by His Sister* (New York: G. P. Putnam's Sons, 1938), 118.

Samuel Arnold, who, with Michael O'Laughlen, had been recruited by Booth for the conspiracy to capture Lincoln in a meeting at Barnum's Hotel in Baltimore some time shortly before 15 August 1864, wrote that "I received a letter which I destroyed, stating that he was laid up with erysipelas in his arm, and he did not make his appearance until sometime in January." See "The Confession of Samuel Arnold," in Louis J. Weichmann, *A True History of the Assassination of Abraham Lincoln and the Conspiracy of 1865*, ed. Floyd E. Risvold (New York: Alfred A. Knopf, 1975), 381. In a diary entry dated 28 August Junius Brutus Booth, Jr., noted that "John Booth ill 3 weeks with Erysepalas in the Right Elbow—had Dr. Smith." Junius Brutus Booth, Jr., diary, 1864, Folger Shakespeare Library, Washington, D.C.

To Isabel Sumner
New York City, [27 or 28 August 1864]

Dearest Isabel

I am so sorry I have just recd: your note and not two hours ago had a gash cut in my arm about two inches long I am sure I will be in bed all day tomorrow I hope not though, and will try and meet you But if you will only make it a day or two later I may (God willing) be quite well Excuse this Bless you

John

Autograph letter signed, Taper Collection.

"Might Makes Right":
The Conspiracy against Abraham Lincoln

By November 1864 John Wilkes Booth had given himself over entirely to his grand scheme of saving the Confederacy by capturing Lincoln and carrying him south as a hostage. The story of Booth's activities in the months before the assassination, the failure of his plot to abduct Lincoln, the assassination itself, and the assassin's flight, capture, and death has been told many times. No further recapitulation will be attempted here. Nevertheless, the documents that follow trace events leading to and following from the murder of Abraham Lincoln.

November 1864 saw one of the Civil War's great turning points—the election of President Lincoln to a second term. Lincoln had won on a platform of fighting the war through to victory and ending slavery forever by means of an amendment to the Constitution—terms that encompassed the extinguishment of the Confederate States of America. It is tempting to look back on Lincoln's reelection on 8 November as the day the South actually lost the Civil War. But to the Confederate high command, and to a defiant Confederate partisan named John Wilkes Booth, the Southern cause seemed far from lost. These men believed that the South could still prevail in its gigantic struggle for independent nationhood. It was probably shortly after Lincoln's reelection that Booth wrote two of the most significant of his letters to survive, the "to whom it may concern" letter and that to his "dearest beloved Mother." These two documents provide the clearest and most forceful statements of the political convictions that had led him to take up arms for the Confederacy.

He began the "to whom it may concern" letter with an angry challenge, "Right, or wrong, God, judge me, not man," and his words still quiver with barely controlled fury. "I have ever held the South were right," Booth insisted. "The very nomination of Abraham Lincoln four years ago, spoke plainly—war, war upon Southern rights and institutions. His election proved it." He ended with a stark promise he would soon keep when he vowed "to triumph or die": "It is either extermination or slavery for *themselves* (worse than death) to draw from. I would know *my* choice." But if Booth was willing to accept extermination, he was not obliged to welcome it; he would first do all he could to forestall Northern success. Booth's convictions could justify killing as well as capture; in any event, an attempt at capture could easily result in the death of Lincoln, a vigorous "Western" man who could be expected to resist his assailants.

◇◇

Recruited by the Confederate secret service for the mission in a meeting at Boston's Parker House Hotel on 26 July 1864, Booth had traveled to Canada in the fall, consulting with Confederate agents in Montreal from 18 to 27 October. He talked for hours with George N. Sanders, a former Pierce administration diplomat who had joined a plot to assassinate French Emperor Louis Napoleon in 1853. Sanders had since dedicated himself to Confederate victory; his motto was said to be "death to tyrants!"

Booth was back in Washington on 9 November, where he checked into the National Hotel. A week later he opened an account with the Washington office of Jay Cooke and Company, Bankers. He deposited $1,500. While in Montreal he had deposited $400 in the Ontario Bank, also buying a £63 bill of exchange for an additional few hundred dollars. He now had funds in place to finance his conspiracy and, if need be, to escape abroad, into the Confederacy, or within the United States itself. The source of Booth's substantial deposits cannot be established. He had not been acting. His oil investments had only lost money. The timing, however, suggests that he had been given the cash, some of it in U.S. gold coin, by the spies in Montreal.[1]

In November and December Booth made several trips to southern Maryland. His reputation as a wealthy actor made it easy to pass off his rides along the backroads of the Confederate "Secret Line" as an investor's search for property. He was actually scouting his escape route and meeting with Confederate agents, introductions to whom he had secured in Montreal. He began buying supplies—weapons, rations, and boats to cross the Potomac.

On 25 November, Booth was in New York City to appear in a special production of *Julius Caesar* with his brothers Junius Brutus and Edwin. Wilkes played Marc Anthony, Edwin the assassin Brutus, while Junius Brutus Booth played Cassius. Proceeds from the benefit went to purchase the statue of Shakespeare that still stands in Central Park. Although a second Shakespeare statue benefit was planned for April 1865, the November performance would be the only time the three brothers appeared on stage together. That same night a gang of saboteurs financed by Confederate headquarters in Canada tried to burn down New York by simultaneously setting fire to more than twenty Manhattan hotels. They failed, but news of the operation sent the city into an uproar the next day. That morning the Booth brothers quarreled bitterly about Lincoln and the war. Junius said the fire-setters should be tracked down and lynched. He declared Southern defeat certain. Edwin told his younger brother that he had voted for Lincoln and that he prayed for

Union victory. John, who had met the leader of the arsonists in Montreal a month before, argued that the destruction of New York City would have been a legitimate act of war and fitting retribution for the many acts of Northern barbarism in the South. He also claimed that Lincoln meant to crown himself king of the United States.[2]

◇◇

The year 1864 ended, and the great war entered its final months. Now an unexpected complication arose. Booth found himself entangled in an romance with Lucy Lambert Hale, whose father was Senator John Parker Hale, a New Hampshire abolitionist. The senator and family had checked into Booth's Washington hotel in January 1865. By March, Booth and Lucy Hale were said to be engaged to be married. But the Confederate spy did not allow his love for a Yankee (if love it was) to come between him and his ambition to win the war by seizing the president or, later, his determination to exact vengeance on the man to whom "our country owed all her troubles."[3]

Booth had recruited his first two conspirators, Samuel Arnold and Michael O'Laughlen, in August 1864. In January he enlisted John Harrison Surratt, a Confederate courier who traveled between Canada and Richmond, where he sometimes met with Confederate Secretary of State Judah P. Benjamin, the man who exercised a large measure of control over his government's secret service operations. In the weeks that followed, more men joined the conspiracy: Thomas Harbin, a Confederate agent in southern Maryland; George A. Atzerodt; David Herold; Lewis Powell; and others unknown to history. (Booth could not persuade two of his actor friends to volunteer.)

Booth then began a protracted period of waiting characterized by both tedium and frantic efforts to keep his gang together and discover a way to capture the president. He was also running out of money. Arnold later recalled that "the month of January passed, and as yet nothing had been accomplished. February ushered itself in only to be a repetition of the former month, as Booth through riotous living and dissipation was compelled to visit the City of New York for the purpose of replenishing his squandered means. His absence continued nearly the entire month, caused by the great difficulty experienced in borrowing money. . . . During the Entire Month of February the project was at a stand still and seeming apathy, seldom meeting with Booth."[4]

On 4 March John Wilkes Booth attended Lincoln's second inauguration at the east front of the Capitol, coming close enough to the president, he would later claim, to have killed him then. Had Booth bothered to listen to the address he probably would have been infuriated by the extraordinary meditation on history in which Abraham Lincoln proposed that the vast struggle that had consumed hundreds of thousands of lives was God's "true and righteous" punishment of the entire American nation for 250 years of slavery. On 15 March Booth gathered his followers for the stormy late-night dinner party at which they argued over the mission's diminishing prospects for success. The party broke up at five in the morning after the conspirators exchanged a round of drunken death threats. Two days later, what had promised to be the team's best chance of catching Lincoln ended in a humiliating fiasco, the result of Booth's failure to check newspaper accounts of the president's daily schedule. It seemed to confirm all the doubts and objections hurled across the table in the private room at Gautier's Restaurant. Some of the conspirators now deserted their leader. On 18 March the actor made his final stage performance in *The Apostate.* His next appearance would be on the Ford's Theatre stage on the night of 14 April. But on 31 March Booth told Arnold and O'Laughlen that he had abandoned his "project" against Lincoln, that he planned to return to acting.

◇◇

Recent studies of the Lincoln assassination have presented compelling evidence that a secret mission to blow up the White House and wipe out the president and his cabinet in early April was approved by Confederate President Jefferson Davis.[5] The critical role was assigned to an explosives expert named Thomas F. Harney, a sergeant in the clandestine Confederate Torpedo Bureau. Harney left Richmond about 31 March. He was to be inserted into Washington by a unit of John S. Mosby's irregular cavalry, which often operated behind enemy lines. But on 10 April the force was attacked by federal cavalry outside Washington. Harney, who, the Union commander reported "had brought ordnance to Colonel Mosby and joined his command," was captured.[6]

There would be no explosion at the White House. Moreover, Grant's army had entered Richmond on 3 April; Jefferson Davis was in full flight with a few remnants of the Confederate government. Lee had surrendered on 9 April. Lincoln's death could no longer wrest victory from the North. But Booth, it is argued, knew of the proposed mining of the White House and decided to approximate its results by orchestrating the murders of the president, vice president, the secretary of state, and perhaps General Grant and other cabinet officers.

It has yet to be proven, however, that Booth did know of the Confederate mission to destroy the White House. Atzerodt reported that Booth had told him of the plan of "a party in New York who would get the prest." by mining the Executive Mansion.[7] He said nothing about the plan originating in Richmond. Had Booth simply not told Atzerodt what he knew of the true origins of the plot? Or had he repeated idle talk or rumors of an entirely different conspiracy he had learned about in New York? It is not clear what the Confederate secret service would gain by informing Booth of an operation whose success depended on complete secrecy and in which Booth himself had apparently not been assigned a part. Research may yield new truths about the role of the Confederate government in conspiracies against Lincoln, but it seems likely that death will continue to guard the secrets John Wilkes Booth once possessed.

---

1. Stanley Kimmel, *The Mad Booths of Maryland* (Indianapolis: Bobbs-Merrill, 1940), 189; James O. Hall, quoted in Jim Kushlan, "Collectible: A Paper Link to a Conspiracy," *Civil War Times Illustrated* 30 (Sept.–Oct. 1991): 15. Booth eventually wrote seven checks on the Jay Cooke account; see "Summary List of John Wilkes Booth Documents," 30.

2. William A. Tidwell, with James O. Hall and David Winfred Gaddy, *Come Retribution: The Confederate Secret Service and the Assassination of Lincoln* (Jackson: University Press of Mississippi, 1988), 202; Kimmel, *Mad Booths of Maryland,* 192–93.

3. JWB may have valued Lucy most for the entry he hoped she could provide to high Republican circles in Washington. He also bragged to a friend about Lucy's wealth. Testimony of Samuel K. Chester, Lincoln Assassination File, National Archives, 599-4-162ff.

4. Samuel Bland Arnold, *Defence and Prison Experiences of a Lincoln Conspirator* (Hattiesburg, Miss.: The Book Farm, 1943), 43–4.

5. Tidwell, with Hall and Gaddy, *Come Retribution,* 416–21; William A. Tidwell, *April '65: Confederate Covert Action in the American Civil War* (Kent: Kent State University Press, 1995), 8–9, 160–75, and passim.

6. Tidwell, with Hall and Gaddy, *Come Retribution,* 420.

7. See Introduction, note 39.

To J. Dominic Burch
Washington, D.C., 14 November 1864

Washington, Nov. 14th

J. D. Burch, Esq.

Dear Sir.

Hope I shall see you again ere long. Our *friend* of the *stage* last friday never left what I gave to his charge. You know *what* I had to take from my carpetbag. It's not worth more than $15, but I will give him $20 rather than lose it. As it has saved my life two or three times. He has left the city. If you would be kind enough to get it from him and send it to me I will reimburse you for any outlay. And will never forget you. If you should ever recover it, either send, or give it to *our friend*, co. Fayette st. where if you wish you can write me.

Remember me to all the friends I met while in your country.

I am yours truly

J. Wilkes Booth.[1]

Transcription of autograph letter signed in the David Rankin Barbee Papers, Georgetown University Library.

1. The letter was transcribed by David Rankin Barbee on 9 June 1936 from the original then in the possession of Susie C. Burch, Baltimore, Maryland. The following memorandum is included with the transcription in the Barbee Papers:

> Memo. of an interview David Rankin Barbee had with Mr. James Burch, 1011 Cathedral Street, and with his mother, Mrs. Susie Burch, 2743 North Calvert Street, Baltimore, in relation to a letter written by John Wilkes Booth to J. D. Burch, this 9th day of June, 1936.
>
> J. Dominic Burch, to whom Booth wrote this letter, lived at Bryantown, Maryland, in 1864. His father, Henry Burch, who was the uncle of my father, the late Dr. W. Balsell Burch, of Baltimore, kept the tavern or hotel at Bryantown. In November 1864, Booth made a trip into Southern Maryland, stopping at the hotel in Bryantown. He found himself among a group of Southern people whose sympathies were all for the Confederacy. His purpose in visiting that region was said to be to organize his plans for kidnapping President Lincoln, and among the persons he met to whom he became very much attached, and who returned his friendship was Dominic Burch. Booth and Burch were very nearly the same age. While in around Bryantown Booth became suspicious that agents of the Federal Government were spying on him. He possessed a fine revolver, which he valued highly, and he felt that if it became known that he had this revolver he might be arrested. So he gave it to the driver of the stage coach, with directions to leave it with some one

either in Washington or Baltimore. The stage driver failed to do this, and Booth wrote Dominic Burch this letter, with a view to repossessing the weapon. When Booth killed Lincoln, it is understood that every person who had received a letter from him burned such letter or letters. Dominic Burch, however, kept his, and hid it under a stone in the fireplace in his father's city house on St. Paul Street, Baltimore. After the war he came to Baltimore to live. He was a sickly man and never married, but lived to the great age of ninety years. My father, Dr. Burch, attended him professionally through the years, and from him learned the history of the Booth letter. At his death the letter came into the possession of our family.

"To Whom It May Concern"
[Philadelphia, November] 1864[1]

1864

My Dear Sir[2]
  You may use this, as you think best, but as some, may wish to know ~~the when, the who~~ and ~~the why~~, and as I know not, *how,* to direct, I give it. (In the words of your Master)

"To whom it may concern"[3]
  Right, or wrong, God, judge me, not man. For be my motive good or bad, of one thing I am sure, the lasting condemnation of the north.
  I love peace more than life. Have loved the Union beyond expression. For four years have I waited, hoped and prayed, for the dark clouds to break, And for a restoration of our former sunshine, to wait longer would be a crime. All hope for peace is dead, my prayers have proved as idle as my hopes. God's will be done. I go to see, and share the bitter end.
  I have ever held the South were right. The very nomination of Abraham Lincoln four years ago, spoke plainly—war, war upon Southern rights and institutions. His election proved it. "Await an overt act." Yes till you are bound and plundered. What folly, the South were wise. Who thinks of argument or patience when the finger of his enemy presses on the trigger. In a *foreign war,* I too could say "Country right or wrong," but in a struggle *such as ours* (where the brother tries to pierce the brothers heart) for God's sake choose the right. When a country ~~such as ours~~ ^like this^ spurns *justice* from her side, She forfeits the allegiance of every honest freeman, and ^should^ leave him untrammeled by any fealty soever, to act, as his conscience may approve.
  People of the north, to hate tyranny to love liberty and justice, to strike

at wrong and oppression, was the teaching of our fathers. The study of our early history will not let *me* forget it, And may it never.

This country was formed for the *white* not for the black man. And looking upon *African slavery* from the same stand-point, ~~as~~ held by those noble framers of our Constitution. I for one, have ever considered *it,* one of the greatest blessings (both for themselves and us,) that God even bestowed upon a favored nation. Witness heretofore our wealth and power. Witness their elevation in happiness and enlightment above their race, elsewhere. I have lived among it most of my life and have seen *less* harsh treatment from Master to Man than I have beheld in the north from father to son. Yet Heaven knows *no one* would be willing to do, *more* for the negro race than I. Could I but see a way to still better their condition, But Lincoln's policy is only preparing the way for their total annihilation. The South *are not, nor have they been fighting* for the continuance of slavery, the first battle of Bull-run did away with that idea. Their causes *since* for *war* have been as *noble,* and *greater far than those that* urged our *fathers on. Even* should we allow, they were *wrong* at the beginning of this contest, *cruelty and injustice,* have made the wrong become the *right.* And they stand *now,* (before the wonder and admiration of the *world*) as a ∧noble∧ band of patriotic heroes. Hereafter, reading of *their deeds,* Thermopylae will be forgotten.

When I aided in the capture and ~~the g~~ execution of John Brown,[4] (Who was a murderer on our Western Border, and who was fairly *tried* and *convicted,*—before an impartial judge & jury—of treason,—And who by the way has since been made a God—I was proud of my little share in the transaction, for I deemed it my duty And that I was helping our common country to perform an act of justice. But what was a crime in poor John Brown is now considered (by themselves) ∧as∧ the greatest and only virtue, of the whole Republican party. Strange transmigration, *vice* to become a *virtue.* Simply because *more* indulge in it. I thought then, *as now,* that the abolitionists, *were the only traitors* in the land, And that the entire party, deserved the fate of poor old Brown. Not because they wish to abolish slavery, but on account of the means they have even endeavored to use, to effect that abolition. If Brown were living, I doubt if he *himself,* would set slavery, against the Union. Most, or many, in the North do, And openly curse the Union, if the South are to return and retain a *single right* guaranteed them by every tie which we once *revered as sacred.* The south can make no choice. It is either extermination or slavery for *themselves* (worse than death) to draw from. I would know *my* choice.

I have, also, studied hard to discover upon what grounds, the rights of a state to Secede have been denied, when our very name (United States) and our Declaration of Independence, *both* provide for secession. But there is no time for words. I write in haste. I know how foolish I shall be deemed, for undertaking such a step, as this, Where on the one side, I have many friends, and everything to make me happy. Where my profession *alone* has gained me an income of *more than* Twenty thousand dollars a year. And where my great personal ambition in my profession has such a great field for labor. On the other hand—the south have never bestowed upon me one kind word. A place now, where I have no friends, except beneath the sod. A place where I must either become a private soldier or a beggar. To give up all of the *former* for the *latter,* besides my mother and sisters whom I love so dearly, (although they so widely differ with me in opinion) seems insane, But God is my judge I love *justice,* more than I do a country, that disowns it. More than fame and wealth. More (Heaven pardon me if wrong) more than a happy home. I have never been upon a battlefield, but, O my countrymen, could you all but see the *reality* or effects of this horrid war, as I have seen them (in *every State,* save Virginia) I know you would think like me. And would pray the Almighty to create in the northern mind a sense of *right* and *justice* (even should it possess no seasoning of mercy.) and that he would dry up this Sea of blood between us,—which is daily growing wider. Alas, poor Country, Is she to meet her threatened doom. Four years ago, I would have given a thousand lives, to see her remain (as I had always known her) powerful and unbroken. And even now I would hold my life as naught, to see her what she was. O my friends, if the fearful scenes of the past four years had never been enacted, and if what has been had been but a frightful dream, from which we could now awake, with what overflowing hearts could we bless our God And pray for his continued favor. How I have loved the *old flag* can never, now, be known. A few years since and the entire world could boast of *none* so pure and spotless. But I have of late been seeing and hearing of the *bloody deeds* of which She has *been made, the emblem.* And would shudder to think how changed she had grown. O How I have longed to see her break from the mist of blood and death that now circles round her folds, spoiling her beauty and tarnishing her honor.[5] But no, day by day has she been draged deeper and deeper into cruelty and oppression, till now (in my eyes) her once bright red stripes look like *bloody gashes* on the face of Heaven. I look now upon my early admiration of her glories as a dream. My love (as things stand today) is for the South alone. Nor, do I deem it a dishonor in attempting to make for her a prisoner of this man, to whom she owes so much of misery. If success attends me, I go penniless to her side. They say she has found *that* "last ditch" which the north have so long derided, and been endeavoring to force her in, forgetting they are our brothers, and that its impolitic to goad an enemy to madness. Should I reach her in safety and find it true, I will proudly beg permission to triumph or die in that same "ditch" by her side,[6]

A Confederate, ~~At present~~ doing duty *upon his own responsibility.*

J Wilkes Booth

Autograph manuscript signed, National Archives.

1. It may have been shortly after Lincoln's reelection that Booth wrote these two important letters: this one and that to his "dearest beloved Mother" (which follows). The letters were "lost" for more than 110 years in the files of the Justice Department in National Archives, where James O. Hall, a Lincoln assassination expert, rediscovered them in 1977. Booth had left both letters with his sister Asia in Philadelphia, probably during his last meeting with her on 10 February 1865. William A. Tidwell, with James O. Hall and David Winfred Gaddy, *Come Retribution: The Confederate Secret Service and the Assassination of Lincoln* (Jackson: University Press of Mississippi, 1988), 405.

Asia recalled that her brother "said, taking a large packet from his breast, 'Lock this up in your safe for me. I may come back for it, but if anything should happen— to me—open the packet *alone* and send the letters as directed, and the money and papers give to their owners.' It was not unusual to speak thus of possible accidents, for in these reckless times the travel was rough and incessant, and a traveling actor's life is one of exposure to danger. . . . Together we unfastened the heavy door, then unbarred the inner iron one, then entered the room of stone and iron, and I stooped and placed the packet in the iron safe." Asia Booth Clarke, *The Unlocked Book: A Memoir of John Wilkes Booth by His Sister* (New York: G. P. Putnam's Sons, 1938), 126.

In a private letter to a friend about a month after her brother's death, Asia wrote, "I can give you no idea of the desolation which has fallen upon us. The sorrow of his death is very bitter but the disgrace is far heavier. Already people are asserting that it is [a] political affair, the work of a bloody rebellion, the enthusiast's love of country, etc., but I am afraid to us it will always be a *crime*. Junius [Brutus Booth, Jr.] and John Clarke have been today confined in the Old Capitol [Prison], Washington—for no complicity or evidence. Junius wrote an innocent letter from Cincinnati which by wicked misconstruction has been the cause of his arrest. He begged [John Wilkes Booth] to quit the oil business and attend to his profession, not knowing that *oil* signified conspiracy in Washington, as it has since been proven that all engaged in the plot passed themselves off as oil merchants. [As did Samuel B. Arnold and Michael O'Laughlen; see notes for JWB to Michael O'Laughlen, 27 February 1865.] John Clarke was arrested for having in house a package of papers upon which he had never laid his hands or eyes, but after the occurrence I produced them, thinking it was a will put here for safe keeping. John took them to the U.S. Marshall who reported to headquarters. Hence this long imprisonment for two entirely innocent men" (Asia Booth Clarke to Jean Anderson, 22 May 1865, Peale Museum, Baltimore).

Asia retrieved the packet from her safe on 18 April. Her husband turned the "to whom it may concern" letter over to U.S. Marshall William Milward, who allowed it to be published in the 19 April edition of the *Philadelphia Inquirer*.

2. This letter is apparently addressed to John Sleeper Clarke (1835–79), the Philadelphia comedian and husband of JWB's sister Asia. Although they had known each other from their Baltimore schooldays, JWB and Clarke were no longer friendly. As he had with his brother Edwin, JWB had quarreled with Clarke over the war. With his brother-in-law, the disagreement had gone beyond quarreling. Clarke told of an incident in a railroad car when he had made a remark disparaging Jefferson Davis. "As the words were uttered Booth sprang up and hurled himself at Clarke in a wild tempest of fury, catching him by the throat. Other passengers tried to interfere, but Booth held his hold, to all appearances bent on strangling his brother-in-law. He swung Clarke from side to side with maniac strength while his grip tightened. His face was drawn and twisted with rage. Slowly his anger left him, none to soon for Clarke. . . . Booth stood over him with a dramatic gesture. 'Never, if you value your life,' he said, tensely, 'never speak in that way to me again of a man and a cause I hold sacred.'" George S. Bryan, *The Great American Myth* (New York: Carrick and Evans, 1940; repr., with an introduction by William Hanchett, Chicago: Americana House, 1990), 141–42.

3. "Your Master" is Abraham Lincoln, who, on 18 July 1864, had directed a letter to the Confederate "peace emissaries" in Canada, Clement Clay, James Holcombe, and Jacob Thompson: "To Whom it may concern: Any proposition which embraces the restoration of peace, the integrity of the whole Union, and the abandonment of slavery, and which comes by and with an authority that can control the armies now at war against the United States will be received and considered by the Executive government of the United States, and will be met by liberal terms on other substantive and collateral points; and the bearer, or bearers thereof shall have safe-conduct both ways." In *The Collected Works of Abraham Lincoln*, ed. Roy P. Basler (New Brunswick: Rutgers University Press, 1953), 7:451.

In the summer of 1864 most observers agreed that Abraham Lincoln had little chance of winning a second term as president. Lincoln himself reckoned that he would be "beaten, and . . . *badly* beaten." James M. McPherson, *Battle Cry of Freedom: The Civil War Era* (New York: Oxford University Press, 1988), 771. The tide of war seemed to have turned against the North, and the November election promised to be a referendum on the president's military leadership. All summer Grant's Army of the Potomac had slugged it out with Lee's Army of Northern Virginia in a series of brutal battles. The war's most sustained and bloody fighting saw sixty-five thousand Union soldiers killed, captured, or wounded. These horrific casualties seemed to have gained Grant nothing but costly stalemate—a trench warfare siege of Lee's army outside Richmond. Meanwhile, in the West, Sherman's offensive was stalled short of Atlanta. People who lived in the North had begun to despair that the cost of winning the war was more than they could endure. And peace in the summer of 1864 clearly meant Southern independence.

The Republicans themselves were divided. Some hoped to find another candidate. Nevertheless, in June the Republican Party renominated Abraham Lincoln. The platform called for the unconditional surrender of the Confederacy and an amendment to the Constitution to outlaw slavery in the United States forever. The Democrats' platform, in contrast, advocated a negotiated peace and the protection of slavery in the South. The Democratic nominee was Gen. George B. McClellan. In one of the most bitter presidential campaigns in American history, the Democrats accused Lincoln of stubbornly fighting an unwinnable war and sacrificing the lives of hundreds of thousands of white men to gain the freedom of black slaves.

The Confederates sensed their great opportunity. They embarked on a sophisticated propaganda campaign aimed at convincing Northerners that the main obstacle to peace and the reunion of the country was Lincoln himself. The "Niagara Falls peace conference" of July 1864 was one episode in this Southern propaganda effort. The Confederate secret service had found an unwitting ally in the person of Horace Greeley, the mercurial editor of the New York *Tribune*. In early July, Greeley was told that "two Ambassadors of [Jefferson] Davis & Co" had arrived in Canada "with full & complete powers for a peace." (In fact the men had no authority whatever to negotiate in the name of the Confederate government.) Greeley urged Lincoln to bring the Southerners to Washington for talks. Lincoln responded by declaring that he remained ready to consider a proposal, from those in authority in Richmond, which encompassed his "indispensable terms": peace, the restoration of the Union, and the abolition of slavery. The president also sent his private secretary, John Hay, to meet with Greeley and the Confederate agents in Niagara Falls, Canada. At this meeting on 18 July, Hay gave Clay and Holcombe Lincoln's letter addressed "to whom it may concern." The Confederate government and Lincoln's opponents in the North were quick to use the exchange to make it appear that only Lincoln and his stubborn insistence on emancipation stood in the way of ending the war and reuniting the two warring sections. Southern men such as Booth were enraged by Lincoln's refusal to negotiate with the Confederate emissaries; particularly galling was the refusal of the churlish Yankee president to even to address them in terms of respect. James G. Randall and Richard N. Current, *Lincoln the President: Last Full Measure* (New York: Dodd, Mead, 1955), 156–65; James M. McPherson, *Battle Cry of Freedom: The Civil War Era* (New York: Oxford University Press, 1988), 760–69.

4. See notes for "[Draft of a Speech], Philadelphia, late December 1860" for a discussion of JWB's involvement with the execution of John Brown in 1859. In a passionate condemnation of Abraham Lincoln in 1864, JWB compared John Brown and Lincoln, telling his sister that Lincoln "is walking in the footprints of old John Brown, but no more fit to stand with that rugged old hero—Great God! no. John Brown was a man inspired, the grandest character of the century! *He* is Bonaparte in one great move, that is, by overturning this blind Republic and making himself a king. This man's re-election which will follow his success, I tell you—will be a reign!" Clarke, *The Unlocked Book*, 124.

JWB tended to exaggerate his role in the suppression of John Brown's rebellion in 1859. He was present at Brown's execution on 2 December 1859, having gone to Charles Town with the Richmond Grays on 19 November. He returned to Richmond with the unit on 4 December. He did not, however, participate in the skirmish in which Brown and his followers were captured by federal troops in Harpers Ferry on 18 October 1859. JWB apparently told Asia Booth Clarke, however, that he been in on the capture of Brown: "He left Richmond," Asia wrote, "and unsought enrolled himself as one of the party going to search for and capture John Brown. He was exposed to dangers and hardships; he was a scout, and I have been shown a picture of himself and others in their scout and sentinel dresses. He was a witness of the death of old John Brown. He acknowledged him a hero when he saw him die, and felt a throb of anguish as he beheld the old eyes straining their anxious sight for the multitude he vainly thought would rise to rescue him. 'He was a brave old man; [JWB told his sister] his heart must have broken when he felt himself deserted.'" Clarke, *The Unlocked Book*, 113.

5. Booth is reported to have shouted "one more stain on the old banner" just before he was shot by federal soldiers on 26 April 1865. Bryan, *The Great American Myth*, 265.

6. During the final months of the Civil War, some Confederates vowed to "die in the last ditch" before surrendering to the Yankees and their "nigger allies."

To Mary Ann Holmes Booth
[Philadelphia, November] 1864

Dearest beloved Mother

Heaven knows how dearly I love you. And may our kind Father ^in Heaven^ (if only for the sake of my love) watch over, *comfort* & protect you, in my absence. May he soften the blow of my departure, granting you peace and happiness for many, many years to come. God ever bless you.

I have always endeavored to be a good and dutiful son, And even now would wish to die sooner than give you pain. But dearest Mother, though, I owe you all, *there* is another duty. A noble duty for the sake of liberty and humanity due to my Country—For, four years I have lived (I may say) A *slave* in the north (A favored slave its true, but no less hateful to me on that account.) Not daring to express my thoughts or sentiments, even in my own home Constantly hearing every principle, dear to my heart, denounced as treasonable, And knowing the vile and savage acts committed on my countrymen their wives & helpless children, that I have cursed my wilful idleness, And begun to deem myself a coward and to despise my own existence. For four years I have borne it mostly for your dear sake, And for you alone, have I also struggled to fight off this desire to begone, but it seems that uncontrollable fate, moving me for its ends, takes me from you, dear Mother, to do what work I can for a poor oppressed downtrodden people. May that same fate cause me to do that work well. I care not for the censure of the north, so I have your forgiveness, And I feel I may hope it, even though you differ with me in opinion. I may by the grace of God, live through this war dear Mother, if so, the rest of my life shall be more devoted to you, than has been my former. For I know it will take a long lifetime of tenderness and care, to atone for the pang this parting will give you. But I cannot longer resist the inclination, to go and share the sufferings of my brave countrymen, holding an unequal strife (for every right human & divine) against the most ruthless enemy, the world has ever known. You can answer for me dearest Mother (although none of you think with me) that I have not a *single selfish motive* to spur me on to this, nothing save the sacred duty, I feel I *owe the cause I love.* the cause of the South. The cause of liberty & justice. So should I meet the *worst,* dear Mother, in struggling for such holy rights. I can say "Gods' will be done" And bless him in my heart for not permitting me, to outlive, our dear bought freedom. And for keeping me from being longer a hidden lie among my country's foes. Darling Mother I can not write you, you will understand the deep regret, the forsaking your dear side, will make me suffer, for you have been the best, the noblest, an example for all mothers. God, God bless you. As I shall ever pray him to do. And should the last bolt strike your son, dear Mother, bear it patiently And think at the best life is but short, and *not at all times happy.* My Brothers & Sisters (Heaven protect them) will add my love and duty to their own, and watch you with care and kindness, till we meet again. And if *that happiness* does not come to us on earth, then may, O May it be with God. So then dearest, *dearest* Mother, *forgive* and pray for me. I feel that I am right in the justness of my cause, And that we shall, *ere long,* meet again. Heaven grant it. Bless you, bless you. Your loving son will never cease to hope and pray for such a joy.

Come weal or woe, with never ending love and devotion you will find me ever your affectionate son

John.

Autograph letter signed, National Archives.

To Junius Brutus Booth, Jr.
Washington, D.C., 17 January 1865

P.S. I play Romeo for Avania Jones's Ben[efit] Friday[1]

Washington, Jan 17th

Dear Brother
    I have just recd yours from Philada in which you complain of my not

writing. I wrote you some days ago to Phila and I know my letter must have been waiting you yet by yours you had not recd it. I directed to Chesnut St Theatre. I therein stated why I had not written before. You ask me what I am doing.[2] Well a thousand things. Yet no more, hardly than what I could attend to if I was at home. But dear brother you must not think me childish when I say that the old feeling roused by our loving brother[3] has not yet died out. I am sure he thinks I live upon him. And its only for dear Mother that I have gone there at all when in New York, and as I cannot live in that city without him at home and as this season I would be home all the time, I thought it best not to be in the City at all, and as I like this place next, and my bus[iness] at present calls me here. I thought I would here make my stand. I hope you recd my last, it was a little better than this,[4] as this is in haste. Give my love to all. When does John[5] come here. if I was him I would put it off till March as all's dull now. I dont know how the Phila papers will use you but if they are as kind to you as to me, why god help you say I.

Your loving brother,

John

I recd Joe's letter

Autograph letter signed, Andre de Coppet Collection, Princeton University Library.

1. JWB played Romeo in the penultimate performance of his career at Grover's Theatre in Washington on 20 January 1865. The performance was a benefit for actress Avonia Stanhope Jones (1839–67). JWB had to go on in a borrowed costume, having left his theatrical wardrobe in Canada for shipment to the Confederacy. Of his performance, the *National Intelligencer* gushed: "No such *Romeo* ever trod the boards. What perfect acting! We have never seen a *Romeo* bearing any near comparison with the acting of Booth. His death scene was the most remarkable and fearfully natural that we have seen for years upon the stage. His elocution was faultless."

But JWB devoted himself more to conspiracy than the drama in January 1865. Early in the month, he enlisted John Surratt. On 14 January Surratt traveled to Port Tobacco, where he and Confederate agent Thomas Harbin recruited George Andrew Atzerodt to ferry the captive Lincoln across the Potomac to Virginia. With money furnished by JWB, Surratt purchased a boat. Atzerodt took charge of the boat, concealing it near the river, ready for use. Surratt also recruited David Herold. In Baltimore, on 11 January, Booth divided with Samuel Arnold and Michael O'Laughlen the contents of a trunk filled with weapons and equipment needed for the operation. The trunk, Arnold later testified, contained "two guns (makes unknown) cap Cartridges, which were placed in the gun stock. (Spencer rifles I think called). Revolver Knive belts cartridge Boxes caps canteen all fully fixed out which were to be used in case of pursuit and two pairs of handcuffs to handcuff the President. His trunk being so heavy he gave the Pistol Knives and handcuffs to Michael O'Loughlin and myself to have shipped or bring to Washington to which place he had gone." Arnold and O'Laughlen shipped the weapons and drove to Washington in a horse and buggy Booth had bought. Surratt Society, eds., *From War Department Files: Statements Made by the Alleged Lincoln Conspirators under Examination 1865* (Clinton, Md.: Surratt Society, 1980), 20.

In late January or early February Booth recruited Confederate veteran Lewis Thornton Powell. Powell—also known as Lewis Paine or Payne, Mr. Wood, and Mr. Mosby—had served with John Singleton Mosby's elite partisan cavalry command. He may have been acting under Confederate orders when he joined the conspiracy. William A. Tidwell, with James O. Hall and David Winfred Gaddy, *Come Retribution: The Confederate Secret Service and the Assassination of Lincoln* (Jackson: University Press of Mississippi, 1988), 339.

2. JWB is responding to his family's criticism of his having apparently abandoned his acting career. In early February, Samuel Arnold later testified, "Booth told me he had received a letter from his mother in which she stated she had fearful dreams about him. She sent his brother Junius Brutus to Washington to persuade him to come home so Booth told me." Samuel Bland Arnold, *Defence and Prison Experiences of a Lincoln Conspirator* (Hattiesburg, Miss.: The Book Farm, 1943), 21. "In order to prevent Junius from insisting on his return to New York, Wilkes had told him that he held a commission in the Confederate army, but asked him to keep this information from the family." Stanley Kimmel, *The Mad Booths of Maryland* (Indianapolis: Bobbs-Merrill, 1940), 200.

On 26 April 1865 Junius Brutus Booth, Jr., then under arrest, testified that, in a letter written to JWB a few days before the assassination, he had "urged him to have nothing to do with the rebellion. Knowing his sympathy was for the South I was very much afraid he might go over the lines, and I begged of him not to be so foolish. I told him to follow his profession; to give up oil speculating; and that I was expecting to meet him in New York City, Saturday, [April 22, when the three Booth brothers were again to perform for the benefit of the Shakespeare statue in Central Park] to play with his two other brothers. I then said if he wished I would go with him to the oil regions and see how wells were being sunk there. I told him that this rebellion was now all over; Richmond had fallen; Lee had surrendered; Johnston would do the same shortly, and all there would be left would be a few bands of guerrillas to rove over the country, and these would very soon be routed out. . . . We have always been fearful of J. Wilkes, knowing his sympathy for the South, and have again and again advised him to have nothing to do with it. We tried to get him away from Washington, knowing that here he would see so much of military life, and besides being so close to Southern soil."

In a second statement, Junius swore that he "found his brother Wilkes strongly in sympathy with the Southern cause and endeavored by frequent and earnest arguments to dissuade him from his views on that subject. Believes that his brother Edwin and brother-in-law J. S. Clarke made similar efforts but were equally unsuccessful. Told his brother that his views of a Southern independence would never be realized and begged him for his own and his family's sake not to meddle in the family quarrel, as it might be styled, and only obtained a promise from him that he would not join the rebel army." Stanley Kimmel, *The Mad Booths of Maryland* (Indianapolis: Bobbs-Merrill, 1940), 369–70.

3. Edwin Booth. Their disagreements over the Civil War and Lincoln (for whom Edwin had voted in 1864) had finally resulted in the estrangement of the two brothers. Edwin told Adam Badeau that "he had long and violent discussions with his brother at this time. Wilkes declared his wish for the success of the Rebellion so decidedly that Edwin finally told him he should go elsewhere to make such sentiments known; that he was not at liberty to express them in the house of a Union man." Adam Badeau, "Dramatic Reminiscences," *St. Paul and Minneapolis Pioneer Press,* 20 February 1887.

4. The previous letter of JWB to Junius Brutus Booth, Jr., alluded to here does not survive.

5. John Sleeper Clarke.

To Orlando Tompkins
Washington, D.C., 9 February 1865

Feb 9th
Washington D.C.

Dear Orlando[1]

You will say I never write without I want something. That may be so, nevertheless I think of you all the same. And as I kno, you are aware of my hatred to letter writing and can therefore excuse it. I will say no more in extenuation of my fault. So to the point Would you be kind enough to ask Case[2] to send me *without a moments delay one dozen* of my *card photghs.* The ones I want are *those seated, with cane & Black* cravat He knows the ones I liked the best. Tell him to send them at once to New York No 28 East 19th St as I hope to be there day after tomorrow, only, to stay a day or two. This is very important As there are several parties whom I would like to give one.[3] So please attend to it upon the receipt of this—and I will do more than this for you. How are you all: And how is Boston. remember me to all. That Oil Company Joe S- and myself started in your city has gone up fine. Stock to day instead of being $1000, is $15000, per share Please attend to above. With best wishes for *you all,* and kind regards to Case

I remain
Yours

J. Wilkes Booth

P.S. By the way I never acknowledged the receipt of that deed. Thank you, all right.

Yours *John*

I return to this city in about a week, stop at National Hotel, an will get any letter sent to Fords Theatre.

Yours[4]

Autograph letter signed, private collection.

1. Orlando Tompkins was a stockholder in the Boston Theatre, which he managed from 1862 to 1878.

2. The Boston firm of Silsbee, Case and Company made two *carte de visite* portraits of JWB at a single sitting. The photographs were subsequently published by Case and Getchell and Black and Case. The better-known of the two photographs is sometimes called the "wanted poster view" because "this photo of Booth was widely copied after the assassination, and was mounted directly onto many of the wanted posters that were put out by the government." Richard J. S. Gutman and Kellie O. Gutman, *John Wilkes Booth Himself* (Dover, Mass.: Hired Hand Press, 1979), 31, 70.

3. "The suspicion lingers that these photographs were somehow to be used for identification purposes connected with the Lincoln operation." William A. Tidwell, with James O. Hall and David Winfred Gaddy, *Come Retribution: The Confederate Secret Service and the Assassination of Lincoln* (Jackson: University Press of Mississippi, 1988), 404.

4. The day he wrote this letter, JWB checked out of the National Hotel, where he had lived during most of January, and left Washington for Philadelphia and New York. (The New York address to which he asked Tompkins to send the photographs was that of Edwin Booth.) JWB and his sister Asia Booth Clarke met for the last time in Philadelphia on 10 February. It was probably during this visit that he gave her the packet of papers to lock in her safe; included were his undated letter to "dearest beloved Mother" and the "to whom it may concern" letter (Tidwell, with Hall and Gaddy, *Come Retribution*, 405). He left Philadelphia for New York the next day. An entry in Junius Brutus Booth, Jr.'s diary dated 13 February 1865 reads, "In NY. JW came on for a few days." An entry dated 18 February reads, "In NY. John returned to Washington." Junius Brutus Booth, Jr., diary, 1865, Boston University Library.

In a letter to Asia Booth Clarke, headed "New York—Tuesday [14] Feb 1865," Junius Brutus Booth, Jr., reported that "John sat up all Mondays night [13 February] to put Miss Hales valentine in the mail—and slept on the sofa—to be up early & kept me up last night till 3½ AM—to wait while he wrote her a long letter & kept me awake by every now and then useing me as a dictionary—John says that he will remain here till Wednesday." Asia Booth Clarke, *The Unlocked Book: A Memoir of John Wilkes Booth by His Sister* (New York: G. P. Putnam's Sons, 1938), 198–200.

After his return from Montreal in October 1864 Booth had become entangled in an romance with Lucy Lambert Hale, the daughter of the New Hampshire abolitionist Senator John Parker Hale. Hale, with his wife and two daughters, had checked into

Booth's Washington hotel—the National—in January 1865. By March, Booth and Lucy Hale were apparently engaged to be married. It was from Lucy that the actor obtained a ticket to the stands at Lincoln's inauguration on 4 March 1865; he may have attended one of the inaugural balls with her that night. Senator Hale, who had failed to win reelection in June 1864, had been named by Lincoln to be ambassador to Spain on 10 March. He was confirmed by the Senate that month and made plans to sail for Europe with his family.

It is unlikely the ambassador-designate knew of his youngest daughter's engagement. But the Booths apparently did know. "The secret you have told me," Mary Ann Booth wrote to her favorite son, "is not exactly a secret, as Edwin was told by someone, you were paying great attention to a young lady in Washington—Now my dear boy, I cannot advise you how to act—you have so often been dead in love and this may prove like the others, not of any lasting impression—you are aware that the woman you make your wife you must love and respect beyond all others, for marriage is an act that cannot be recalled without misery if so entered into. . . . You are old enough and have seen so much of the world, to know all this, only a young man in love does not stop to reflect and like a child with a new toy—only craves the possession of it—think and reflect—and if the lady in question is all you desire—I see no cause why you should not try to secure her—her father, I see he has his appointment, would he give his consent." Stanley Kimmel, *The Mad Booths of Maryland* (Indianapolis: Bobbs-Merrill, 1940), 346–47.

After the assassination, Asia Booth Clarke wrote that her brother "was engaged to Miss Hale. They were devoted lovers and she has written broken-hearted letters to Edwin [Booth] about it. Their marriage was to have been in a year, when she promised to return from Spain for him, either with her father or without him. That was the decision only a few days before the fearful calamity. Some terrible oath hurried him to this wretched end" (Asia Booth Clarke to Jean Anderson, 22 May 1865, Peale Museum, Baltimore).

Photographs of five women were found on Booth's body by the men who killed him. One was of Lucy Hale. When the identity of Lincoln's assassin was revealed, there was a wild Republican scramble to obscure all traces of the love affair. On 22 April 1865, the New York *Tribune* reported that "the unhappy lady—the daughter of a New England Senator—to whom Booth was affianced, is plunged in profoundest grief; but with womanly fidelity, is slow to believe him guilty of this appalling crime, and asks, with touching pathos, for evidence of his innocence." A story denying the report of the romance appeared in the *New York Times* on 26 April. Lucy Hale's suitors are said to have also included Robert Todd Lincoln, Oliver Wendell Holmes, Jr., and President Lincoln's private secretary, John Hay. She eventually married Navy Secretary and New Hampshire Senator William E. Chandler (1835–1917). She died in 1915. Richmond Morcom, "They All Loved Lucy," *American Heritage* 21 (Oct. 1970): 12–15.

To John Parker Hale Wentworth
Baltimore, 21 February 1865

Baltr: Barnums Hotel Feb. 21 1865.
John Wentworth, Esq., National Hotel, Washington[1]

I am here. Will you keep promise to-day or tomorrow. Let me know. I cannot stay.

J. Wilkes Booth

Ans[wer]:

Telegram, printed form filled out and signed, Benjamin F. Butler Papers, Library of Congress.

1. Californian John Parker Hale Wentworth was a nephew of Senator John P. Hale and the first cousin of Hale's daughter Lucy, to whom Booth was said to have been secretly engaged. "On his way back to Washington from New York on 21 February 1865, Booth stopped off at Barnum's Hotel in Baltimore. From there he sent a telegram to 'John Wentworth.'. . . One speculation about this telegram is that Booth wanted Wentworth to help arrange with Senator John P. Hale to get him an official pass to be in the Capitol stands at the second inauguration of President Lincoln. Such a pass was secured and given to Booth by Miss Hale. What Booth hoped to accomplish by attending the inauguration is uncertain, but one inflated account is that he sought to press his way to the president that day and was restrained by a heroic police officer, John W. Westfall, who thus saved Lincoln's life. The story is not very convincing." William A. Tidwell, with James O. Hall and David Winfred Gaddy, *Come Retribution: The Confederate Secret Service and the Assassination of Lincoln* (Jackson: University Press of Mississippi, 1988), 408.

Booth did attend the ceremony. Actor Samuel Knapp Chester testified at the trial of the conspirators that on April 7 his friend Booth had said, "What an excellent chance I had to kill the President, if I had wished, on inauguration day!" Benn Pitman, comp., *The Assassination of President Lincoln and the Trial of the Conspirators* (New York: Moore, Wilstach, and Baldwin, 1865; facsimile edition edited by Philip Van Doren Stern, New York: Funk and Wagnalls, 1954), 45. JWB checked back into the National Hotel, Washington, on 22 February.

To Michael O'Laughlen
Washington, D.C., 27 February 1865

Feb 27th: 1865.
M. Olaughlen Esq[1]
no 57 North Exeter St:
Baltimore Md

As you could not stay here to see me, I will be in Baltimore tomorrow. See me there Both. Sure.

J Wilkes Booth

Telegram, printed form filled out and signed, Benjamin F. Butler Papers, Library of Congress.

1. Booth had attended a Baltimore grammar school with T. William O'Laughlen and his younger brother Michael (1840–67). The O'Laughlen family home, to which this telegram was directed, was across the street from the Booths' Baltimore town-house at 62 North Exeter. O'Laughlen had served in the Confederate army but had crossed the lines and taken the oath of allegiance to the United States on 16 June 1863. O'Laughlen and Samuel Bland Arnold (1834–1906) were recruited by JWB at Barnum's Hotel, Baltimore, in a meeting that took place during the first two weeks of August 1864. Arnold was another boyhood friend; he and JWB had attended the same boarding school—St. Timothy's Hall in Catonsville, Maryland.

O'Laughlen and Arnold spent many months waiting for a chance to capture Lincoln. They lived in Washington and Baltimore. Although both men became increasingly impatient with Booth, they had a jolly time of it, drinking with friends in taverns while passing themselves off as salesmen of oil stocks. On 10 February they began living together at a Washington boardinghouse, where JWB called to see them three or four times a week. Surratt Society, eds., *From War Department Files: Statements Made by the Alleged Lincoln Conspirators under Examination 1865* (Clinton, Md.: Surrat Society, 1980), 20–22; Benn Pitman, comp., *The Assassination of President Lincoln and the Trial of the Conspirators* (New York: Moore, Wilstach, and Baldwin, 1865; facsimile edition edited by Philip Van Doren Stern, New York: Funk and Wagnalls, 1954), 222.

O'Laughlen was to spend the night of the assassination drinking in a series of Washington saloons; he put away ten ales and did not get to bed until three o'clock the morning of 15 April. The next day O'Laughlen returned to Baltimore, where he was arrested on 17 April. Convicted in July as an accomplice in the assassination, Michael O'Laughlen was sentenced to life imprisonment. He died during an outbreak of yellow fever at Fort Jefferson in 1867.

Autograph Manuscript Signed
Washington, D.C., 5 March 1865

Now, in this hour, that we part,
I will ask to be forgotten, *never*
But in thy pure and guileless heart
Consider me thy friend, dear Eva.

J Wilkes Booth[1]

Autograph manuscript signed, published in auction catalog: Parke-Bernet, the Oliver R. Barrett Lincoln Collection sale, 19, 20 February 1952.

1. JWB's verse is followed by this couplet from John Greenleaf Whittier's poem "Maude Muller," apparently in the hand of Lucy Hale: "'For of all sad words from tongue or pen / The saddest are these—it might have been.' / March 5th, 1865 / In John's room."

The Parke-Bernet catalog described the manuscript as "four-line verse in the autograph of John Wilkes Booth, signed 'J. Wilkes Booth'; written on an envelope. Below it is a four-line verse in another hand, followed by 'March 5th 1865. In John's room.' AN INTERESTING MEMENTO. The two verses described above are inscribed on the verso of an envelope. The recto of the envelope is franked in the upper right hand corner 'Jno. Conness, U.S.S.' (Senator from California, 1863–7), and below is a three-line quotation with note reading 'The above, though quoted, are the real sentiments of your friend, who trusts that the acquaintance and friendship formed will never be forgotten by either. Jno. P.H.W.'"

Of this document, Lincoln assassination researcher James O. Hall has written: "On 5 March 1865, two people were with John Wilkes Booth in his room at the National Hotel in Washington. One was John Parker Hale Wentworth, a nephew of Senator John Parker Hale, New Hampshire, who had just vacated his senate seat. Hale would go on to be ambassador to Spain. The other person in the room was a lady. Who was she? There have been many guesses as to the identity of the lady who wrote the Whittier quotation. Over time it has generally been assumed that she was Miss Lucy Hale, the younger of the two daughters of Senator Hale and a first cousin of John Parker Hale Wentworth. Further, that the side-shot picture of a young woman, found on Booth when he was shot, is that of Miss Lucy Hale. Still, there was a nagging question of absolute proof as to the identity of the woman in Booth's room on 5 March 1865." Hall then describes his successful effort to acquire undoubted examples of Lucy Hale's handwriting for purposes of comparison and concludes that "the writing in all cases is clearly in the same hand. Taken with other evidence, it follows that Lucy Hale was the woman in Booth's room on 5 March 1865" (James O. Hall to John Rhodehamel, 5 December 1989).

To Michael O'Laughlen
Washington, D.C., 13 March 1865

Washington, March 13, 1865[1]

Mr. O'Laughlin

57 North Exeter Street, Baltimore, Md.

Don't fear to neglect your business. You had better come at once.[2]

J. Booth.

Telegram, published in Benn Pitman, comp., The Assassination of President Lincoln and the Trial of the Conspirators *(New York: Moore, Wilstach, and Baldwin, 1865; facsimile edition edited by Philip Van Doren Stern, New York: Funk and Wagnalls, 1954), 223.*

1. Although written on a telegram form bearing the printed date "1864," the telegram was sent on this date in 1865.

2. O'Laughlen and Samuel Arnold took a train for Washington on 14 March. On 15 March, JWB arranged for John Surratt and Lewis Powell to take in a play from the state box at Ford's Theatre. This was the box usually occupied by President Lincoln when he attended Ford's; it was the box that the Lincolns would occupy on 14 April. "The purpose was for Surratt and Powell to become acquainted with the layout" of the theater in which Booth had considered capturing Lincoln. William A. Tidwell, with James O. Hall and David Winfred Gaddy, *Come Retribution: The Confederate Secret Service and the Assassination of Lincoln* (Jackson: University Press of Mississippi, 1988), 413.

After the play, Booth, Surratt, Paine, Arnold, O'Laughlen, and David Herold and George A. Atzerodt met at Gautier's, an expensive Pennsylvania Avenue restaurant, where Booth had reserved a private room for a midnight dinner. Arnold recounted the meeting:

> We were then formally introduced. Oysters, liquors and cigars were obtained. Booth then remarked that these were the parties engaged to assist in the abduction of the President. Whereupon the plan of abducting him from the Theatre was introduced and discoursed upon, Booth saying that if it could not be done from the lower box it could from the upper one. He set forth the part he wanted each to perform. He and Payne alias Mosby were to seize him in the box, O'Laughlin and Herold to put out the gass I was to jump upon the stage and assist them as he was lowered down from the box. Surratt and Atzerodt alias Port Tobacco were to be on the other side of the Eastern Branch to act as pilots and to assist in conveying him to the boats which had been purchased by Booth. Booth said everything was in readiness. The gist of the conversation during the meeting was whether it could or could not be accomplished in the manner as proposed. After listening to Booth and others comment I firmly protested and objected to the whole scheme & told them of its utter impracticability. I stated that prisoners were now being exchanged

and the object to be obtained by the abduction had been accomplished, that patriotism was the motive that prompted me in joining the scheme not ambition. That I wanted a shadow of a chance for my life and I intended having it. Then an angry discussion arose between Booth and myself in which he threatened to shoot me. I told him two could play at that game and before them all expressed my firm determination to have nothing to more to do with it after a week. About 5 o'clock in the morning the meeting broke up. (Samuel Bland Arnold, *Defence and Prison Experiences of a Lincoln Conspirator* [Hattiesburg, Miss.: The Book Farm, 1943], 22)

Arnold had thus given Booth an ultimatum, one he repeated the next day: if another week passed without an attempt to capture Lincoln, Arnold would sever his ties with the conspiracy. See also the Surratt Society, eds., *From War Department Files: Statements Made by the Alleged Lincoln Conspirators under Examination 1865* (Clinton, Md.: Surrat Society, 1980), 20–22.

But on 17 March, just two days after the meeting at Gautier's, Booth learned that Lincoln planned to attend an afternoon performance of the play *Still Waters Run Deep* at Campbell Hospital. John Surratt described the fiasco that followed:

Days, weeks and months passed without an opportunity presenting itself for us to attempt the capture. . . . One day we received information that the President would visit the Seventh Street Hospital for the purpose of being present at an entertainment to be given for the benefit of the wounded soldiers. The report only reached us about three quarters of an hour before the time appointed, but so perfect were our communications that we were instantly in our saddles on the way to the hospital. This was between one and two o'clock in the afternoon. It was our intention to seize the carriage, which was drawn by a splendid pair of horses, and to have one of our men mount the box and drive direct for southern Maryland via Benning's bridge. We felt confident that all the cavalry in the city could never overhaul us. We were all mounted on swift horses, besides having thorough knowledge of the country, it being determined to abandon the carriage after passing the city limits. Upon the suddenness of the blow and the celerity of our movements we depended for success. By the time the alarm could have been given and horses saddled, we would have been on our way through southern Maryland towards the Potomac river. To our great disappointment, however, the President was not there but one of the government officials—Mr. Chase, if I mistake not. . . . It was certainly a bitter disappointment, but yet I think a most fortunate one for us. It was our last attempt. We soon after this became convinced that we could not remain much longer undiscovered, and that we must abandon our enterprise. Accordingly, a separation finally took place. (Louis J. Weichmann, *A True History of the Assassination of Abraham Lincoln and of the Conspiracy of 1865*, ed. Floyd E. Risvold [New York: Alfred A. Knopf, 1975], 432)

Although it makes a fine story, Booth and his men did not actually intercept a carriage they thought to be Lincoln's on the road from the hospital, as many writers have carelessly asserted. Rather, Booth learned from an actor friend that the president had not attended the play. William Hanchett, "The Ambush on the Seventh Street Road," in Surratt Society, eds., *In Pursuit of . . . Continuing Research in the Field of the Lincoln Assassination* (Clinton, Md.: Surratt Society, 1990), 151–61. After the humiliating failure of the 17 March attempt, Arnold deserted Booth, O'Laughlen returned to Baltimore, and Surratt went back to his dangerous work as a Confederate courier. The next day, 18 March, John Wilkes Booth made his final stage performance in *The Apostate,* a benefit for his friend John McCullough.

To Louis J. Weichmann[1]
Washington, D.C., 23 March 1865

New York, 23 March 1865[2]
To Wickmann Esq., 541 H Street

Tell John to telegraph number and street at once.[3]

J. Booth.

Telegram, published in Benn Pitman, comp., The Assassination of President Lincoln and the Trial of the Conspirators *(New York: Moore, Wilstach, and Baldwin, 1865; facsimile edition edited by Philip Van Doren Stern, New York: Funk and Wagnalls, 1954), 121.*

1. Louis J. Weichmann (1842–1902), a War Department clerk who boarded at Mrs. Surratt's house, knew nearly all of the members of Booth's circle of conspirators. He was a key prosecution witness at the 1865 trial that resulted in death sentences for David Herold, George Atzerodt, Lewis Powell, and Mary Surratt, and life imprisonment for Samuel Arnold, Michael O'Laughlen, and Dr. Samuel A. Mudd. Weichmann's account of his involvement with the conspirators is found in *A True History of the Assassination of Abraham Lincoln and of the Conspiracy of 1865,* ed. Floyd E. Risvold (New York: Alfred A. Knopf, 1975).

2. JWB was in New York City for two or three days. An entry in Junius Brutus Booth, Jr.'s diary dated 25 March 1865, but probably written 22 March, reads: "John came on to see Miss H[al]e." Junius Brutus Booth, Jr., diary, 1865, Boston University Library.

3. "Weichmann could not understand [the telegram]. But when John Surratt saw the telegram, it made sense to him. Booth wanted to know the Washington address of the Herndon House, kept by Martha Murray. Powell was to come from New York and board there." William A. Tidwell, with James O. Hall and David Winfred Gaddy, *Come Retribution: The Confederate Secret Service and the Assassination of Lincoln* (Jackson: University Press of Mississippi, 1988), 415.

To Michael O'Laughlen,
Washington, D.C., 27 March 1865[1]

Washington, D.C., 27 March 1865.[2]
To M. O'Laughlin Esq., 57 North Exeter Street, Baltimore, Md.:

Get word to Sam.[3] Come on, with or without him, Wednesday morning. We sell that day sure. Don't fail.

J. Wilkes Booth.

Telegram, published in Benn Pitman, comp., The Assassination of President Lincoln and the Trial of the Conspirators *(New York: Moore, Wilstach, and Baldwin, 1865; facsimile edition edited by Philip Van Doren Stern, New York: Funk and Wagnalls, 1954), 223.*

1. Although written on a printed telegraph form bearing the printed date "1864," the telegram was sent from the Metropolitan Hotel, Washington, on this date in 1865.
2. An entry in Junius Brutus Booth, Jr.'s diary, dated 27 March 1865, but probably written about 23 March, reads: "John left [New York] for Washington at 11½ am. Little thought it would be the last time I should see him." Junius Brutus Booth, Jr., diary, 1865, Boston University Library.
3. Sam Arnold. In his confession on 18 April, Arnold stated that, in response to this summons from Booth through O'Laughlen, he had come from the family farm near Hookstown to Baltimore to meet Booth. There Arnold learned that Booth and O'Laughlen had already left for Washington. He then wrote to Booth, emphatically refusing to be drawn back into the conspiracy. Surratt Society, eds., *From War Department Files: Statements Made by the Alleged Lincoln Conspirators under Examination 1865* (Clinton, Md.: Surratt Society, 1980), 22. In a letter dated "Hookstown, Balto. Co., March 27, 1865" and signed "SAM," Arnold wrote:

Dear John:
Was the business so important that you could not remain in Balto. till I saw you? I came as soon as I could, but found that you had gone to W[ashingto]n. I called also to see Mike, but learned from his mother that he had gone with you and had not returned. I concluded, therefore, he had gone with you. How inconsiderate you have been! When I left you, you stated that we would not meet in a month or so. Therefore, I made application for employment, an answer to which I shall receive during the week. I told my parents I had ceased with you. Can I, then, under existing circumstances, act as you request? You know full well that the G[overnmen]t suspicions something is going on there; therefore the undertaking is becoming more complicated. Why not, for the present, desist, for various reasons, which, if you look into, you can readily see, without my making any mention thereof. You, nor anyone, can censure me for my present course. You have been its cause, for how can I come now after telling them I had left you? Suspicion rests upon me now from my whole family, and even parties in the county. I will be compelled to leave home any how, and

how soon I care not. None, no not one, were more in favor of the enterprise than myself, and to-day would be there, had you not done as you have—by this I mean, manner of proceeding. I am, as you well know, in need. I am, you may say, in rags, whereas to-day I ought to be well clothed. I do not feel right stalking about with means, and more from appearances a beggar. I feel my dependence; but even all this would and was forgotten, for I was one with you. Time more propitious will arrive yet. Do not act rashly or in haste. I would prefer your first query, "go and see how it will be taken in R[ichmon]d, and ere long I shall be better prepared to again be with you." (Benn Pitman, comp., *The Assassination of President Lincoln and the Trial of the Conspirators* [New York: Moore, Wilstach, and Baldwin, 1865; facsimile edition edited by Philip Van Doren Stern, New York: Funk and Wagnalls, 1954], 236)

This letter was discovered in Booth's trunk at the National Hotel the night of the assassination. Arnold, who had already been identified as an acquaintance of Booth by informants in Baltimore, was arrested on 17 April. The next day he made a full confession of his part in the scheme to capture Lincoln. Arnold's letter "furnished the first and most important clue to the Government and was one of the direct means of unearthing the Conspiracy." Louis J. Weichmann, *A True History of the Assassination of Abraham Lincoln and of the Conspiracy of 1865*, ed. Floyd E. Risvold (New York: Alfred A. Knopf, 1975), 125. After his conviction and sentence to life imprisonment at hard labor in July 1865, Arnold called Lincoln's assassination "the cowardly act of a dishonored wretch, coward at heart, who had no soul." Surratt Society, eds., *In Pursuit of . . . Continuing Research in the Field of the Lincoln Assassination* (Clinton, Md.: Surratt Society, 1980), 35. Arnold was pardoned by Andrew Johnson in 1869.

To Mary Ann Holmes Booth
Washington, D.C., 14 April 1865

April 14 2 A.M.

Dearest Mother:[1]

I know you expect a letter from me, and am sure you will hardly forgive me. But indeed I have nothing to write about. Everything is dull; that is, has been till last night. (The illumination.)[2]

Everything was bright and splendid. More so in my eyes if it had been a display in a nobler cause. But so goes the world. Might makes right. I only drop you these few lines to let you know I am well, and to say I have not heard from you. Excuse brevity; am in haste. Had one from Rose.[3] With best love to you all, I am your affectionate son ever,

John

Letter published in the New York Herald, *30 April 1865, 1; reprinted in George S. Bryan,* The Great American Myth *(New York: Carrick and Evans, 1940; repr., with an introduction by William Hanchett, Chicago: Americana House, 1990), 148.*

1. One actress remembered the bond that existed between JWB and his mother: "The love and sympathy between him and his mother were very close, very strong. No matter how far apart they were, she seemed to know, in some mysterious way, when anything was wrong with him. If he were ill, or unfit to play, he would often receive a letter of sympathy, counsel, and warning, written when she could not possibly have received any news from him. He has told me this, himself." Ann Hartley Gilbert, *The Stage Reminiscences of Mrs. Gilbert* (New York: Scribner's, 1901), 57–61.

Mary Ann Booth feared for the safety of her favorite son in the final weeks of the Civil War. On 28 March 1865 she addressed this letter to him: "My dear Boy: I have just got yours. I was very glad to hear from you, & hope you will write often. I did part with you sadly—& I still feel sad, very much so. June has just left me. He staied as long as he could. I am now quite alone. Rose has not returned yet. I feel miserable enough. I never yet doubted your love & devotion to me—in fact I always gave you praise for being the fondest of all my boys, but since you leave me to grief I must doubt it. I am no Roman mother. I love my dear ones before Country or any thing else. Heaven guard you is my Constant Prayer." Bryan, *The Great American Myth*, 141.

A friend of the family described the scene when Mary Ann Booth received a letter dated 14 April from JWB:

> Outside the newsboys, with strident voice, were calling, "The President's death, and the arrest of John Wilkes Booth." While in answer to these words the mother moaned: "O God, if this be true, let him shoot himself, let him not live to be hung! Spare him, spare us, spare the name that dreadful disgrace!" Then came the sound of the postman's whistle, and with the ring of the doorbell a letter was handed to Mrs. Booth. It was from John Wilkes Booth, written in the afternoon before the tragedy. A half-sheet of a fairly good-sized letter paper. It was an affectionate letter, such as any mother would like to receive from her son, containing nothing of particular moment, but ghastly to read now, with the thought of what the feelings of the man must have been who held the pen in writing it, knowing what overwhelming sorrow the next few hours would bring. (Mrs. Thomas Bailey Aldrich, *Crowding Memories* [Boston: Houghton Mifflin, 1920], 72–73)

2. The city of Washington celebrated the surrender of Lee's Army of Northern Virginia with a "grand illumination" the night of 13 April. "By seven o'clock on Thursday evening, the last candle was burning. . . . Ostentatiously, the City Hall sat dressed in gas jets, with as many as sixty candles apiece in some of its windows; while, from the square, the radiating streets seemed to stretch in unbroken vistas of flame. On the Avenue, the south side vied with the north in grandeur, and Seventh Street was dazzling. 'Union' and 'Grant' were the words the gaslights flashed on every hand. 'Victory brings peace,' proclaimed the transparencies; 'Stand by the flag,' and 'God wills that we remain united.' Lengthy Biblical and patriotic quotations covered many

shops and houses. . . . In all the seven wards, from Rock Creek to the poorhouse, from the Arsenal to the Northern Liberties, there was no section which lacked its patriotic display. At the mansions of the rich and prominent, the great windows were brilliant, and fireworks played on the festooned flags." Margaret Leech, *Reveille in Washington, 1861–1865* (Garden City: Garden City Publishing, 1945), 385. It was hardly a spectacle that could be expected to please John Wilkes Booth.

3. JWB's sister, Rosalie Booth.

To Andrew Johnson[1]
Washington, D.C., 14 April 1865

Don't wish to disturb you; are you at home?

J.Wilkes. Booth.[2]

Autograph note signed on visiting card, National Archives.

1. Booth's note may have been for Vice-President Andrew Johnson or for Johnson's secretary, William A. Browning. JWB met Johnson (then military governor of Tennessee) and Browning in Nashville during his two-week engagement at Wood's Theatre, which had opened 1 February 1864. JWB gave the unreliable George A. Atzerodt the assignment of assassinating Johnson. The purpose of this note may have been to establish Johnson's whereabouts that night, when Atzerodt was to make his attack.

2. The fact that Booth had directed this note to Johnson was later to arouse suspicion that the vice president was involved in the plot to kill Abraham Lincoln. The accusation was raised at the Johnson impeachment proceedings in 1867. The year before, Mary Lincoln had written *"that,* miserable inebriate Johnson, had cognizance of my husband's death—*Why,* was *that card* of Booth's, found in his box, some acquaintance certainly existed—I have been deeply impressed, with the harrowing thought, that *he,* [Johnson] had an understanding with the conspirators & *they,* knew *their man.* Did not Booth, say, 'There is one thing, he would not tell.' There is said, to be honor, among thieves. No one ever heard, of Johnson, regretting my sainted husband's death, he never wrote me a line of condolence, and behaved in the most brutal way." Mary Todd Lincoln to Sally Orne, 15 March 1866, in *Mary Todd Lincoln: Her Life and Letters,* ed. Justin G. Turner and Linda Levitt Turner (New York: Alfred A. Knopf, 1972), 345.

A special Assassination Committee established by the 40th Congress in 1867, however, found no evidence of Johnson's involvement in the plot against Lincoln. William Hanchett, *The Lincoln Murder Conspiracies* (Urbana: University of Illinois Press, 1983), 83–85.

To the Editors of the National Intelligencer
Washington, D.C., 14 April 1865

Washington, D.C., April 14, 1865.[1]

To My Countrymen: For years I have devoted my time, my energies, and every dollar I possessed to the furtherance of an object. I have been baffled and disappointed. The hour has come when I must change my plan. Many, I know—the vulgar herd—will blame me for what I am about to do, but posterity, I am sure, will justify me.[2] Right or wrong, God judge me, not man. Be my motive good or bad, of one thing I am sure, the lasting condemnation of the North. I love peace more than life. Have loved the Union beyond expression. For four years have I waited, hoped and prayed for the dark clouds to break and for a restoration of our former sunshine. To wait longer is a crime. My prayers have proved as idle as my hopes. Gods will be done. I go to see and share the bitter end. This war is a war with the constitution and the reserve rights of the state. It is a war upon Southern rights and institutions. The nomination of Abraham Lincoln four years ago bespoke war. His election forced it. I have ever held the South were right. In a foreign war I too could say "country, right or wrong." But in a struggle such as ours (where the brother tries to pierce the brother's heart) for God's sake chose the right. When a country like this spurns justice from her side she forfeits the allegiance of every honest freeman, and should leave him untrammeled by any fealty soever to act as his conscience may approve.

People of the North, to hate tyranny to love liberty and justice, to strike at wrong and oppression, was the teaching of our fathers. The study of our early history will not let me forget it, and may it never.

I do not want to forget the heroic patriotism of our fathers, who rebelled against the oppression of the mother country.

This country was formed for the white, not for the black man. And, looking upon African slavery from the same standpoint as the noble framers of our constitution, I, for one, have ever considered it one of the greatest blessings, both for themselves and us, that God ever bestowed upon a favored nation. Witness, heretofore, our wealth and power; witness their elevation and enlightenment above their race elsewhere. I have lived among it most of my life, and have seen less harsh treatment from master to man than I have beheld in the North from father to son. Yet, Heaven knows no one would be willing to do more for the negro race than I, could I but see a way to still better their condition. But Lincoln's policy is only preparing the way for their total annihilation. The South are not, nor have they been, fighting for the continuation of slavery. The first battle of Bull Run did away with that idea.

Their causes for the war have been as noble and greater far than those that urged our fathers on. Even should we allow that they were wrong at the beginning of this contest, cruelty and injustice have made the wrong become the right, and they stand now before the wonder and admiration of the world as a noble band of patriot heroes. Hereafter reading of their deeds Thermopylae would be forgotten.

When I aided in the capture and execution of John Brown (who was a murderer on our western border, and who was fairly tried and convicted before an impartial judge and jury of treason, and who, by the way, has since been made a God.) I was proud of my little share in the transaction, for I deemed it my duty. and that I was helping our common country to perform an act of justice, but what was a crime in poor John Brown is now considered (by themselves) as the greatest and only virtue of the whole Republican party.

Strange transmigration! Vice to become a virtue, simply because more indulge in it. I thought then, as now, that the Abolitionists were the only traitors in the land, and that the entire party deserved the same fate as poor old Brown. Not because they wished to abolish slavery. but on account of the means they have ever endeavored to use to effect that abolition. If Brown were living I doubt whether he himself would set slavery against the Union. Most, or nearly all the North, do openly curse the Union if the South are to return and retain a single right guaranteed to them by every tie which we once revered as sacred. The South can make no choice. It is either extermination or slavery for themselves (worse than death) to draw from. I know my choice, and hasten to accept it. I have studied hard to discover upon what grounds the right of a State to secede has been denied, whether our very name, United States, and the Declaration of Independence both provide for secession. but there is now no time for words. I know how foolish I shall be deemed for undertaking such a step as this, where on the one side I have many friends and every thing to make me happy, where my profession alone has gained me an income of more than twenty thousand dollars a year, and where my great personal ambition in my profession has been a great field for labor. On the other hand, the South have never bestowed upon me one kind word; a place now where I have no friends, except beneath the sod; a place where I must either become a private soldier or a beggar. To give up all of the former for the latter, besides my mother and sisters whom I love so dearly (although they so widely differ with me in opinion), seems insane; but God is my judge.

I love justice more than I do a country that disowns it; more than fame and wealth; more (heaven pardon me if wrong) more than a happy home. I have never been upon a battlefield, but oh! my countrymen, could you all but see the reality or effects of this horrid war. As I have seen them in every state save Virginia, I know you would think like me, and would pray the Almighty to create in the Northern mind a sense of right and justice (even should it possess no seasoning of mercy) and that he would dry up the sea of blood between us which is daily growing wider. Alas, I have no longer a country. She is fast approaching her threatened doom. Four years ago, I would have given a thousand lives to see her remain (as I had always known her) powerful and unbroken. And even now I would hold my life as naught, to see her what she was. Oh! my friends, if the fearful scenes of the past four years had never been enacted, or if what has been had been but a frightful dream, from which we could now awake, with what overflowing hearts could we bless our God and pray for his continued favor.

How I have loved the old flag can never now be known. A few years since and the entire world could boast of [none] so pure and spotless. But I have of late been seeing and hearing of the bloody deeds of which she has been made the emblem. And would shudder to think how changed she had grown. Oh! how I have longed to see her break from the mist of blood and death so circled around her folds, spoiling her beauty and tarnishing her honor. But no; day by day has she been dragged deeper and deeper into cruelty and oppression, till now (in my eyes) her once bright red stripes look like bloody gashes on the face of heaven. I look now upon my early admiration of her glories as a dream. My love (as things stand today) is for the South alone, and to her side I go penniless.

Her success has been near my heart, and I have labored faithfully to further an object which would more than have proved my unselfish devotion. Heartsick and disappointed I turn from the path which I have been following into a bolder and more perilous one. Without malice I make the change. I have nothing in my heart except a sense of duty to my choice. If the South is to be aided it must be done quickly. It may already be too late. When Caesar had conquered the enemies of Rome and the power that was his menaced the liberties of the people, Brutus arose and slew him. The stroke of his dagger was guided by his love of Rome. It was the spirit and ambition of Caesar that Brutus struck at.

"Oh that we could come by Caesar's spirit,
And not dismember Caesar!

But, alas!
Caesar must bleed for it."[3]

I answer with Brutus:

He who loves his country better than gold or life.[4]

John W. Booth

Text of letter written and destroyed on 14 April 1865, reconstructed from memory by John Matthews with the help of Philadelphia journalist Frank A. Burr, and published in the Washington Evening Star *on 7 December 1881.*[5]

1. A newspaper reporter provided this account of Booth writing his letter to the *National Intelligencer* on the afternoon of 14 April: "At about 4 P.M., he . . . made his appearance at the counter [of the National Hotel], . . . and with a nervous air called for a sheet of paper and an envelope. He was about to write when the thought seemed to strike him that someone around him might overlook his letter, and, approaching the door of the office, he requested admittance. On reaching the inside of the office, he immediately commenced his letter. He had written but a few words when he said earnestly, 'Merrick, is the year 1864 or '65?' 'You are surely joking, John,' relied Mr. M., 'you certainly know what year it is.' 'Sincerely, I am not,' he rejoined, and on being told, resumed writing. It was then that Mr. M. noticed something troubled and agitated in Booth's appearance, which was entirely at variance with his usual quiet deportment. Sealing the letter, he placed it in his pocket and left the hotel." New York *Tribune,* 17 April 1865; quoted in Philip Van Doren Stern, "Introduction," in *The Assassination of President Lincoln and the Trial of the Conspirators,* comp. Benn Pitman (New York: Moore, Wilstach, and Baldwin, 1865; facsimile edition edited by Philip Van Doren Stern, New York: Funk and Wagnalls, 1954), ix–x.

2. Booth seems to have believed that this letter would help to justify his action. He was bitterly disappointed a few days later to learn that it was not published. He alluded to the letter twice in the diary he kept while in hiding after the assassination. In the entry headed 14 April he wrote, "This night (before the deed), I wrote a long article and left it for one of the Editors of the National Inteligencer, in which I fully set forth our reasons for our proceedings." In the entry headed 21 April he added, "The little, the very little I left behind to clear my name, the Govmt will not allow to be printed."

3. *Julius Caesar,* II, i, 169.

4. See also the two variant closing paragraphs provided in the following note.

5. The story of Booth's lost letter to the *National Intelligencer* is a curious one. On the afternoon of the day he killed Lincoln, Booth apparently wrote the letter to the Washington newspaper justifying the murderous action he intended to take at Ford's that evening. But the only person who ever saw the letter was Booth's actor friend John Matthews (or Mathews). Afraid of being implicated in the assassination, Matthews destroyed it. Matthews had reason to be fearful. He had known

Booth most of his life; the two had shared a Baltimore childhood before becoming actors. During the winter of 1864–65, Booth had tried to recruit Matthews for the conspiracy to capture Lincoln. Matthews had not at that time reported his friend's plot to the authorities. Now, moments after Lincoln had been shot, he found himself in possession of a document that might have saved the president. Matthews burned the letter.

Although John Matthews testified in 1867 that he had been unable to recall the full text, in 1881 he and Philadelphia journalist Frank A. Burr managed to "reconstruct" the letter. The reconstructed text was published in a long article by Burr entitled "Lincoln's Last Night," which appeared in the *Philadelphia Press* on 3 and 4 December 1881. It was reprinted in the *Washington Evening Star* on 7 December 1881, which is the source of the preceding text. Except for the opening and closing paragraphs, the reconstructed text is nearly identical to that of the "to whom it may concern" letter Booth had written in the fall of 1864 and left in Philadelphia with his sister, Asia Booth Clarke. The letter had been widely published by the time John Matthews undertook to reconstruct the 14 April letter in 1881.

It seems most unlikely that Matthews would be able to remember so exactly a 1,500–word document sixteen years after reading it through twice. The best explanation is that Matthews simply copied the text of the "to whom it may concern" letter (James O. Hall to John Rhodehamel, 27 June 1994). Matthews was called as witness and questioned about Booth's letter before the House Judiciary Committee in the impeachment investigation of President Andrew Johnson in 1867. His testimony was published in "Impeachment of the President," *House Report Seven* (serial set 1314), 40th Cong., 1st sess. (1867), 782–85:

Washington, D.C., Monday, July 1, 1867.
John Mathews sworn and examined.
By Mr. Boutwell:

Q. Where do you reside?
A. I am residing at present in Rochester, New York.
Q. Did you know John Wilkes Booth?
A. I did.
Q. When did you last see him?
A. I saw him last on the night of the assassination of Mr. Lincoln, a few minutes before the occurrence; I saw him on the stage of the theatre; I was engaged that night in playing a part of the piece that was performed.
Q. When had you last seen him previously to that?
A. The same day, about three o'clock in the afternoon, on Pennsylvania avenue, near Willard's. . . .
Q. What was the nature of the conversation?
A. I met him coming down the avenue on horseback; he stopped, and we spoke of the prisoners—Lee's officers, who had been brought in prisoners in a body, and had just passed by. Said I, "John, have you seen the prisoners?" "Yes, Johnny," said he, "I have." Then said he, placing his hand on his forehead, "Great God! I have no longer a country!" He then said to me. . . . "Johnny, I wish to ask you a favor; will you do it for me?" I said, "Of

course." Said he, "I have a letter which I wish you to deliver to the publishers of the National Intelligencer to-morrow morning, unless I see you in the mean time. I may leave town to-night, and it will not be much trouble for you to deliver that letter." I said, "Certainly, I will.". . .

Q. Did you deliver the letter to the National Intelligencer?

A. No, sir.

Q. Have you it in your possession?

A. No, sir.

Q. What did you do with it?

A. After the assassination, we all [the cast of *Our American Cousin*] retired to the dressing rooms. . . . it was said that nobody could leave the house— that we were all under arrest. The excitement was great. . . . There were shouts of "burn" and "hang" and "lynch.". . . When taking off my coat the letter which Booth had given me dropped out of the pocket. I had forgotten all about it. I said, "Great God! there is the letter John gave me in the afternoon." It was in an envelope, sealed and stamped for the post office. I opened it, and glanced hastily over the letter. I saw it was a statement of what he was going to do. I read it very hurriedly. It was written in a sort of patriotic strain, and was to this effect: That he had for a long time devoted his money, his time, and his energies to the accomplishment of an end; that a short time ago he had been worth so much money—twenty or thirty thousand dollars, I think—all of which he had spent furthering this enterprise; but that he had been baffled. It then went on: "The moment has come at last when my plans must be changed. The world may censure me for what I am about to do; but I am sure posterity will justify me." Signed. "Men who love their country better than gold or life: J. W. Booth,—Payne,—Atzerodt, and—Herold.". . .

Q. Did you make a copy of the letter?

A. No, sir. I am sorry I did not.

Q. What did you do with it?

A. I burned it up.

Q. How many times did you read it over?

A. Perhaps a couple of times. It was written on two sides of a sheet of paper. I thought to myself, "What shall I do with this letter? It could only convict him, and that has been done already, because people in the house have recognized him. If this paper is found on me I will be compromised—no doubt lynched on the spot. If I take it to the newspaper office it will be known. I will be associated with the letter, and suspicions will grow out of it that can never be explained away, and I will be ruined." I therefore burned it. . . .

Q. You have stated the contents of the letter. Do you mean to be understood as having stated fully and exactly what was written in that letter?

A. Yes, sir; the substance without the exact words, but nearly those. The letter made an impression on my memory at the time.

Q. What is your profession?

A. I am an actor.

Q. You are accustomed to commit words to memory?

A. Yes, sir; I have to do so to a very inordinate degree, sometimes.

Q. Since the destruction of the letter, have you ever written out, from your memory, the contents of that letter?

A. I have frequently striven to do so. I have set down to do so, but I could not get the commencement of the letter—the starting of it. . . .

In a letter to the *National Intelligencer*, published on 18 July 1867, Matthews provided this account of the "Booth Letter":

Much has been said been said in the public press in regard to the missing letter of John Wilkes Booth. As I am the person to whom the letter was entrusted, I know its contents and the circumstances attending its delivery into my hands better than any person now living. It was the afternoon of Good Friday, April 14, 1865, at about 4 o'clock, that I met John Wilkes Booth (on horseback) on Pennsylvania avenue, at the triangular enclosure between Thirteenth and Fourteenth streets. We met, shook hands, and passed the compliments of the day. It so happened that the officers of Lee's army had just passed up in a body. I asked Booth, "Johnny, have you seen Lee's officers, just brought in?" He replied, "Yes, Johnny, I have"; then placing his hand upon his forehead, exclaimed, "Great God, I have no longer a country." Observing his paleness, nervousness, and agitation, I remarked, "John, how nervous you are, what is the matter?" to which he replied, "Oh, no, it is nothing," and continued with, "Johnny, I have a little favor to ask of you, will you grant it?" "Why certainly, Johnny," I replied; "what is it?" He then stated, "Perhaps I may have to leave town to-night, and I have a letter here which I desire to be published in the NATIONAL INTELLIGENCER; please attend to it for me, unless I see you before ten o'clock to-morrow; in that case I will see to it myself." At that moment I observed General Grant riding by in an open carriage, carrying also his baggage. Seeing this, I called Mr. Booth's attention to him, and said, "Why, Johnny, there goes Grant. I thought he was to be coming to the theatre this evening with the President." "Where?" he exclaimed. I pointed to the carriage; he looked toward it, grasped my hand tightly, and galloped down the avenue after the carriage. . . . Now for the contents of the letter. It was written on a sheet of commercial note paper, covering three pages. The first two pages were written in the spirit and style of the Philadelphia letter ["to whom it may concern"] and it was only at the concluding paragraph that anything was said bearing upon what had transpired, which was to this effect and in these words:

For a long time I have devoted my energies, my time and money, to the accomplishment of a certain end. I have been disappointed. The moment has arrived when I must change my plans. Many will blame me for what I am about to do, but posterity, I am sure, will justify me. Men who love their country better than gold and life.

John W. Booth, Payne, Herold, Atzerodt.

John Wilkes Booth's Diary[1]
Zekiah Swamp and Nanjemoy Creek,
Charles County, Maryland,
17 and 22 April 1865

April 13th   14 Friday the Ides[2]

Until to day nothing was ever *thought* of sacrificing to our country's wrongs. For six months we had worked to capture. But our cause being almost lost, something decisive & great must be done. But its failure is owing to others, who did not strike for their country with a heart. I struck boldly and not as the papers say. I walked with a firm step through a thousand of his friends, was stopped, but pushed on. A Col- was at his side.[3] I shouted Sic semper *before* I fired.[4] In jumping broke my leg. I passed all his pickets, rode sixty miles that night, with the bones of my leg tearing the flesh at every jump.[5] I can never repent it, though we hated to kill: Our country owed all her troubles to him, and God simply made me the instrument of his punishment. The country is not what it *was*. This forced union is not what I *have* loved. I care not what *becomes* of me. I have no desire to out-live my country. This night (before the deed), I wrote a long article and left it for one of the Editors of the National Inteligencer,[6] in which I fully set forth our reasons for our proceedings. He or the Govmt[7]

Friday 21—[8]
After being hunted like a dog through swamps, woods, and last night being chased by gun boats till I was forced to return wet cold and starving, with every mans hand against me, I am here in despair. And why; For doing what Brutus was honored for, what made Tell[9] a Hero. And yet I for striking down a greater tyrant than they ever knew am looked upon as a common cutthroat. My action was purer than either of theirs. One, hoped to be great himself. The other had not only his countrys but his own wrongs to avenge. I hoped for no gain. I knew no private wrong. I struck for my country and that alone. A country groaned beneath this tyranny and prayed for this end. Yet now behold the cold hand they extend to me.[10] God *cannot* pardon me if I have done wrong. Yet I cannot see any wrong except in serving a degenerate people. The little, the very little I left behind to clear my name, the Govmt will not allow to be printed. So ends all. For my country I have given up all that makes life sweet and Holy, brought misery on my family, and am sure there is no pardon in Heaven for me since man condemns me so. I have only *heard* what has been done (except what I did myself) and it fills me with

horror.[11] God try and forgive me and bless my mother. To night I will once more try the river with the intent to cross, though I have a greater desire to return to Washington and in a measure clear my name which I feel I can do. I do not repent the blow I struck. I may before God but not to man.

I think I have done well, though I am abandoned, with the curse of Cain upon me. When if the world knew my heart, *that one* blow would have made me great, though I did desire no greatness.

To night I try to escape these blood hounds once more. Who who can read his fate. God's will be done.

I have too great a soul to die like a criminal. Oh may he, may he spare me that and let me die bravely.

I bless the entire world. Have never hated or wronged anyone. This last was not a wrong, unless God deems it so. And its with him, to damn or bless me. And for this brave boy[12] with me who often prays (yes before and since) with a true and sincere heart, was it a crime in him, if so why can he pray the same I do not wish to shed a drop of blood, but "I must fight the course" Tis all thats left me.

Autograph manuscript, National Park Service, Lincoln Museum at Ford's Theatre, Washington, D.C.; transcription from William Hanchett, "Booth's Diary," Journal of the Illinois State Historical Society 72 (Feb. 1979): 39–56.

1. The two diary entries were written by Booth in his *Pocket Diary, 1864,* a datebook printed and sold by St. Louis, Missouri, stationer James M. Crawford. Booth may have acquired the diary when he was in St. Louis in January 1864. The pocket diary begins with twenty-four printed pages offering the sort of information often found in almanacs—train schedules, tide charts, and dates of astronomical events. The printed tables are followed by sixty blank pages headed by printed dates, from "Saturday June 11, 1864" through "Thursday December 29, 1864," then two blank pages headed "Memoranda" and eighteen blank pages headed "Cash Account." Twenty-seven leaves, or fifty-four pages, those dated from 1 January through 10 June 1864, have been torn out of the diary. Stubs of twenty-five leaves are present; the removal of the two other leaves can be inferred from date headings of the blank diary pages. An additional sixteen leaves have been removed from different places in the last half of the book. Booth was apparently in the habit of tearing out diary leaves on which to write notes and letters. The two 24 April 1865 letters to Dr. Richard H. Stewart that follow were both written on leaves torn from the diary. The diary, which has been displayed for many years at Ford's Theatre, measures about six by three and one-half inches in its leather, threefold cover. The leather cover contains pockets for miscellaneous papers, as well as a leather loop for a pencil and smaller pockets labeled for notes and tickets. The photographs of the five women Booth carried were found in the diary pockets. Hanchett, "Booth's Diary," 50.

2. The text of the two entries is taken from the transcription in Hanchett, "Booth's

Diary," 39–56. The first entry is written on two pages bearing the printed dates "SAT-URDAY, JUNE 11, 1864" through "THURSDAY 16." At the top of the second page, Booth has crossed out the printed day, month, and year dates of "TUESDAY, JUNE 14, 1864" and written "April 1865" to yield April 14, 1865. "The Ides" is, of course, an allusion to the assassination of Julius Caesar. The entry was probably written on 17 April 1865. Hanchett, "Booth's Diary," 53.

3. The officer with Lincoln was not a colonel. Maj. Henry Rathbone (1837–1911) and his stepsister, Clara Harris, were the young couple who accompanied the Lincolns to the performance of *Our American Cousin* at Ford's Theatre the night of the assassination. After shooting Lincoln with his single-shot pistol, Booth struck at Rathbone with a knife, inflicting a serious wound to the officer's left arm. Booth then jumped out of the box to the stage twelve feet below. Rathbone later married Clara Harris. In 1894, while living in Germany, Rathbone went mad and murdered his wife. He died in a German asylum.

4. There is confusion about the words Booth may have shouted before and after firing the shot that killed Lincoln. Most authorities agree that he cried out *"Sic Semper Tyrannis!"* (thus always to tyrants) after he leaped to the stage. Some of the audience thought they also heard him shout "the South is avenged!" Timothy S. Good, *We Saw Lincoln Shot: One Hundred Eyewitness Accounts* (Jackson: University Press of Mississippi, 1995), passim.

5. Booth rode only thirty miles on the first night of his flight from Washington. Because he had sustained a simple, rather than a compound, fracture, no jagged piece of bone would have been "tearing at the flesh" as he rode. It is doubtless true, however, that the assassin was in great pain. In a statement made under interrogation on 21 April 1865, Dr. Samuel A. Mudd (1833–83) said, "On examination, I found there was a straight fracture of the [fibula] about two inches above the ankle. My examination was quite short, and I did not find the adjoining bone fractured in any way. I do not regard it a particularly painful or dangerous wound; there is nothing resembling a compound fracture. I do not suppose I was more than three-quarters of an hour in making the examination of the wound and apply the splint. He continued to suffer, and complained of severe pain." Surratt Society, eds., *From War Department Files: Statements Made by the Alleged Lincoln Conspirators under Examination 1865* (Clinton, Md.: Surratt Society, 1980), 25. Dr. Mudd also made the crutches the crippled assassin was still using when he was killed on 26 April. Mudd was a Confederate agent who had probably been party to the conspiracy to capture Abraham Lincoln. For helping Booth and aiding his escape, Mudd was sentenced to life imprisonment at hard labor. President Andrew Johnson pardoned him in 1869.

6. Booth refers to his letter of 14 April 1865, "To My Countrymen."

7. The first entry ends here in midsentence; perhaps Booth had been interrupted by a visit from Thomas A. Jones, the Charles County Confederate Signal Corps agent who brought food and newspapers to David Herold and him during the five nights and six days they hid out a clearing in Zekiah Swamp. Booth probably intended to charge (as he did in the entry dated 21 April) that the newspaper editor or the government had suppressed the "long article" of justification he had written. The remaining two-thirds of this page contains a daily calendar drawn up by Booth to

keep track of the date because the pocket diary itself was for 1864. It continued through 18 June. The last date to be crossed off was 25 April.

8. The second entry was written on three pages bearing the printed dates "THURS-DAY, JUNE 23, 1864" through "FRIDAY, JULY 1." Research indicates that this entry was actually written on 22, not 21, April. Booth and Herold had first tried to get across the two-mile-wide Potomac River dividing Maryland from Virginia on the night of 21 April. They set off at about ten o'clock in a little fishing boat provided by Jones. Confederate agents on the Virginia side had been alerted to help the fugitives. But, despite rowing most of the night, they did not reach Virginia. Booth and Herold's little boat may have been pushed off-course by wind and tides, and the men may have been frightened by the presence of two federal patrol boats. Morning found them on the Maryland shore at Nanjemoy Creek, several miles upstream of their starting point. Fed and sheltered by Confederate sympathizers, the fugitives waited for the return of darkness to try the river crossing again. Leaving about sunset on 22 April, they did reach Virginia on the second attempt, probably arriving in the early-morning hours of 23 April. William A. Tidwell, with James O. Hall and David Winfred Gaddy, *Come Retribution: The Confederate Secret Service and the Assassination of Lincoln* (Jackson: University Press of Mississippi, 1988), 454–57; William A. Tidwell, "Booth Crosses the Potomac: An Exercise in Historical Research," *Civil War History* 36 (Dec. 1990): 325–33.

9. The Roman statesman Marcus Junius Brutus (ca. 78–42 B.C.) was one of the assassins of Julius Caesar; William Tell was a fifteenth-century Swiss patriot and killer of the Austrian tyrant Gessler.

10. It was from the papers Jones brought that Booth learned that the murder of Lincoln was widely condemned in the South as well as the North. The passages Booth wrote in his pocket diary are informed by his shock at Southern reaction to the assassination. Jones recalled that the assassin "never tired of the newspapers. And there—surrounded by the sighing pines—he read the world's just condemnation of his deed and the price that was offered for his life." Thomas A. Jones, *J. Wilkes Booth: An Account of His Sojourn in Southern Maryland after the Assassination of Abraham Lincoln, His Passage Across the Potomac, and His Death in Virginia* (Chicago: Laird and Lee, 1893), 97.

11. Booth probably meant that newspaper accounts of Lewis Powell's attack on William H. Seward's home horrified him. Booth had ordered Powell to kill Lincoln's secretary of state. In his attack on Seward, Powell wounded four other men (including two of Seward's sons) he encountered in the house. Powell himself said he regretted injuring the four who were not the target of his assassination mission.

12. David Herold.

To Dr. Richard H. Stewart[1]
"Cleydael," King George County, Virginia, 24 April 1865

My Dea[r Sir:]
    Forgive me, but I have some little pride. I cannot to blame you for want

of hospitality. You know your own affairs. I was sick, tired, with a broken limb, and in need of medical advice. I would not have turned a dog from my door in such a plight. However, you were kind enough to give us something to eat, for which I not only thank you, but, on account of the rebuke and manner in which, to [. . .] It is not the substance, but the way in which kindness is extended that makes one happy in the acceptance thereof. The sauce to meat is ceremony. Meeting were bare without it.[2] Be kind enough to accept the enclosed five dollars (although hard to spare) for what we have rec'd.

Most respectfully, your obedient servant.

Letter in House Judiciary Committee, "Impeachment of the President," House Report Seven (serial set 1314), 40th Cong., 1st sess. (1867), 676–77.

1. Dr. Richard H. Stewart was one of King George County's most prominent citizens. Thoroughly Southern in sympathies, he was a cousin of Robert E. Lee and had been imprisoned twice by federal authorities who correctly suspected he was collaborating with the Confederates. He would be arrested again because of his brief encounter with John Wilkes Booth and David Herold. Dr. Stewart testified that the two men, with a local guide, had arrived at his house late in the afternoon of 23 April. It was already dark. Stewart came out to meet them. Herold asserted that they were Marylanders who needed lodging for the night and treatment for Booth's broken leg. Herold claimed that Dr. Mudd had recommended Dr. Stewart to them. Stewart refused to help. He had no room to put them up, he said, and he did not know Dr. Mudd. Stewart, who thought the story of the broken leg was a ruse to win his sympathy, would do no more than give the fugitives a meal in his kitchen before hustling them out of the house and sending them on their way. Booth was furious at the treatment they received. It seemed but one more example of the "cold hand" extended to the assassin of the arch-tyrant by a "degenerate people." On a leaf torn from his pocket diary, Booth composed this stinging little note in which he intended to enclose $5 in payment for the meal. But Booth reconsidered. His funds were getting short, and he decided that $5 was more than he could afford, even for so theatrical a gesture. He put the first letter back in his pocket and wrote a second, enclosing $2.50. Besides the amount offered in payment for the meal, the two letters differ slightly in wording. The first, unsent, letter was found on Booth after he was shot; the second was obtained by investigators from Dr. Stewart, who had saved it because it tended to prove he had given no help to Booth and Herold. Stanley Kimmel, *The Mad Booths of Maryland* (Indianapolis: Bobbs-Merrill, 1940), 240–42.

2. *Macbeth*, III, iv, 36.

To Dr. Richard H. Stewart
"Cleydael," King George County, Virginia, 24 April 1865

Dear Sir: Forgive me, but I have some little pride. I hate to blame you for your want of hospitality: you know your own affairs. I was sick and tired, with a broken leg, in need of medical advice. I would not have turned a dog from my door in such a condition. However, you were kind enough to give me something to eat, for which I not only thank you, but, on account of the reluctant manner in which it was bestowed, I feel bound to pay for it. It is not the substance, but the manner in which kindness is extended that makes one happy in the acceptance thereof. The sauce to meat is ceremony; meeting were bare without it. Be kind enough to accept the enclosed two dollars and a half (though hard to spare) for what we have received.

Yours respectfully,

Stranger

April 24, 1865.

Letter House Judiciary Committee, "Impeachment of the President," House Report Seven *(serial set 1314), 40th Cong., 1st sess. (1867), 676–77.*

BIBLIOGRAPHY

Abbott, Martin. "Southern Reaction to Lincoln's Assassination." *Abraham Lincoln Quarterly* 7 (Sept. 1952): 111–27.

Aldrich, Mrs. Thomas Bailey. *Crowding Memories.* Boston: Houghton Mifflin, 1920.

Archer, Stephen M. *Junius Brutus Booth: Theatrical Prometheus.* Carbondale: Southern Illinois University Press, 1992.

Arnold, Samuel Bland. *Defence and Prison Experiences of a Lincoln Conspirator.* Hattiesburg, Miss.: The Book Farm, 1943.

The Assassination and History of the Conspiracy. Cincinnati: J. R. Hawley, 1865. Reprint. New York: Hobbs, Dorman, 1965.

Badeau, Adam. "Dramatic Reminiscences." *St. Paul and Minneapolis Pioneer Press,* 20 Feb. 1887.

———. "Edwin Booth On and Off Stage." *McClure's Magazine* (Aug. 1893).

Baker, Lafayette C. *History of the United States Secret Service.* Philadelphia: L. C. Baker, 1867.

Bates, David Homer. *Lincoln in the Telegraph Office.* New York: Century, 1907.

Bigelow, John. *Retrospections of an Active Life.* 5 volumes. New York: Baker and Taylor, 1909.

Bowman, Walter P., and Robert H. Ball. *Theatre Language: A Dictionary of Terms.* New York: Theatre Arts Book, 1961.

Brennan, John C. "The Confederate Plan to Abduct President Lincoln." In Surratt Society, eds., *In Pursuit . . . Continuing Research in the Field of the Lincoln Assassination,* 141–50. Clinton, Md.: Surratt Society, 1990.

———. "Confederate Spy: Captain Thomas Nelson Conrad." *Surratt Society News* (June 1977).

———. "General Bradley T. Johnson's Plan to Abduct President Lincoln." *Chronicles of St. Mary's* 22 (Nov.–Dec. 1974) 421–25.

Brooks, Noah. *Washington in Lincoln's Time.* New York: Rinehart, 1958.

Brown, T. Allston. *History of the American Stage, Containing Biographical Sketches of Nearly Every Member of the Profession Who Has Appeared on the American Stage, from 1733 to 1870.* New York: Dick and Fitzgerald, 1870.

Bryan, George S. *The Great American Myth.* New York: Carrick and Evans, 1940. Reprint. Introduction by William Hanchett. Chicago: Americana House, 1990.

Buchanan, James. *The Works of James Buchanan.* 12 volumes. Edited by John B. Moore. Philadelphia: J. P. Lippincott, 1910.

Carpenter, Francis B. *Six Months at the White House.* New York: Hurd and Houghton, 1867.

The Circular of the Milton Boarding School, Situated in Baltimore County, MD. Baltimore, 1859.

Clark, Champ. *The Assassination, Death of a President.* Alexandria: Time-Life Books, 1987.

Clarke, Asia Booth. *Booth Memorials: Passages, Incidents, and Anecdotes in the Life of Junius Brutus Booth (the Elder).* New York: Carleton, 1867.

———. *The Elder and the Younger Booth.* Boston: James R. Osgood, 1882.

———. *The Unlocked Book: A Memoir of John Wilkes Booth by His Sister.* New York: G. P. Putnam's Sons, 1938.

Clarke, James W. *American Assassins: The Darker Side of Politics.* Princeton: Princeton University Press, 1982.

Conrad, Thomas N. *A Confederate Spy.* New York: J. Ogilvie Publishing, 1892.

———. *The Rebel Scout.* Washington: National Publishing, 1904.

Craven, Avery. "Southern Attitudes toward Abraham Lincoln." *Papers in Illinois History 1942.* Springfield: State Historical Society, 1944.

Crook, William H. *Through Five Administrations.* Compiled and edited by Margarita Spalding Gerry. New York: Harper and Brothers, 1910.

Cuthbert, Norma B., ed. *Lincoln and the Baltimore Plot, 1861, from Pinkerton Records and Related Papers.* San Marino: Huntington Library, 1949.

Davis, Michael. *The Image of Lincoln in the South.* Knoxville: University of Tennessee Press, 1971.

Davis, Varina Howell. *Jefferson Davis: A Memoir by His Wife.* New York: Belford, 1890.

DeWitt, David Miller. *The Assassination of Abraham Lincoln, and Its Expiation.* New York: Macmillan, 1909.

———. *The Judicial Murder of Mary E. Surratt.* Baltimore: John Murphy, 1893.

Dodels, Jeannie Clarke. "John Wilkes Booth's Secession Crisis Speech of 1860." In *John Wilkes Booth, Actor: The Proceedings of a Conference Weekend in Bel Air, Maryland, May 1988,* 48–52. Edited by Arthur Kincaid. North Leigh, Oxfordshire: Published privately, 1989.

———. "Water on Stone: A Study of John Wilkes Booth's Political Draft Preserved at the Players Club NYC." Unpublished ms. Copy in possession of Louise Taper.

Dolson, Hildegarde. *The Great Oil Dorado.* New York: Random House, 1959.

Doster, William E. *Lincoln and Episodes of the Civil War.* New York: G. P. Putnam's Sons, 1915.

Eisenschiml, Otto. *In the Shadow of Lincoln's Death.* New York: Wilfred Funk, 1940.

———. *Why Was Lincoln Murdered?* Boston: Little, Brown, 1937.

Ellsler, John A. *The Stage Memories of John A. Ellsler.* Edited by Effie Ellsler Weston. Cleveland: The Rowfant Club, 1950.

Ferguson, William J. *I Saw Booth Shoot Lincoln.* Austin: Pemberton Press, 1969.

Foner, Eric, ed. *Nat Turner.* Englewood Cliffs: Prentice-Hall, 1971.

Fowler, Robert H. *Album of the Lincoln Murder.* Harrisburg: Stackpole Books, 1965.

Garrett, Richard Baynham. "A Chapter of Unwritten History . . . Account of the Flight and Death of John Wilkes Booth." *Virginia Magazine of History and Biography* 71 (Oct. 1963): 387–407.

Gilbert, Ann Hartley. *The Stage Reminiscences of Mrs. Gilbert.* New York: Scribner's, 1901.

Goldsborough, William W. *The Maryland Line in the Confederate States Army.* Baltimore: Kelly, Piet, 1869.

Good, Timothy S. *We Saw Lincoln Shot: One Hundred Eyewitness Accounts.* Jackson: University Press of Mississippi, 1995.

Graham, Franklin. *Histrionic Montreal: Annals of the Montreal Stage.* Montreal: J. Lovell and Son, 1902.

Grossman, Edwina Booth. *Edwin Booth: Recollections by His Daughter.* New York: Century, 1894.

Gutman, Richard J. S., and Kellie O. Gutman. *John Wilkes Booth Himself.* Dover, Mass.: Hired Hand Press, 1979.

Hall, James O. *Notes on the John Wilkes Booth Escape Route.* Clinton, Md.: Surratt Society, 1980.

———. *The Surratt Family and John Wilkes Booth.* Clinton, Md.: Surratt Society, n.d.

Hanchett, William. "The Ambush on the Seventh Street Road." In Surratt Society, eds., *In Pursuit of . . . Continuing Research in the Field of the Lincoln Assassination,* 151–61. Clinton, Md.: Surratt Society, 1990.

———. "Booth's Diary." *Journal of the Illinois State Historical Society* 72 (Feb. 1979): 39–56.

———. *The Lincoln Murder Conspiracies.* Urbana: University of Illinois Press, 1983.

Head, Constance. "John Wilkes Booth as a Hero Figure." *Journal of American Culture* 5 (Fall 1982): 22–28.

———. "John Wilkes Booth, 1864: Prologue to Assassination." *Lincoln Herald* 85 (Winter 1983): 254–62.

———. "John Wilkes Booth in American Fiction." *Lincoln Herald* 82 (Fall 1980): 256.

———. "J.W.B: His Initials in India Ink." *Virginia Magazine of History and Biography* 90 (July 1982): 359–66.

Headley, John W. *Confederate Operations in Canada and New York.* New York: Neale Publishing, 1906.

Hensel, W. U. *The Christiana Riot and the Treason Trials of 1851.* Lancaster: New Era Printing, 1911.

Holding, Charles E. "John Wilkes Booth Stars in Nashville." *Tennessee Historical Quarterly* 23 (March 1964): 73–79.

House Judiciary Committee. "Impeachment of the President." *House Report Seven* (serial set 1314), 40th Cong., 1st sess. Washington, D.C.: Government Printing Office, 1867.

Jones, Thomas A. *J. Wilkes Booth: An Account of His Sojourn in Southern Maryland after the Assassination of Abraham Lincoln, His Passage Across the Potomac, and His Death in Virginia.* Chicago: Laird and Lee, 1893.

Katz, Jonathan. *Resistance at Christiana: The Fugitive Slave Rebellion, Christiana, Pennsylvania, September 11, 1851.* New York: Thomas Y. Crowell, 1974.

Kauffman, Michael W. "Booth's Escape Route: Lincoln's Assassin on the Run." *Blue and Gray Magazine* 7 (June 1990): 8–21, 38–61.

———. "John Wilkes Booth and the Murder of Abraham Lincoln." *Blue and Gray Magazine* 7 (April 1990): 9–25, 46–62.

———, ed. *Samuel Bland Arnold: Memoirs of a Lincoln Conspirator.* Bowie, Md.: Heritage Books, 1995.

Kendall, John S. *The Golden Age of the New Orleans Theater.* Baton Rouge: Louisiana State University Press, 1952.

Kimmel, Stanley. *The Mad Booths of Maryland.* Indianapolis: Bobbs-Merrill, 1940.

———. *Mr. Lincoln's Washington.* New York: Bramhall House, 1957.

Kincaid, Arthur, ed. *John Wilkes Booth, Actor: The Proceedings of a Conference Weekend in Bel Air, Maryland, May 1988.* North Leigh, Oxfordshire: Published privately, 1989.

Kinchen, Oscar A. *Confederate Operations in Canada and the North.* North Quincy, Mass.: Christopher Publishing House, 1970.

Kirkland, Edward Chase. *The Peacemakers of 1864.* New York: Macmillan, 1927.

Kirkham, James F., Sheldon G. Levy, and William J. Crotty. *Assassination and Political Violence: A Report to the National Commission on the Causes and Prevention of Violence.* New York: Praeger Publishers, 1970.

Kline, Mary-Jo. *A Guide to Documentary Editing.* Baltimore: Association for Documentary Editing, 1987.

Kunhardt, Dorothy Meserve, and Philip B. Kunhardt. *Twenty Days.* New York: Castle Books, 1965.

Kushlan, Jim. "Collectible: A Paper Link to a Conspiracy." *Civil War Times Illustrated* 30 (Sept.–Oct. 1991): 15.

Lamon, Ward Hill. *Recollections of Abraham Lincoln.* Edited by Dorothy Lamon Teillard. Washington: Teillard, 1911. Reprint. Lincoln: University of Nebraska Press, 1994.

Lattimer, John K. "Good Samaritan Surgeon Wrongly Accused of Contributing to President Lincoln's Death: An Experimental Study of the President's Fatal Wound." *Journal of the American College of Surgeons* 182 (May 1996): 431–48.

———. *Kennedy and Lincoln: Medical and Ballistic Comparisons of Their Assassinations.* New York: Harcourt Brace Jovanovich, 1980.

Laughlin, Clara E. *The Death of Lincoln: The Story of Booth's Plot, His Deed and the Penalty.* New York: Doubleday, Page, 1909.

Lee, Robert E. *The Wartime Papers of Robert E. Lee.* Edited by Clifford Dowdey and Louis H. Manarin. Boston: Little, Brown, 1961.

Leech, Margaret. *Reveille in Washington, 1861–1865.* Garden City: Garden City Publishing, 1945.

Lewis, Lloyd. *Myths after Lincoln.* New York: Readers Club, 1941.

Lincoln, Abraham. *Collected Works of Abraham Lincoln.* Edited by Roy P. Basler. 9 volumes. New Brunswick: Rutgers University Press, 1953.

Lockridge, Richard. *Darling of Misfortune, Edwin Booth.* New York: Century, 1932.

Logan, John A. *The Great Conspiracy.* New York: A. R. Hart, 1886.

Loux, Arthur F. "The Accident-Prone John Wilkes Booth." *Lincoln Herald* 85 (Winter 1983): 263–67.

———. "John Wilkes Booth Day by Day." Unpublished ms.

Luthin, Reinhard. *The Real Abraham Lincoln.* Englewood Cliffs: Prentice-Hall, 1960.

Mahoney, Ella V. *Sketches of Tudor Hall and the Booth Family.* Bel Air, Md.: Franklin Printing, 1925.

Marshall, John A. *American Bastille: A History of the Illegal Arrests and Imprisonment of American Citizens during the Late Civil War.* Philadelphia: Thomas W. Hartley, 1877.

May, John F. "The Mark of the Scalpel." *Records of the Columbia Historical Society* 13 (1910): 49–68.

McGlinchee, Claire. *The First Decade of the Boston Museum.* Boston: Bruce Humphries, 1940.

McPherson, James M. *Battle Cry of Freedom: The Civil War Era.* New York: Oxford University Press, 1988.

Mearns, David C., ed. *The Lincoln Papers.* 2 volumes. Garden City: Doubleday, 1948.

Miers, Earl Schenck, editor-in-chief. *Lincoln Day by Day: A Chronology.* 3 volumes. Washington: Lincoln Sesquicentennial Commission, 1960.

Miller, Ernest C. *John Wilkes Booth in the Pennsylvania Oil Region.* Meadville, Pa.: Crawford County Historical Society, 1987.

Morcom, Richmond. "They All Loved Lucy." *American Heritage* 21 (Oct. 1970): 12–15.

Morris, Clara. *Life on the Stage: My Personal Experiences and Recollections.* New York: McClure, 1901.

Neely, Mark E., Jr. *The Abraham Lincoln Encyclopedia.* New York: McGraw-Hill, 1982.

———. "The Assassination" in "The Lincoln Theme since Randall's Call: The Promises and Perils of Professionalism." *Papers of the Abraham Lincoln Association* 1 (1979): 10–70.

Nevins, Allan. *The War for the Union.* 4 volumes. New York: Charles Scribners Sons, 1959–71.

Nicolay, Helen. *Lincoln's Secretary: A Biography of John G. Nicolay.* New York: Longmans, Green, 1949.

Nicolay, John G., and John Hay. *Abraham Lincoln: A History.* 10 volumes. New York: Century, 1890.

Oberholtzer, Ellis P. *Abraham Lincoln.* Philadelphia: Geo. W. Jacobs, 1904.

———. *Philadelphia: A History of the City and Its People.* Philadelphia: S. J. Clarke, 1912.

Official Records of the Union and Confederate Armies: The War of the Rebellion. 130 volumes. Washington: Government Printing Office, 1880–1901.

Official Records of the Union and Confederate Navies. 30 volumes. Washington: Government Printing Office, 1894–1914.

Oggel, L. Terry, ed. *The Letters and Notebooks of Mary Devlin Booth.* New York: Greenwood Press, 1987.

Oldroyd, Osborn H. *The Assassination of Abraham Lincoln.* Washington: O. H. Oldroyd, 1901.

Pitman, Benn, comp. *The Assassination of President Lincoln and the Trial of the Conspirators: Compiled and Arranged by Benn Pitman.* New York: Moore, Wilstach, and Baldwin, 1865. Facsimile edition edited by Philip Van Doren Stern. New York: Funk and Wagnalls, 1954.

Poore, Ben Perley, ed. *The Conspiracy Trial for the Murder of the President.* Boston: J. E. Tilton, 1865. Reprint. New York: Arno Press, 1972.

———. *Perley's Reminiscences of Sixty Years in the National Metropolis.* 2 volumes. Philadelphia: Hubbard Brothers, 1886.

Randall, James G., and Richard N. Current. *Lincoln the President: Last Full Measure.* New York: Dodd, Mead, 1955.

Raymond, Henry J. *The Life and Public Services of Abraham Lincoln.* New York: Derby and Miller, 1865.

Rhodehamel, John H., and Thomas F. Schwartz. *The Last Best Hope of Earth: Abraham Lincoln and the Promise of America.* San Marino: Huntington Museum, 1993.

Richardson, James D., ed. *Messages and Papers of Jefferson Davis and the Confederacy.* 2 volumes. New edition. New York: Chelsea House-Robert Kector, 1966.

Roscoe, Theodore. *The Web of Conspiracy: The Complete Story of the Men Who Murdered Lincoln.* Englewood Cliffs: Prentice-Hall, 1959.

Ruggles, Eleanor. *Prince of Players: Edwin Booth.* New York: W. W. Norton, 1953.

Ruggles, M. B. "Pursuit and Death of John Wilkes Booth: Major Ruggles's Narrative." *Century Magazine* 39 (Jan. 1890).

Ruling of the Circuit Court of Baltimore City, 26 May 1995. Case Number 94297044/ CE187741. Copy in the possession of John Rhodehamel.

Samples, Gordon. *Lust for Fame: The Stage Career of John Wilkes Booth.* Jefferson, N.C.: McFarland, 1982.

Sandburg, Carl. *Abraham Lincoln: The War Years.* 4 volumes. New York: Harcourt, Brace, 1939.

———. *Lincoln Collector: The Story of Oliver R. Barrett's Great Private Collection.* New York: Harcourt, Brace, 1949.

Skinner, Otis. *Footlights and Spotlights: Recollections of My Life on Stage.* Indianapolis: Bobbs-Merrill, 1924.

Smith, Gene. *American Gothic: The Story of America's Legendary Theatrical Family— Junius, Edwin, and John Wilkes Booth.* New York: Simon and Schuster, 1992.

Sobel, Bernard, ed. *The Theatre Handbook and Digest of Plays.* New York: Crown, 1940.

Stern, Philip Van Doren. *The Man Who Killed Lincoln.* New York: Literary Guild, 1939. Revised edition. New York: Dell Publishing, 1955.

Stoddard, William O. *Inside the White House in War Times.* New York: Charles L. Webster, 1890.

Surratt, John H. "Lecture on the Lincoln Conspiracy." *Lincoln Herald* 51 (Dec. 1949): 20–33.

Surratt Society, eds. *From War Department Files: Statements Made by the Alleged Lincoln Conspirators under Examination 1865.* Clinton, Md.: Surratt Society, 1980.

———, eds. *In Pursuit of . . . Continuing Research in the Field of the Lincoln Assassination.* Clinton, Md.: Surratt Society, 1990.

Taylor, Frank F. *Philadelphia in the Civil War 1861–1865.* Philadelphia: Published by the City, 1913.

Thomas, Benjamin R., and Harold Hyman. *Stanton: The Life and Times of Lincoln's Secretary of War.* New York: Alfred A. Knopf, 1962.

Tidwell, William A. *April '65: Confederate Covert Action in the American Civil War.* Kent: Kent State University Press, 1995.

———. "Booth Crosses the Potomac: An Exercise in Historical Research." *Civil War History* 36 (Dec. 1990): 325–33.

Tidwell, William A., with James O. Hall and David Winfred Gaddy. *Come Retribution: The Confederate Secret Service and the Assassination of Lincoln.* Jackson: University Press of Mississippi, 1988.

Tompkins, Eugene. *The History of the Boston Theatre: 1854–1901.* Boston: Houghton Mifflin, 1908.

Townsend, George Alfred. "How Wilkes Booth Crossed the Potomac." *Century Magazine* (April 1884).

———. *Katy of Catoctin; or, The Chain-breakers, a National Romance.* New York: Appleton, 1886.

———. *The Life, Crime, and Capture of John Wilkes Booth.* New York: Dick and Fitzgerald, 1865.

Trial of John H. Surratt. 2 volumes. Washington: French and Richardson, 1867.

Turner, Justin G., and Linda Levitt Turner, eds. *Mary Todd Lincoln: Her Life and Letters.* New York: Alfred A. Knopf, 1972.

Turner, Thomas Reed. *Beware the People Weeping: Public Opinion and the Assassination of Abraham Lincoln.* Baton Rouge: Louisiana State University Press, 1982.

Weichmann, Louis J. *A True History of the Assassination of Abraham Lincoln and of the Conspiracy of 1865.* Edited by Floyd E. Risvold. New York: Alfred A. Knopf, 1975.

Weigley, Russell F., ed. *Philadelphia: A Three-Hundred-Year History.* New York: W. W. Norton, 1982.

While Lincoln Lay Dying. A Facsimile Reproduction of the First Testimony Taken in Connection with the Assassination . . . as Recorded by Corporal James Tanner. Philadelphia: Union League of Philadelphia, 1968.

Wilmeth, Don B. "The American Theatre in Transition." In *John Wilkes Booth, Actor: The Proceedings of a Conference Weekend in Bel Air, Maryland, May 1988,* 19–25. Edited by Arthur Kincaid. North Leigh, Oxforshire: Published privately, 1989.

Wilson, Francis. *John Wilkes Booth: Fact and Fiction of Lincoln's Assassination.* Boston: Houghton Mifflin, 1929.

Wilson, Rufus Rockwell. *Lincoln in Caricature.* New York: Horizon Press, 1953.

Winter, William. *Vagrant Memories.* New York: George H. Doran, 1915.

INDEX

JOHN RHODEHAMEL is Norris Foundation Curator of American History at the Huntington Library, San Marino, California, where he served as co-curator of the 1993 exhibition "'The Last Best Hope of Earth': Abraham Lincoln and the Promise of America." Editor of the Library of America's *George Washington, Writings* (1977), he is currently preparing an edition of the Civil War diary of Gideon Welles, Lincoln's secretary of the navy.

LOUISE TAPER and her husband Barry H. Taper have assembled one of the finest private collections of original documents and artifacts of Abraham Lincoln and his family. Her original concept inspired the Huntington Library's exhibition "'The Last Best Hope of Earth': Abraham Lincoln and the Promise of America." The Tapers also have the largest extant collection of autograph manuscripts of John Wilkes Booth. Louise Taper serves on the boards of the Huntington Library, the Abraham Lincoln Association, and the Manuscript Society.